Eleanor's Odyssey

ELEANOR'S ODYSSEY

AN OLD SALT PRESS BOOK, published by Old Salt Press, a Limited Liability Company registered in New Jersey, U.S.A.

For more information about our titles, go to *www.oldsaltpress.com*

First published in 2014

ISBN 978-0-9941152-0-1 (digital edition)
ISBN 978-0-9941152-1-8 (paperback edition)

A catalogue record for this book is available from the National Library of New Zealand.

Eleanor's Odyssey

Journal of the Captain's Wife on the East Indiaman

Friendship

1799-1801

Edited and with a commentary by

Joan Druett

Also by Joan Druett

NON FICTION

The Elephant Voyage

Tupaia, Captain Cook's Polynesian Navigator

Island of the Lost

In the Wake of Madness

Rough Medicine

She Captains

Rough Medicine

She Captains

Hen Frigates

The Sailing Circle (with Mary Anne Wallace)

Captain's Daughter, Coasterman's Wife

She Was a Sister Sailor

Petticoat Whalers

Fulbright in New Zealand

Exotic Intruders

WIKI COFFIN MYSTERIES

A Watery Grave

Shark Island

Run Afoul

Deadly Shoals

The Beckoning Ice

PROMISE OF GOLD TRILOGY

Judas Island

Calafia's Kingdom

Dearest Enemy

OTHER FICTION

A Love of Adventure

Contents

Note

Eleanor Reid's journal was published as a serial in *The Asiatic Journal and Monthly Register for British and Foreign India, China, and Australia*: volume 8 (July-December, 1819), pages 237, 344, 452, and 555; volume 9 (January-June, 1820), pages 37, 130, 255, 451, and 564; and volume 10 (July-December, 1820), pages 40, 249, 454, and 575. The introduction to the first episode runs, "In this number we commence a series of extracts from an unpublished MS with which we have been favoured, bearing the following title: *Cursory Remarks, on board the ship Friendship, H. R—, commander; or, the Occurrences of a Voyage from Ireland to New South Wales, the South Sea, the Spice Islands, and Bengal, and thence back to Europe; performed in the years 1799, 1800 and 1801.*" Those three volumes of the *Asiatic Journal* are readily available on the internet and in a number of libraries, including the State Library of New South Wales, where I did most of my research. The first part of the journal, from Cork to Port Jackson, has also been printed as *The Voyage of the ship* Friendship *from Cork to Botany Bay 1799-1800,* edited by Col Graham, Perry McIntyre and Anne-Maree Whitaker (Sydney: 2000), and is available for sale from the PR Ireland website.

For this edition, the entire journal has been transcribed. Spelling and sentence punctuation have been retained, but long paragraphs have been split up for easier reading. Eleanor Reid indulged in the Georgian fancy of substituting initials with dashes for personal names; where the names are known, they are substituted without square brackets, for easier reading. However, square brackets are used for inserted explanatory words. In the commentaries and index, the abbreviation "HEIC" is used for "Honourable East India Company," where convenience dictates. In the index, the term "HEIC regular ship" generally means a ship that was built in England specifically for the Company; "HEIC extra ship" was one contracted by the Company for a specific voyage or part-voyage; and HEIC country ship" means a vessel that was built in India to Company specifications, and employed exclusively in the Orient, being forbidden to sail to Europe, or, indeed, anywhere west of the Cape of Good Hope.

As this book is published digitally as well as in print, footnotes have been avoided. Instead, the journal is divided into sections, and each part is preceded by a discursive commentary, giving background to what Eleanor found on board and in exotic ports. The final commentary sketches out what the future held for Hugh and Eleanor Reid. The sources are listed in the bibliography. The illustrations are mostly from old books and periodicals, those which could be traced being also included in the bibliography. Original sketches were contributed by Ron Druett, and the maps were created by the editor.

Waterford Quay, from Ireland, its scenery & character *(1843)*

One

Ireland and the Atlantic : June to October, 1799

The day dawned mistily, the way it does in southern Ireland in the summer. As the early light started to glisten on the roof tops, the captain of the Honourable East Indies Company extra ship *Friendship* strode along the waterfront of Waterford Harbour. Then he stood on the quay, waiting for the packet boat to come from Milford Haven. It was running late, as it was scheduled to make port at daybreak every morning of the week—every morning, that is, except Wednesday.

Time went by. Behind the captain drays rattled back and forth over the planks and cobbles of the mile-long quay, many heading for the bridge that led to Kilkenny. The smoke from cooking fires drifted in the air, carrying a hint of breakfast bacon, and the deep waters of the Suir River rippled past the hulls of moored craft. Bells tolled from the ancient tower of Christ Church cathedral, sending gulls shrieking into the cool morning air, but still he waited. With luck, his young wife would be on board when the packet arrived.

The packet came into sight, driven hard, as usual—not only was the Milford-Waterford service notorious for rough passages, but French privateers were troubling the Irish Sea. The people who gathered on the waterfront always looked for signs of combat, inspecting the boat's hull and rigging for shot-holes, but though battered by wind and waves, she was otherwise unscathed. She heeled sharply as she made for her berth, but the wharf men were as capable as always, snatching flung ropes as they curled through the air. Then, at last, the vessel came to a still, folding her wings at the dock. The passengers at the rail drooped miserably as the plank was lowered. Obviously, those who had survived the overnight battering had succumbed to the jolt and jerk of the tidal race at the entrance into the river, sixteen miles downstream, because most had handkerchiefs pressed to their mouths.

The crowd thinned out as the passengers trailed onto shore. The captain's wife was not there. Captain Hugh Reid turned and headed for his boat. Tomorrow he might be luckier.

The Honourable East India Company ship was lying at anchor in the middle of the river. Only six years old, she was a splendid sight, sitting quietly on her reflection now that the dawn breeze had dropped. She was Hugh Reid's first command, so it was natural that he should regard her with vast affection as the ship's boat was rowed about the grand, galleried stern, and along the varnished starboard side. The *Friendship*'s fine appearance belied her several faults, however, as well as a chequered past.

Built by the famous Rotherhithe builders, John and William Wells, at their Acorn shipyard, and launched on August 26, 1793, the *Friendship* had been rated at just 341 tons when first registered by Oldham and Co., her managing owners at the time. Designed as a bulk carrier, she had just two decks above, and a seventeen-foot hold below. Two voyages to Jamaica had followed, probably for sugar, but then this career had come to a sudden end.

West Indiaman

The date was October 27, 1796. The *Friendship* was on the way home from the Cape of Good Hope on her third voyage, heavily laden with a cargo of wheat. Her captain, Thomas Black, was carrying important despatches from the governor, as well as a number of passengers. Everything was going well until a shout from aloft warned him that disaster was at hand. A vessel was bearing fast down upon them—a ship that proved to be the 14-gun French privateer *La Voiture*.

Black crowded on all his canvas, firing his six twelve-pounder guns as he fled, but the *Friendship* was seriously out-sailed, out-gunned and out-manned. Forty minutes later, the corsair was within musket range, and one of the passengers, Lieutenant Fitzgerald, was spun around by a ball through the head. Black threw the weighted despatch bag overboard, and hauled down his flag. The *Friendship* was boarded by a prize crew, and joined the sad little fleet of English merchantmen that *La Voiture*, with her consort, *L'Hirondelle*, had captured already.

A week later, as the two privateers were escorting their prizes into Bordeaux, and Captain Black was glumly calculating the ransom Oldham & Co. would have to pay to get their property back, the Frenchmen were ambushed by a three-ship armada—HMS *Cerberus*, HMS *Diana*, and HMS *Magnanime*. It was the privateers' turn to be out-gunned. On 13 November Captain John Drew of *Cerberus* wrote to Admiral Kingsmill, "On the 4th I retook the ship *Friendship*, from the Cape of Good Hope."

It was just one part of a successful exercise—"the 5th took *L'Hirondelle*, a French cutter privateer, carrying 10 six pounders, and fifty-three men, but had thrown 6 of her guns overboard in the chace; and on the 6th, retook the *Jackson Junior*, from Jamaica." The *Friendship* sailed into

Plymouth on the morning of November 16, 1796, with a master who was understandably shaken by the experience. As Black reported to the ship's owners, an equally heavily loaded Cape ship had managed to run away from the privateer on the very same day that the *Friendship* had been seized.

So Oldham & Co. cut their losses by selling the slow ship to the Mangles brothers of Wapping. These were merchants who specialized in far-ranging Oriental voyages, which is the most likely reason that instead of sending her out at once, they had her rebuilt, envisaging her as an "extra" ship that could be leased to the East India Company. John Wells was again the shipwright, but this time the shipyard was different, as the Wells brothers had sold the Rotherhithe operation, and moved to Blackwall, where they were in partnership with Perry and Green. There, they cut the *Friendship* in half amidships, pulled her two halves apart, then bridged the gap in the middle with scarfed planks, which were duly caulked and coppered to match the rest. After they had finished she was about a third longer than she had been before—when she was re-registered, she was 118 feet long, with a 96-foot keel, and was rated at 430 tons.

The refurbished *Friendship* had also gained another deck—a grand one, designed for the accommodation of passengers. Once the new part of her hull was planked, tarred and caulked, and the bottom coppered, the Wells brothers' shipwrights raised a poop over the quarterdeck. This deck was embellished with a veranda-like gallery, which ran round the stern above the serried windows of the Great Cabin, so that the passengers could promenade and take the air. Finally, the *Friendship* was re-rigged so that the spanker boom of the mizzen mast cleared the roof of the poop, with provision made for awnings to shade the open decks from the tropical sun. No longer a humble freight-carrier, she had metamorphosed into a relatively small but definitely splendid East Indiaman.

East Indiaman

In February 1797, while the rebuilding was still underway, the Mangles brothers negotiated a contract with the Honourable East India Company for carrying freight at the rate of £24 per ton "builder's measurement" for one voyage—a total of £10,320. John Newham, who had been Black's chief mate, was promoted to captain, and on May 11 the *Friendship* set off for Calcutta. On August 3, 1798 the ship arrived safely back at Gravesend, and Hugh Reid was commissioned to be her commander next voyage.

Snaring the captaincy of even an extra East Indiaman was potentially very profitable, because of the benefits that came with the job. As well as his ten-pound monthly pay, John Newham had been allowed to carry a private cargo—a privilege that was known as his indulgence. This took up a space in the holds that was either five per cent of the chartered tonnage, or thirty tons, whichever was the greater. He also kept whatever money he made from carrying passengers from one port to another. Altogether, it could have added up to as much as £20,000, enough for him to retire in comfort.

Reid's upcoming voyage was a little different. As the managing owners, John and James Mangles, had negotiated a contract with the Transport Board for the *Friendship* to carry Irish convicts to New South Wales, the contract with the East India Company would not commence until after the ship left Sydney. The terms of the arrangement are not known, but if the calculated return was on the basis of the ship's tonnage, then it was ten shillings per month, while if it was per prisoner, it was £18 per head; either way, the amount would have been in the region of £2,000, of which Captain Reid was due five percent, on top of his ten-pound monthly pay.

Added to that was his private venture, which included choice foodstuffs such as hams, wines and cheeses, and was calculated to find a good market in the luxury-starved settlement, if not at some port before they arrived. Then, after leaving Port Jackson, Hugh Reid would get five per cent of whatever the Mangles brothers had negotiated with the East India Company, plus what he made out of his home-bound indulgence and any passengers he carried. And, if his thirty tons of free freight was made up of silks, muslins, spices, indigo dye, and the intricately woven shawls in moth-like colours that were all the vogue in this, the Georgian Age, he would end up with a very nice sum of money indeed.

All the officers of the *Friendship*, down to the boatswain and the surgeon, had indulgences of their own, which might be a lot smaller than the captain's, but were still significant. Altogether, their private cargo would add up to more than eighty tons, which was quite a cut out of the owners' share of the ship. The *Friendship*, however, had a cargo space that was much more capacious than her above-water appearance hinted. When first built, her 17-foot hold had been designed to carry as much freight as possible, and now she was lengthened she could load even more. Her deep sides also meant that she was ideal for carrying a human cargo—in this case the Irish convicts Captain Reid was contracted to carry to Port Jackson.

As he clambered over the gangway, a smell of sulphur and whitewash drifted up from the lowest deck—the orlop—where a gang of seamen was fumigating the cages. There were a few poor fellows incarcerated there already, as convicts had been trickling on board since May 20, the day the ship had arrived at Waterford. So far, there were five prominent rebels—John Brannen, Matthew Sutton, William Bates, Roger McGuire and James Fahey—in their number, but the complete prisoner list was still unknown to Reid, because the Irish government's agent for transports afloat, Commander Richard Sainthill, was in Cork.

What Hugh Reid did know was that he would be rewarded with a gratuity, perhaps as much as fifty pounds, if he delivered the prisoners in good health. But what state would they be in when they boarded the ship?

Would the poor creatures be carrying some ghastly disease? Looking over the rail at the misty spires and towers of Waterford port, it was hard to believe that less than a half-day's ride from this peaceful scene, thousands of people had been slaughtered in a battle that had commenced at dawn on June 5, 1798, almost exactly one year before. Or that thousands more were incarcerated in grim conditions while they awaited transportation—that most of the men filing on board the *Friendship* had been held in the notorious New Geneva Barracks, where the dripping heads of the executed were spiked on the outer walls.

The 1798 Irish Rebellion had its genesis in the Society of United Irishmen, which had been founded in Belfast, back in October 1791. The original ideals, which had been inspired by the American and French revolutions, had been lofty ones, including religious freedom for all, greater representation in parliament, more opportunities in commerce, and "a cordial union among all the people of Ireland." Hotheads, however, had taken over, and the popular goal had become the complete ousting of the British, along with their Irish loyalists. In 1796, deputies had gone to Paris to persuade the French to send over an invading army, a bold move that ended in abject failure, as the French fleet was repelled by both the Royal Navy and the elements, being scattered by a midwinter storm. It was disastrous in other ways, too, as the authorities, terrified by the close shave with revolution, had savagely cracked down. It had become a capital offence to deliver an oath of allegiance to the United Irishmen, and being seen taking the oath guaranteed a sentence of transportation. House-to-house raids were accompanied by cross-examination and torture. Panic-stricken men and women conspired to give evidence against each other, and upright, innocent citizens were flogged, hanged, and imprisoned.

As reports of atrocities raged, more uprisings followed. Mail coaches were waylaid in a campaign to destroy lines of communication, and village after village was invaded. The rebels often lacked guns and ammunition, but in close quarters, standing shoulder to shoulder, they were deadly with their sharpened pikes. In May 1798 they took Wexford, then turned their attention to nearby New Ross, a town surrounded by medieval walls that stood on the confluence of the Barrow and Nore rivers, and formed the gateway to Kilkenny and Munster. After repelling a British cavalry charge, the rebels swept into the city through the Three Bullet Gate, burning whole streets of thatched houses as they went.

For hours success seemed theirs, but then ammunition ran out, while any military order collapsed in a frenzy of pillage and rape. When the British forces counter-attacked, the rebels fell back and ran. Massacres followed, as shocking acts of revenge were committed by both sides.

Hundreds were hanged, often with no trial. Leading revolutionaries surrendered, agreeing to voluntary exile to Botany Bay to avoid trial and sentencing. Thousands of others were incarcerated in brutal circumstances, often on the flimsiest of grounds—and Hugh Reid was due to carry 176 of these bitter men to the other side of the world.

As it turned out, there were some real criminals in the consignment. Commander Sainthill's list included eleven soldiers who had behaved in an "unsoldierly" fashion by deserting in the hour of battle, along with five layabouts who were transported for being idle and disorderly. There were four murderers, one looter, and a fellow who had been sentenced to life for hamstringing a sheep. The majority of Hugh Reid's convicts, however, were United Irishmen, many of them well-educated men who had been energized by the writings of philosophers. Almost all of these had been held at the Geneva Barracks, confined in filthy, overcrowded conditions, so that their clothes and skins were crawling with typhus-carrying body lice when they trailed onto the *Friendship*.

It was an explosive complement, a bitter mix of farmers and labourers with a history of great grudges, and eloquent academics with the ability to exploit their rancour. Not only did this pose a challenge, but Hugh Reid must have been grimly reminded of the bloody uprising on his last voyage to Port Jackson, when he had been first officer of the extra ship *Marquis Cornwallis*, and the captain had been a shady adventurer by the name of Michael Hogan.

Mutiny had simmered from the day in June 1795 when the military guard had taken up their berths on board. At the time, the ship was at Portsmouth, loading gear and provisions, and Hugh Reid was in charge. As he watched from the quarterdeck, twenty-six soldiers from the New South Wales Corps marched up the quay from the Chatham Barracks, led by two ensigns, one sergeant and one corporal. After they had sullenly filed on board, the barracks officer who had escorted them to the ship came aft, to deliver a quiet word that the troops were rebellious. Sergeant Ellis, the officer said, was the worst, setting the privates a very bad example.

Hugh Reid passed on the warning to the ensign in charge, John Brabyn, but Brabyn merely shrugged it off.

No soldier wanted to go to New South Wales, he said. It was a virtual life sentence for no crime committed, so complaining was only natural. Accordingly, on August 7, the *Marquis Cornwallis* sailed from Portsmouth to Cork without anyone asking any more questions about the quality of the guard. Then, after 233 prisoners, including seventy women, had come on board, Captain Michael Hogan arrived to take over the ship, accompanied by his wife and two children. If Hugh Reid told him about the problem, he shrugged it off, too. And so, on August 7, the convict transport took her departure.

Just one month later, Hogan was handed a secretly scribbled note, and over the next two days three of the prisoners—Patrick Hines, William Mouton, and Francis Royal—revealed that a plot was afoot. Sergeant Ellis was the leader and instigator, they said. He planned to kill and confine the officers and crew, seize the *Marquis Cornwallis,* and sail her to America.

The men accused as ringleaders were brought on deck and cross-examined. Severe punishments followed, but did not put an end to the affair—as the *Derby Mercury* reported on January 21, 1796, "An Officer on board the *Marquis Cornwallis* East-Indiaman writes as follows to his brother in London, from St. Helena, under the date October 22." Hugh Reid was most likely the writer, and his brother, London merchant Thomas Reid, was most probably the man who passed the sensational letter to the papers, which ran as follows:

> *On the 11th September we discovered a most desperate plot formed by the men convicts, who, to the number of one hundred and sixty three, are the most horrid ruffians that ever left the kingdom of Ireland. They were on the point of putting the*

captain, officers, and ship's company to death, when one of them, either through fear of punishment or from a hope of reward, discovered [revealed] the whole affair.

It was a common practice for Capt. Hogan and the officers of the deck to go down and see that their births were clean twice a week, at which time they were to watch an opportunity to seize the captain, surgeon, and such other officers as went down with them, whom they were to put to death with their own swords, and force their way upon deck, where they were to be assisted by the serjeant, corporal, and some of the private soldiers, who were to dispatch the officers upon deck, and also to supply the convicts with arms.

We got upon deck the ringleaders, to the number of forty, who, after a severe punishment, confessed the whole. We thought this might put a stop to any further proceedings; but in this we were much mistaken. About two nights after they made an attempt to break out. They began by strangling the man [William Mouton] who discovered the plot, whilst the rest were to force down the bulkhead, force their way upon deck, put those not in the plot to death, and take possession of the ship, or die in the attempt.

The captain and officers did all in their power to appease them by fair words, and also by threats; but all would not do. They were desperate. Capt. Hogan rushed down the fore hatchway, followed by Mr. Richardson and three more of the officers and myself, armed with a pair of pistols and cutlass each, where began a scene which was not by any means pleasant. We stuck together in the hatchway and discharged our pistols amongst them that were most desperate, who, seeing their comrades drop in several places, soon felt a damp upon their spirits. Their courage failed them, and they called out for quarter. I broke my cutlass in the affray, but met with no accident myself. There were none killed upon the spot, but seven have since died of their wounds. The serjeant was severely punished, and is since dead.

Sergeant Ellis was in handcuffs and leg-irons when he died, which led to accusations of ill-treatment. Captain Hogan was exonerated in the magisterial inquiry that followed the ship's arrival at Port Jackson, but it shadowed his career from then on.

Altogether, the grim story was a very good reason for Eleanor Reid to feel reluctant to come to Waterford, as Hugh Reid must have been acutely aware. Yet still he expected her to join him, despite the disadvantages and difficulties of taking a young wife to sea

The last time Captain Hugh Reid had seen Eleanor was early May, when they had been married for just seven months. Traditionally, it was while the ship was lying in the Thames at Gravesend, carrying out the last of her loading and provisioning, that friends, associates and family came on board to say their farewells—a hard time for private conversation.

At that time of year, it meant pushing through the social set who were following the fashion for spending sunny Spring days gossiping and flirting at the tables set up outside the timber-framed waterfront taverns. And it was crowded on board, too. Captain Hugh Reid's brother, Thomas Reid, a wine and spirit merchant of Wapping, would have been one of the throng in the big poop cabin, along with his wife, Helen—not only did Thomas have a share in the *Friendship*, but his business was the supply of grog to the ships. There were other merchants with an interest in seeing the ship safely away, too, such as the Hill brothers, Almon and John, who did great business stocking ships with hard bread, and who invested in whaleships as well as merchantmen. And Eleanor's many relatives would have been there—her parents, William and

Janet Barclay, her brothers, William, Andrew, and George Dallas Barclay, and her sisters, Margaret and Jane, along with Margaret's intended husband, Richard Porter.

The lavish hospitality was supplied by the *Friendship*'s managing owners, John, James, Robert, Timothy, and Thomas Mangles, so the noise would have been loud, and the laughter infectious. The hub-hub on the decks was complicated, too, by the business of getting the ship ready for sea, with ropes and bags and boxes flung about, and seamen turning up belatedly. So it was not a good time for Reid to extract a promise from Eleanor to join him in Waterford, especially as her parents expected her to stay at their home in St Martin's, London, while he was away on voyage. But somehow he had managed it, even though he must have known that he was asking a great deal.

Bull and Mouth, from Real Life in London

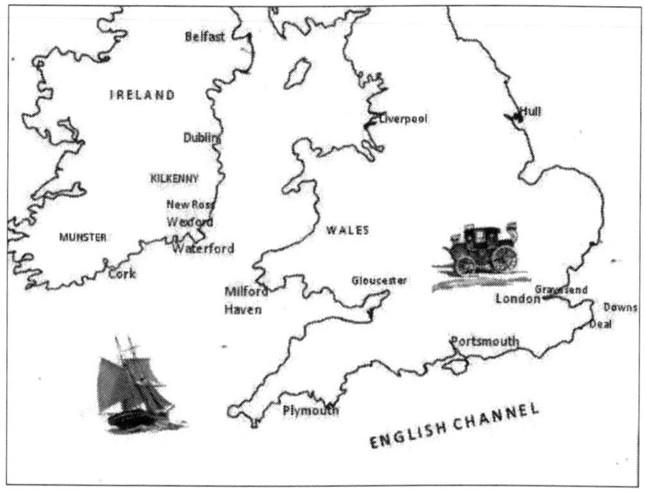

Getting from London to Waterford, Ireland, was quite a challenge for a young woman who was travelling alone, even if Eleanor did have the respectability of a ring on her wedding finger. First, she had to get herself and her luggage to the coaching inn Bull and Mouth in St Martin's-le-Grand. There it would take luck, along with the outlay of as much as two guineas, to snare one of the four seats inside the stage that was headed for the Welsh packet port of Milford Haven. Then, after she was finally settled inside the draughty carriage, she had a slow, uncomfortable forty-nine-hour ride ahead of her. The roads were rutted and rock-strewn, and the coach was so ponderous that every time it arrived at the bottom of a hill the passengers had to get out and walk. Indeed, the male passengers were expected to form up behind and help push.

It was an undoubtedly dangerous journey, too. Despite the blunderbuss-armed guard on the bench alongside the driver, there was a real risk of a hold-up by the highwaymen who infested the countryside. The staging posts, where the horses were changed, were often rough and suspect, being the focus of thieves and pickpockets, though at least it was a chance for the battered passengers to buy a mug of porter or a glass of Madeira, and snack on a pie. If the coaching inn was respectable, it was also possible to negotiate with the driver for the luggage to be offloaded, and reserve a bed for the night. But, hopefully, Eleanor would not opt for that, as it meant gambling that there would be a seat in the next night's coach.

Close to Milford Haven there was another chance of a decent bed, at the village of Hubberston—but, with luck, Eleanor would have boarded the boat the previous night. That is exactly what happened. When Hugh turned up next dawn, Eleanor ran down the gangplank and into his arms. And this is the moment when her journal begins.

End of June 1799 – Our mutual joy was great at meeting, my sickness and fatigues were all soon forgot, when I joined the *Friendship,* which was lying at the passage of Waterford.

While we remained at this port, alternately residing at Waterford, making excursions to the neighbouring country, or giving days to pleasure in the ship's boats; with a party of ladies and gentlemen, we visited New Ross, where Gen. Johnson had such a desperate encounter with those bands of deluded men, who had raised the standard of rebellion; seven or eight months after the battle, the large graves, where the men and horses had been buried promiscuously, were still fresh.

We were informed by an eye-witness, that when the king's troops had given way, and were driven back over the bridge, the general's personal courage regained the day. He exhorted the soldiers at the bridge to rally and retrieve their honour, and revenge the death of Lord Mountjoy, who fell with many others at the Three-bullet Gate. Seeing them backward, he spurred his charger, saying, "Friends follow me, and enemies return," he then galloped into the heart of the town, where his horse was shot and fell under him. Before he had disentangled his leg from the struggling animal, a rebel ran upon him with a pike to dispatch him; when the general rising on his elbow, darted such a look at the fellow as made him hesitate. At that moment some of the king's cavalry came galloping up the street, on which the rebel fled into a house and escaped with many others by a back way. When the king's troops regained the town they were still fired at from the windows. One of the rebels, observing "he had plenty of powder, but no ball or buttons left" — "Never mind," said another "fire away my jewel! The noise will frighten the horses, and I'll engage they will dismount the trooper."

It was some of the defeated insurgents, taken with arms in their hands, which my husband was destined to convey to New South Wales, who by the lenity of government were allowed to embark without trial. Many men of considerable fortune had been swayed by disaffection to revolt, and were now embarked on board the *Friendship*, viz, Mr. John Brannen, who at one time was sheriff of the county of Wexford; Mr. Francis Lysaght, who joined the ship in his own carriage; Mr. Daniel MacCullam, eminent for his medical skill; Mr. Matthew Sutton, and several others of equal repute.

There was another ship lying here, commanded by Capt. James Stewart, called the *Luz St Ann*, whose destination was also for New South Wales, with people of the same description. The members of this sanguinary association were termed at this time *Croppies*, owing not only to their own hair being reduced to the fashion of the round-heads in Cromwell's day, but to their horses, dogs, and cattle having their ears and tails cropped, as a mark to indicate that their masters were friends to the faction.

July 15—Having got on board the compliment of men ordered by government, the captain received orders from Gen. Johnson to proceed to Cork, under convoy of a cutter, and there receive instructions from Admiral Kingsmill, who commanded on that station: the *Friendship* with the convoy sailed next day, and arrived at Cork on the 18th. The ship anchored about ten in the forenoon, after which my husband waited upon the admiral, and finding there was no likelihood of being soon dispatched, I accompanied him to Cork in the ship's boat. The day being fine, had an interesting view of the country on the banks of this fine river, with many gentlemen's seats on either side, particularly on the right bank, near Cork, called Glanmire.

While we remained at Cork we spent our time very agreeably and had little excursions about the country, and received many hospitable attentions from the neighbouring gentry, particularly from the Jennings, Grahams, and Sainthills families.

About ten days after our arrival a fever broke out amongst the prisoners on board, supposed to have been brought from Geneva Barracks, which appeared so alarming from the occurrence of several deaths, that government ordered the prisoners to be removed into another vessel; also the ship to be whitewashed and fumigated, and new clothing furnished.

It was understood by my esteemed parents and friends that I should return to London after the sailing of the ship; and as the time drew near, many a heartrending emotion struggled in my breast, as I was preparing to separate, perhaps for ever from my husband. Even now I cannot bear to think of the meditated parting.

However, for the mutual happiness of both, it was agreed between us that I should proceed, and share with him the dangers of the voyage, committing ourselves to that Providence whose eye is over us all, and to be found by all those who seek him in sincerity, whether on the ocean or on the land, in a cottage or a palace.

This was indeed a trying voyage, as my husband was the first who engaged to take prisoners without a guard of soldiers appointed by government; he chose as substitutes for the usual military escort, Indian seamen, called Lascars, who did not know the English language, and manned his ship with British seamen.

His reason for manning and guarding the ship in this manner was : in 1795 he had been chief officer of a ship called the *Marquis Cornwallis*, destined on a similar voyage; the soldiers sent on board as a guard had been draughted from different regiments, for desertion and other delinquencies; thus a description of men, the most unfitted to be trusted with arms, were to act as centinels over others scarcely as bad as themselves. These guards were implicated in a mutiny which appeared on board that ship, in which some lives were lost before order was restored.

Capt. R. thought that it would be possible to take the prisoners to the place of their destination without having an occasion intervene for inflicting them punishment, or any severity beyond that of attending to their safe custody; which if accomplished, my narrative of the result would shew.

Our mutual determination not to separate was communicated to my parents, and to my much esteemed brother-in-law, Mr. Thomas Reid, who took a father's interest in all that concerned us.

August 20—The admiral gave notice to prepare for sea; in consequence all was bustle, especially with me, preparing to live on a new element. It may be supposed that I was ignorant of many articles of equipment necessary for the voyage, but the deficiency was kindly made up by one who had had experience.

24th—The signal for sailing was made from his Majesty's ship *Dryad*, and repeated by the *Révolutionnaire* frigate, who was to convoy us; and the ship *Minerva*, Capt. Joseph Salkeld, who also had prisoners on board for New South Wales.

We left Cork harbour with a large fleet who were bound to America and the West Indies. Our party at the cabin table, besides the captain and myself, consisted of Mr. Muirhead, chief-mate, a very good and worthy man; Mr. Macdonald, second mate; Mr. Linton, third mate; Mr. Bryce, surgeon, and a gentleman named Ensign John Maundrel, going out to join the New South Wales corps. On the third day after leaving Ireland, the different convoys separated.

Shark catching, from A Picturesque Voyage to India *(1810)*

Sept. 5 and 6 — We had calms; and as I understood, we could not have calms without sharks, so it happened; for during the night a small one, about 4½ feet long, had been caught by a hook over the stern, intended for a dolphin.

It was shewn in the morning, and as I had never seen one before, was curious in examinating such a voracious animal; the stomach had been taken out before I saw it, and when opened it contained only some fish bones; my expectation had pictured at least to see some human bones: it had three rows of teeth.

At dinner a part of the shark formed one of the dishes at table, of which all but myself partook; they said it was very good. I did not appear to doubt it; it was cut into thin slices and fried, and appeared like slices of crimpt cod. During the calm two small green hawk's-bill turtles were caught asleep upon the surface, they weighed about five or six pounds each.

We were now off the entrance of the straits of Gibraltar, but a considerable way to the westward. These calms were becoming very tedious; but a breeze springing up, soon carried us to the island of Madeira, which place we made on the 11th of September, but were not allowed to have communication with the shore, much to our mortification. The ship's crew had hitherto been healthy, but some of the prisoners had been sickly. Every indulgence consistent with propriety had been shewn them, all of whom, by messes, were alternately admitted upon deck in the day-time. The captain, the only person on board who had made the voyage before, knew well how to prevent any abuses; he caused the rations allowed by government to be stowed up in different parts of the prison, and the provisions to be weighed by their own messes in turn. The surgeon was instructed to distribute tea, sugar, and other little comforts, sent for such as were sick. There had been a considerable quantity of wine sent on board at Cork for the private use of about 12 or 14 of the prisoners who had seen better days, and who indeed were enjoying the comforts of affluence when their untameable discontent plunged them into the vortex of rebellion. The wine was served as they required it, by returning the empty bottles, which was a proper caution, as a bad use might have been made of them; the wine was a great comfort, and no doubt saved some lives amongst them. We now entered what is called the Trade Winds; a wind which blows throughout the year, with little variation, from the N.E. quarter.

14th – The commodore made the signal that he would part company that evening, but would lie too until four o'clock for our letters; in consequence of which all were busy preparing to write to their friends, and amongst the number I was not backward in writing to my much loved and venerable parents. Sent the letters on board and parted with the frigate. We kept company with the *Minerva* until next day, when as she sailed much faster than the *Friendship,* Captain Salkeld thought it eligible to make the best of his way, and left us to pursue the voyage alone.

September 16, 1799 –

No. 1505 Hugh Reid of the Parish of Saint John Wapping in the County of Middlesex Bach[illegible]
Eleanor Barclay of this Parish Spinster a Minor [illegible] were
Married in this Church by Licence [illegible] consent of William Barclay
this Sixteenth Day of September in the Year One Thousand seven Hundred
and Ninety eight By me [illegible] Lawrence Curate
This Marriage was solemnized between Us { H Reid / E Barclay
In the Presence of { Will Barclay / Thos Reid

The unmentioned anniversary

Sept. 18 and 19 – Passed between the Cape De Verd Islands and the Guinea Coast; two of which were seen from the ship on our right hand, one called Sal, and the other Bonavesta. These islands are often visited by ships of different nations on the outward voyage to India.

On the 20th, in the morning, two strange sails were seen to windward; and as they drew close together for communication, their appearance was not at all liked by our officers; however it was judged advisable not to alter our progress or point of sailing, and all were ordered to their stations in case of being attacked; the part assigned to poor me was to accompany the surgeon below. I am afraid I should have been but a poor help indeed; but our apprehensions soon subsided, as they both set their sails and stood from us. It was supposed they were Ginea ships [slavers], from the direction in which they came.

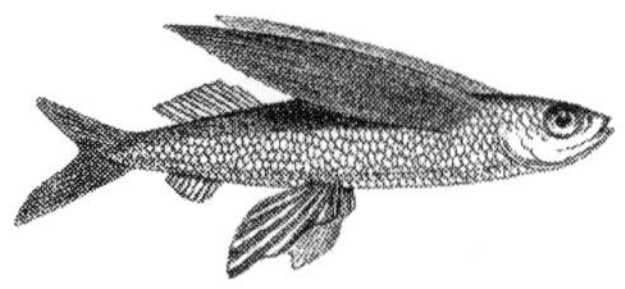

One morning we were agreeably surprised with a voluntary sacrifice to our table, namely, a number of flying fish who had lighted on board during the night. Fear, no doubt, was the cause of these volatile amphibia leaving their fitter element, the deep; the ship penetrating a shoal of them in the dark, caused them to separate in different directions, darting into the atmosphere to escape a supposed danger, by which means some of them dropped on board of us. When fried, they proved a delicious morsel: they resemble the mullet; their fins, or wings as they are called, extend from behind the gills as far as the tail; those that I saw measured from eight to ten inches. They cannot leave the element in a calm; at such times I have often observed them struggling to fly from the dolphin and other fish, without avail, and were devoured; on the contrary, in a breeze, I have seen thousands dart from the water in company, and fly a great distance.

There was another specimen of marine life, found on board in the night, which our officers called squid. These likewise are a prey to the dolphin, bonneto, and albicore. The squid is of a glutinous substance, like a jelly, about four inches long; and when put into a tumbler of water, emitted a dark fluid like ink, which tinged the water so much that the animal was hid from sight. I am told that this property, given by nature, is the only defence it can make against its enemy; that is, by darkening the water around itself in a limited space, then trying to escape in an opposite direction.

We were favoured with the finest weather for seven or eight days after we parted with the frigate, sailing at the rate of from eighty to a hundred and fifty miles in the twenty-four hours. When in latitude about three or four north, the winds became variable and light, with frequent calms; the heat also became oppressive. Great care was observed in ventilating and fumigating the prison; the windsails, with the scuttles, were open night and day.

Notwithstanding this attention, three of the prisoners died of fever, and several of the ship's crew were also attacked. The progress of sickness became very alarming; for, as soon as the first subjects of it became convalescent, others were seized with it. This alternate affliction ran through the major part of the ship's company; however there had been a plentiful supply of all things needful sent on board by government, and the same was administered most seasonably to the sick, which kept the fever under. The prisoners were also permitted to bathe in the morning-watches, which had a salutary effect after a sultry night.

On the 28th of September, after the officers had retired from breakfast, a sudden noise and bustle upon deck surprised me; when the steward coming down, I inquired of him what was the matter? He told me that a tornado was coming on, and that he was sent down by the captain to shut the ports and scuttles in the cabins. I proceeded to the quarter-gallery to see what he meant by a tornado, but had no sooner cast a look towards the east, than I became much alarmed; an immense black cloud was rapidly overcasting the heavens, darting out vivid lightening, while the thunder, at first distant, seemed by its louder detonations fast approaching.

The noise with the people securing the sails, and otherwise preparing to meet the storm, was awful in the extreme. The ship lay quite becalmed, yet at a short distance the tempest made the water fly before it in a white foam. I shall never forget my feelings and apprehensions at this moment; but fortunately my husband came down and told me not to be alarmed, for the squall had given timely warning, and enabled them to get all snug aloft, and that it would be over in half an hour.

He had scarcely done speaking when its fury burst upon us, laying the ship nearly upon its broadside with its force; the mingled tempest of lightning, thunder, wind, and rain made the scene altogether dreadful. I thought it the longest half hour I had ever remembered; but it was upwards of an hour before they again set their sails, and all on board most happy as the lightning had not been attracted to the ship's masts.

As we drew near the equator, the conversation at table turned upon the ceremony which marks the transition to the southern hemisphere. The chief mate asking the doctor if he had crossed the line, the answer was, that he had. It was then inquired, on what voyage, and to what country the ship sailed? He replied, to the Coast of Guinea. However, equivocation on the part of the doctor caused a doubt in the minds of the mates. He was asked, if he had seen the line when he crossed it? He said, he just got a glimpse of it, but as it was near dark at the time, he did not see it distinctly. This was enough to determine them that he should be both ducked and shaved, when Neptune paid the ship a visit.

I should be sorry to traduce the character of any person in these few simple remarks; but for the sake of truth, cannot help giving an outline of this person's qualifications. In the first place, he was most ignorant in his profession as a surgeon, and otherwise illiterate, yet specious and crafty. He had imposed upon the captain by a fair face and false pretensions. The captain, pitying the awkward situation into which he had got, took his part at all times when the officers of the ship were against him; but having discovered his want of skill, was under the necessity of employing one of the prisoners, named MacCullam, who was a professional man, and had seen better days: for the ship surgeon, knowing his own deficiency, gave way to him in everything.

Many jokes now passed about the expected initiation; nothing was said to the doctor, only that Neptune had a very ready method of surely finding out who had passed this part of his dominions, and could not be deceived. On the 8th October, at noon, we were only twenty-eight miles north of the equator, approaching it with a fine breeze. A sharp look-out was kept to see the line before dark; the chief mate fastened a day-glass to the side rails on the deck. All the gentlemen in turn came to take a peep; and amongst the rest, the doctor, who declared that he saw the line, and that it appeared no larger than a silken thread: all looked and saw the same. Mr. Muirhead, the chief mate, put this trick upon the doctor's ignorance and credulity, by placing a small thread across one of the inside glasses of the telescope to create a distinct prospect of the line.

Nothing farther passed until about eight in the evening, when we heard the ship hailed in a most strange manner by a hoarse thundering voice, saying, "*Ho-o – the ship a Ho-oye,*" which was answered by the *Haloo.*

"What ship?" was demanded by the same tremendous voice.

"The *Friendship,*" was answered.

"Very well; tell the captain that after twelve o'clock tomorrow he must prepare all on board who have not crossed into the southern regions before, to prepare to take the oath of allegiance, and go through the usual ceremonies."

An interchange of "Good night," closed the conference. The boatswain, with a speaking-trumpet concealed at the end of the flying jib-boom, had managed, in delivering Neptune's message, to make the sound appear as if emitted from the profound below.

The ship crossed the equator about ten o'clock that night. Next morning some of the sails were taken in, and the ship, as they termed it, made snug. I was cautioned, if I wished to be a spectator of the ceremony, to wear a dress that would not spoilt by salt-water, as no respect would be shewn to any one while Neptune was on board: this hint I followed, being anxious to observe what passed.

About one o'clock the ship was again hailed by the same hoarse voice, desiring them to lie to, as Neptune was coming on board. This order was soon complied with. Presently the screen, formed by a sail on the forecastle, was opened, and presented such a sight as I never shall forget.

Had I not been prepared for the pageantry, and told that some of the seamen were to be the actors, I should not have supposed them to have been earthly beings. A car was drawn towards the quarter-deck, in which were seated two figures representing Neptune and Amphitrite, with their marine attendants. The captain welcomed the sea-deity and his retinue on board, and asked him what refreshment he would take?

Line crossing ceremony aboard La Méduse *(1816), Jules de Caudin*

He answered, "A glass of gin would be very acceptable." After which, he inquired how many mortals were on the list to take the oath of allegiance, and to undergo the ceremony? He expressed a hope that all the prisoners should be shaved and ducked. This the captain compromised, by saying that Neptune's health should be drunk every Saturday night, until we were past the Cape of Good Hope.

The persons who were to be initiated were brought up from below blindfolded, one at a time, and placed over a large tub of water on the main deck; tar was applied to the chin with a blacking brush, which was shaved off by an iron hoop, one side of it was notched, the other not; those who were refractory were shaved with the rough side; they were then plunged backwards in the tub of water, while several buckets full were thrown over them. Some unmeaning jargon, addressed to them by Neptune, finished this great business.

The only persons at our table shaved were a Mr. Maundrel, passenger, and the doctor; the former submitted to it, and escaped pretty well; the latter, who was very refractory, was roughly handled, and had not the captain interfered, would have suffered much more. When the shaving was over, they began to souse each other with water, and I came in for a small share, which made me retreat as soon as possible.

We had experienced for several days much thunder and lightning, with heavy rains and calms; but the variable light breeze about the line we now exchanged for the periodical south-east trade winds, and contrary to the usual practice, we stood to the east towards the Guinea Coast, instead of the Brazil side. The captain gave the mates his reasons for so doing, well knowing from former practice that it would shorten the passage; at the same time, as the track was unfrequented, we should be more likely to avoid the enemy's cruizers.

For several nights past the sea had a very luminous appearance. I sat for hours together in the quarter-gallery, to observe with wonder the strange sight; at times it was like a liquid fire, and cast such a light into the ship passing through it, that we could see to help ourselves to anything wanted in the cabin without a candle.

I had often seen sudden darts as it were of a luminous stream, passing obliquely under the bottom of the ship, leaving a train behind like the shoot of a meteor in the air. This I understood was fish in chace of the smaller species, and had at one time an opportunity of knowing that it was so. A great number of bonnito and albicore had been caught by the hook in the course of the day, and towards night the fish still accompanied the ship; they could be traced in all directions by the luminous appearance they made in the water. One night, when my husband and myself were looking from the gallery, he said if he had the fish-rig he was certain he could strike some of them, at the same time calling upon deck for one to be handed to him over the quarter, when to my great surprise, in the space of half an hour, he speared five bonnetta, each weighing about ten or twelve pounds. These sights were nothing to old sailors, but they excited my surprise.

Several buckets of water were drawn up, in which were seen specimens of this luminous substance; it appeared of a soft glutinous form without motion, and when put into a tumbler with water, retained the same appearance in the dark; it had the power to hide the light for the space of a minute or two, and again let it be shewn. These vicissitudes might be caused by its giving up life on being taken from its element. However, one of these specimens which had been taken out of the glass and put upon paper, had been forgotten in the day, but at night it shone the same as haddocks are seen sometimes to do when hung up after salting. Many small particles also had this luminous appearance for the space of fourteen days.

So many fish were caught, that the poor prisoners sometimes partook of them. The small albicore and the large bonnetto are so nearly alike, that without particularly noticing the fins behind the gills, the difference cannot be distinguished: these fins, on the albicore, are about three times the length of the other, and rather project from the fish; the bonnetto, on the contrary, has these fins short, not exceeding three or four inches, and laying flat to the shoulders of the fish. They resemble large overgrown mackerel, but thicker in proportion to their length; they are coarse fare, and notwithstanding we had them cooked in various ways, found them still unpalatable. The dolphin we found better (when stewed with a proportion of wine and spices) than any of the other fish. As the dolphins we had were caught in the night, I shall not attempt to describe them; when dying they take such a variety of shade and colour, that a description is impossible. The largest we caught measured about four feet in length, and weighed about eleven pounds.

On the morning of the 10th of October, at daylight, we were rather alarmed, by seeing a ship at no great distance. After tacking she again stood towards us. The prisoners were now ordered below; and preparations made for our defence, every man being ordered to quarters. I went as usual to the cockpit. Our ship being a heavy sailer, could not attempt to escape, therefore stood boldly on. As we neared this strange ship, we observed she had Danish colours hoisted, and proved to be of that nation, from Copenhagen, bound to Tranquehar. The *Friendship* having a letter of marque, sent a boat to overhaul her papers; the boat immediately returned with the Danish captain who spoke good English, and informed us that about ten days ago he had been boarded by a French frigate, who had in company an English Guinea ship which they had captured. That the Frenchman had taken many things from him, and had given bills upon his government, which the Dane said he reckoned little better than waste paper. After exchanging civilities, he left us and proceeded on his course.

We were now advancing into the gulph of Guinea, and steering as much to the south as the winds would permit. Many tropical birds appeared about the ship, some of which, called Boobies and Noddies, took up their quarters on the yards at night; the former were about the size of a small duck, they are web-footed and could not rise to fly from the deck; they appeared most stupid birds, were not at all alarmed by any thing near them; they seemed full of vermin, by their constantly picking themselves. The feathers of the Booby are grey, mixed with black; the Noddy is of a sooty colour. They were generally made messengers of the next day, by being sent off with a card (having the ship's name upon it) tied around their necks.

We passed to the night near an island called Annobona, discovered by the Portuguese on a new year's day, from which it takes its name; it was notorious, of old, for being a den for pirates.

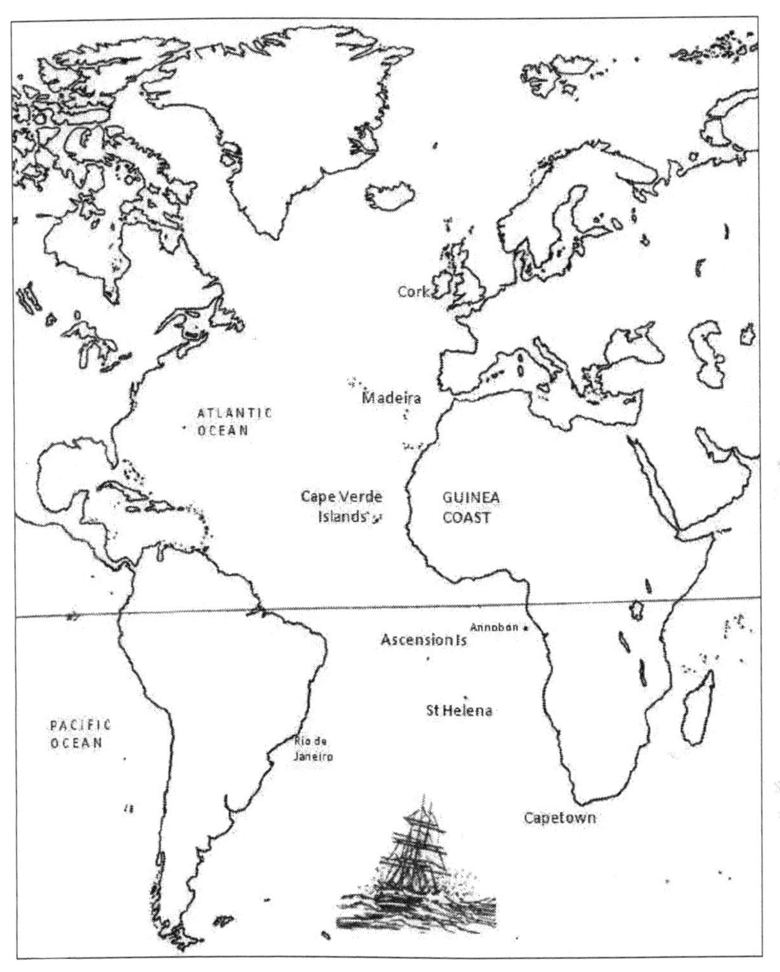
Cork
Madeira
ATLANTIC
OCEAN
Cape Verde
Islands
GUINEA
COAST
Annobon
Ascension Is
St Helena
PACIFIC
OCEAN
Rio de
Janeiro
Capetown

1815.
Costumes anglois et françois.
(52)
1.
2.

Two

To the Indian Ocean : October 1799 to January 1800

Considering that this was her first voyage, and that she was only twenty-one, Eleanor Reid was displaying surprising aplomb. Before the ship had even reached the south Atlantic she had recorded two outbreaks of a virulent fever, a tremendous squall, and two close shaves with what could have been enemy privateers; and yet, while she confessed to being afraid during the storm, and wondered what help she could possibly be if the ship were attacked, she did not quiver, complain or swoon. Instead, this young woman studied the sea and the life within it, at the same time describing interesting or amusing incidents on board. Though a great deal may have been left out when Eleanor edited the sea-letter for publication in the *Asiatic Journal,* still her composure seems remarkable.

At least some of this self-confidence must have been due to the advice she received in Cork "by one who had had experience" of life at sea—whoever that person might have been. It is tempting to speculate that it was Anna Mansfield, wife of the captain of one of the escorting warships, HMS *Dryad.* Anna was a colourful figure, famous for dressing in a version of an officer's uniform complete with epaulettes, a black silk neckerchief, and a round hat with a cockade. Odd as this seems, this kind of eccentricity was not particularly unusual in the eighteenth century Royal Navy. Susannah Losack, whose husband commanded HMS *Jupiter,* currently on the Cape of Good Hope station, wore a naval jacket embellished with two epaulettes over a muslin petticoat—or so observed Lady Anne Barnard, wife of the colonial secretary. Captain George Losack's crew called her "Lady Losack," and accepted her presence on board with good humour. And Captain Mansfield's sailors tolerated Anna Mansfield, too, mainly because she was shrewd enough not to try to interfere with the running of the ship.

So it is easy to imagine that Anna's first recommendation to Eleanor would have been to keep her mouth shut when ship matters were being discussed, along with a strict injunction never to venture forward of the mainmast, that being seamen's territory. Eleanor would certainly not have followed Mrs Mansfield's example in what she chose to wear, though. While the wives of captains in the Royal Navy had the freedom to be as eccentric as they liked, the wife of a captain of a ship in the East Indies trade had to be presentable all day, and elegant in the evening— to look as the wife of a successful shipmaster, adventurer and merchant trader should look. In short, she had to be a credit to her husband.

It was fortunate that an East Indiaman captain's wife was allowed to carry one ton of luggage, because Eleanor needed every ounce of it. On shore, she could expect to be entertained by local nabobs and affluent merchants, and visit palaces, castles, gardens, and waterfalls, and for this she would need walking gowns, visiting gowns, a dance dress, a mantle, a carriage dress, and a riding habit—and her own side-saddle, too.

While these might be packed away while she was at sea, she would still need an extensive shipboard wardrobe. Luckily, the current vogue was for high-waisted, ankle-length day gowns, so her hems did not drag on wet decks. Less elegant were the wooden clogs—pattens—she would have to wear over her dainty satin or velvet shoes, to protect them from mud and rough planks. However, it was common practice for even the most highborn women to wear pattens in the streets, to protect the ballet slipper-style footwear fashionable at the time.

Luckily, too, shady brims were also in style, this being an era when a porcelain complexion was greatly admired, but Eleanor would have needed long, narrow scarves to lash over her hat and tie under her chin when walking the breezy decks—and gloves, to make sure her hands did not become freckled. Naturally, too, she would have shawls, probably lovely Cashmere shawls that Hugh had brought her from India.

The wind would be chilly in the southern ocean, so one or two of the short jackets called spencers would come in handy, along with a serviceable cloak, and even a fur-lined pelisse. Luckily, corset stays were not in fashion, so she was not faced with the problem of keeping a sturdy whalebone-reinforced contraption clean. Instead, a simple linen shift was perfectly adequate for under-clothing, with perhaps a small bust enhancer. If there was a petticoat, it was a single one, made of a light fabric like fine muslin or lawn. And decent women did not wear drawers.

Obviously, the list of "articles of equipment necessary for the voyage" included many other items, such as paper for letter-writing (and list-making), and a journal for her daily diary. While Eleanor does not seem to have been a keen seamstress, she would certainly have carried a sewing kit. It was also sensible to carry small gifts for the people she would meet on shore. Merchant captains' wives often invested in knickknacks that could be traded for foreign curiosities. Eliza Underwood, who sailed with her husband on the *Kingsdown* in 1827, exchanged English bric-a-brac for tropical shells, which found a ready market back home.

While the *Friendship* carried a surgeon (the inept Dr Bryce), it was still advisable to pack a stock of medicines. Ether was the recommended remedy for both sunstroke and seasickness, and Peruvian bark for "intermittent fever"—malaria. Lavender, laudanum, and smelling salts were used widely by women at the time, and so those would be carried, too. A whispered recommendation was to make sure to take "the sponge," which was a finger-like sea-sponge encased in a silk net with a tassel for easy withdrawal, sold by all good apothecaries. Easily washed, it was an ideal menstrual tampon for shipboard use—and, when soaked in vinegar, for contraception, too, though disapproved of by male writers of marriage guides at the time.

Equally delicate was the hint that sea-life was very constipating. As Lady Anne Barnard revealed in her 1797 shipboard diary, many women endured the discomfort of stalled bowels "in silent modesty, because the remedy must be administered by another person." The answer to this embarrassment was a self-administering enema syringe, with a conveniently bent nozzle, which had been introduced to England by a European sophisticate, Lady Christina Theresa Josepha Murray. Lady Christina was a refugee from her husband—she had married James Ogilvy, the seventh Earl of Findlater, when she was just twenty-four, and then found out that he was homosexual. To avoid exposure, he went back to Scotland, while she stayed with her parents in Luxembourg. In 1791, however, this comfortable arrangement had to be reversed, because of an inconvenient court case. Ogilvy disliked the beautiful and disreputable wife of Alexander, Duke of Gordon, and after a copper-sheathed ship named *Duchess of Gordon* was launched, he was overheard quipping, "I aye kent the Duchess had a brass neck and a brazen face, but I niver kent she had a copper arse." The Duchess of Gordon consulted her lawyers, so James Ogilvy fled to Europe, where he introduced English landscape gardens, and Lady Christina fled to London, where she introduced the self-administering enema. As Lady Anne Barnard described, "she bestowed the pattern on a medical Protegé who in *gratitude* gave it her *Ladyships name.*" Though buying a "Lady Findlater" would cost Mrs Reid the enormous sum of two guineas and a half, Lady Anne's recommendation would have been a strong one, "for the duty of suggesting a measure so valuable to future voyagers shall *supercede* all *delicacy.*"

The modesty becoming to a proper female also meant that Eleanor would have made an inspection of the toilet facilities a priority on coming on board. The seamen, prisoners and Lascars used piss-tubs on the berth deck, and relieved their bowels by sitting in the seats of ease bored in the bows, or by going over the side and squatting in the nets that were stretched on either side of the bowsprit. Luckily, Eleanor was not faced with this indignity, as the captain, the officers and the passengers had two toilets, each one in a quarter gallery.

To get to the quarter galleries, Eleanor walked past the ship's wheel to one of the glassed doors in the front wall of the poop. Inside was a grand space that was well illuminated by a skylight above and a splendid sweep of windows at the back, where French doors gave access to the open stern gallery—the ship's veranda. When the ship carried passengers, this poop was divided up for their accommodation. The front half was the cuddy, or dining room, which was furnished with a long table where the most important and affluent passengers ate, presided over by the captain. The sternward half, which was known as the roundhouse, was partitioned off with light wooden screens or sheets of canvas into sleeping cabins.

And, at each end of this roundhouse, there was a quarter gallery. These quarter galleries were elaborately carved and gilded protuberances, each one hanging over a corner of the stern. Both opened onto the stern veranda, while the one on the starboard quarter also had a winding stair that led down to the Great Cabin.

Afterdeck of La Méduse *(1816), Louis Garneray*

Both were furnished with a built-in closet, containing a lavatory that was piped into the sea. Normally, the toilet on the starboard quarter was reserved for the captain and his officers, while the one on the other quarter was for the passengers. On this leg of the voyage, it is very likely that Hugh and Eleanor Reid had the starboard one all to themselves, leaving the water closet in the portside quarter gallery for the use of the officers and the one passenger they carried, the humble Ensign Maundrel.

The Great Cabin ran right across the stern, underneath the roundhouse. This was a magnificent room, a little wider than the poop, and dominated by a sweeping rank of many-paned windows that overlooked the ship's wake. Here Hugh Reid relaxed, posted his books and reports, and kept his charts. As Eleanor's sea letter testifies, on the Atlantic leg of the voyage she and her husband dined here with Dr Bryce, Ensign Maundrel, and the officers.

As was usual, the captain furnished the Great Cabin himself. No expense was spared, a prosperous outward appearance being so important in his trade. As well as the chart desk, its swivelling chair, and the dining table with its own chairs, there was a sideboard where his silver plate was stored in partitioned drawers, and fine china was displayed in racks. A castor hanging from the deckhead held decanters and crystal glasses, which sparkled in the light slanting in the stern windows. The barometer was on the wall over the chart desk. Little embellishments, such as paintings on the walls, depended on the captain's taste—and, in this case, his wife's as well. On some ships, part of this cabin was divided off to make the captain's sleeping room, but Hugh Reid could have established his stateroom up in the poop, by dividing off a space on the starboard side. This seems likely, as Eleanor recorded being out on the stern gallery so often.

Reid also had to bring his own bedroom furniture, but, since he had the Great Cabin for writing and relaxing, this did not need to be extensive. A sturdy washstand, with a folding top to close off the basin, was necessary, along with a little filtering machine to make shipboard water drinkable, and niches for a couple of tumblers. He and Eleanor probably slept on sofa-beds, which were solidly built divans with drawers underneath—unless they had swinging cots, which might be more comfortable, but had the disadvantage of requiring a lot of agility to climb into, while falling out of them was unnervingly easy. Lady Anne Barnard and her husband managed with cots; his was green, and when he was lying there he "looked like young Neptune hung around with sea weed"—or so she told him.

All the space on board had to be flexible, not just to accommodate varying numbers of passengers, but because the ship had to be cleared for action if enemy vessels attacked. This was particularly important on the berth deck, which was often called the gun deck because it was lined with cannon. The area directly forward of the Great Cabin was known as the steerage, and it was here that the mates, the surgeon, and more impecunious passengers slept—though Mr Muirhead might have been allowed the larboard (port) area of the poop on the first part of the voyage. The sleeping cabins in the steerage were even more temporary than those in the poop, as the inner partitions were canvas sheets that were rolled down from overhead beams and lashed to cleats, which were nailed to

Gun deck of La Méduse *(1816), Louis Garneray*

the floor. When danger threatened, and the drum beat to quarters, seamen dashed below to roll up the canvas screens, opening up the length of the deck for battle.

The forward part—the forecastle—was always open, as the Lascars and seamen slept in hammocks, which were "piped up" every morning. After being rolled tightly, they were stowed in nets along the bulwarks of the ship, to absorb the impact of cannon balls that headed that way.

And then there was the third deck, down in the bowels of the ship, just above the cargo holds.

This was the orlop, where the prisoners were kept in cages. It was also the deck where Eleanor was sent when the *Friendship* was being cleared for action. An operating table—often just sea chests shoved together—was set up, and Dr Bryce set out his instruments, while she did her best to help. Then, together with the convict apothecary, Daniel MacCullum, they waited for the crash and scream of battle to start in the unseen decks above.

The atmosphere in the crowded orlop must have been tense. While the more affluent prisoners had been able to negotiate for cabins in the steerage by paying Captain Reid something like 120 guineas, they would have been sent down to the prison as soon as the drum beat for quarters. There, the convicts either crouched on the floor or hunched about their rough deal tables, the whites of their eyes flickering in the darkness, nervous with the knowledge that the *Friendship* was alone and vulnerable in a hostile sea.

Because of Captain Reid's leniency, most of the convicts had been relieved of their crippling irons, which made it a lot easier to feed themselves, and get into their hammocks at night—and also made it possible to swim. But that was of little comfort when everyone was acutely aware that there was no one to come to their aid.

The *Friendship* had been sailing a solitary course ever since September 14, when Captain Mansfield had made the signal that he was about to leave the convoy. While it seems hardhearted to abandon the vulnerable merchantmen without an escort, the *Dryad* and the *Revolutionnaire* had another job to do—hunting down privateers, which is exactly what they did, because just five days later they captured *Cères,* a French corsair that preyed on the West Indies fleet.

After they had gone, the twelve merchant ships had dispersed in bunches, mostly headed for the West Indies. The two convict transports, *Minerva* and *Friendship,* were supposed to stay in company all the way to New South Wales, for mutual protection from natural disasters, as well as privateers. Unfortunately, Captain Joseph Salkeld, who should have been sailing alongside the *Friendship* or just a few miles ahead, had been too impatient to linger. While they had been in convoy, he had been forced to reduce canvas so often to let the sluggish *Friendship* catch up that his temper had frayed.

Consequently, the instant the *Dryad* and *Revolutionnaire* were topgallant-down on the horizon, he had signalled that he refused to keep the company of a ship that sailed so badly. And, with that, he veered off, steering for the Brazilian port of Rio. This meant that the *Minerva* was alone on October 1, when she was chased and fired upon by two ships flying Portuguese flags, but Captain Joseph Salkeld had perfect faith in his speedy ship—justifiably so, because she showed them a clean pair of heels.

Hugh Reid's slow ship, by contrast, was easy prey. As Eleanor testified, her husband had no chance of sailing away from a privateer; his only faint hope was to stand and fight. However, Reid did have the advantage of being a devious and wily man, who had chosen a course that no privateer would have expected a man in his right mind to take.

Ever since 1495, when Vasco da Gama had led his Portuguese fleet on a bold and imaginative track, making a wide swing out into the Atlantic and sailing almost all the way to the coast of Brazil before running south-east to fetch the southern tip of Africa, this swooping course had been the recommended route to the Indian Ocean. Like Salkeld of the *Minerva*, the captains of East Indiamen all sailed as far west as South America before running down their easting to the Cape of Good Hope. So, naturally, that was where the enemy lay in ambush.

Captain Reid broke the rules—he hugged the coast of Africa. Though Eleanor did not realise it when she noted that "contrary to the usual practice, we stood to the east towards the Guinea Coast, instead of the Brazil side," her husband was being crafty. It was not without great peril, as the western coast of Africa was what was known as a lee shore—the prevailing westerlies and the thrust of the waves combined to drive the *Friendship* onto the waiting rocks. Reid, however, believed it was worth the risk. As he explained to his confused officers, "as the track was unfrequented, we should be more likely to avoid the enemy's cruizers."

But the moment when he had to break from cover was inevitable. It came at the end of October, 1799, when he was forced to turn west, to steer for the great rendezvous of East Indiamen, the island of St Helena.

Though just a tiny speck in the remoteness of the south Atlantic, St Helena was maintained by the Honourable East India Company for its two great assets. First was the island's strategic position on the route between England and the treasure house of India, and the second was its remarkable luxuriance.

Ever since its discovery in 1502, captains had been stopping at this handy halfway station so that sailors could go on shore to feast on fruit and greens and get over their scurvy. In 1659, the East India Company formalized this situation by commissioning one of their captains, John Dutton, to "settle, fortify and plant" the uninhabited island, giving him the necessary authority by appointing him the first Governor-in-Chief.

The expedition arrived in May with 400 men, including lots of carpenters and armourers, a portable storehouse, a magazine, and materials to build a fort. Dutton also carried sprouts of yams and potatoes and seedlings of plantains, oranges and lemons that he had picked up in the Cape Verdes, which were speedily planted in hastily cleared plantations. Most pressing, though, was the construction of a fortress, to be called St John. Back then, just as in 1799, England's enemies swarmed in the south Atlantic, and so it was completed before the first month was out.

The embryo settlement survived, despite wars between England and other European powers, a couple of mutinies by the soldiers in the garrison, a handful of incompetent governors, and occasional attempts by the Dutch or the French to storm the island. The plantations produced excellent fruit and vegetables, which were traded for cloth, clothing, and European trinkets, and a straggling village, called Jamestown, was established. Ships called by the hundred, bringing interesting visitors. In 1676, twenty-year-old Edmund Halley arrived, and though yet to be famous as a leading astronomer, he made his mark locally by building a little stone observatory, from which he watched the transit of Mercury. In the 1690s, vineyards were laid down by a governor named Poirier, who was a French Huguenot refugee, and within a couple of decades the press was producing a nectar that rivalled the equally sweet wines produced in the famous Constantia vineyards of the Cape of Good Hope.

Another notable governor was Captain Robert Jenkins, who had lost an ear when his ship was attacked by a Spanish vessel, an outrage that led to the conflict with Spain that was popularly called the War of Jenkins' Ear.

Jenkins took charge of St Helena in 1741, and over the next twenty months built more fortifications, as well as straightening out the corrupt state of civic affairs he found when he arrived. And another noteworthy visitor was Joseph Banks, who arrived in May 1771 on the *Endeavour*. Banks wrote an uncomplimentary report of the place, scoffing about the lack of wheelbarrows and the ill-built houses, but despite this he took a permanent interest in the island. In 1792 one of his protégés, Captain William Bligh of the ill-fated *Bounty*, called there on the way to Jamaica from Tahiti during his second, more successful, breadfruit expedition, and made a presentation of mango and breadfruit plants to the current governor, Sir Robert Brooke, which the island's botanist, Henry Porteous, planted.

This was part of the current passion for wholesale shifting of plants from one country to another, a fashion that owed a lot to Banks himself. After arriving back in England from the *Endeavour* voyage, he had become the King's advisor at the Royal Botanic Gardens at Kew, and it was because of him that the Kew gardens developed from a mere showplace for exotic plants into a centre for serious botanical research. An energetic correspondent, Sir Joseph actively urged explorers and ship captains to send him specimens, and the directors of the Honourable East India Company cooperated with enthusiasm, because it was so easy to see the huge potential in establishing plantations of profitable shrubs and trees in lands that were under the company's control. Indeed, the project was already underway in an informal fashion, as many HEIC planters, explorers, and surgeons were so fascinated with the riot of colourful plant life of India that they were making private collections and establishing their own gardens.

One such man was Colonel Robert Kyd, who founded the Calcutta Botanic Garden in 1786, by turning his private garden into a nursery. After barricading it with a bamboo fence to keep buffalo out, he sent letters to the provinces asking for seeds and sprouts of lucrative plants—black pepper, cardamom, mango, sandalwood, teak, sago, nutmegs and cloves. Banks backed him with huge enthusiasm, seeing the Calcutta garden as the motherlode of Asian plants that would be useful for feeding Jamaican slaves, and also as a nursery for European plants that would help fight famine in India. Other botanical gardens were soon established, and by 1790 fifteen men were involved. As well as Robert Kyd in Calcutta, there were James Anderson in Madras, William Roxburgh at Samulcottah (a town near Madras), Helenus Scott in Bombay, Thomas Dancer, Hinton East and Alexander Anderson in Mauritius and the West Indies—and Henry Porteous in St Helena.

The nursery at St Helena was particularly important. The island was already a halfway house for soldiers to acclimatise themselves to a tropical climate before being posted to India, and at the urging of Robert Kyd, it became a halfway house for the acclimatisation of plants too. As he pointed out to Banks in a letter written in January 1787, sprouts and saplings had been dying before they arrived at their destination, simply because the voyage was so long. The answer was obvious—to set up a garden on St Helena, where they could be cultivated until they produced shoots for carrying onwards. Not only was the island already owned and managed by the East India Company, but its position made it the perfect way-station on the route between India and the Caribbean, and India and England.

The Company directors agreed, and so Henry Porteous, a keen amateur botanist who was keeping a boarding house in Jamestown, was awarded the title of Superintendent of the Honourable East India Company's Lands in St Helena. His qualifications were good, as he was developing an experimental plantation at Orange Grove, near Longwood, where Napoleon was later incarcerated. There, he was cultivating pineaster pines from seeds he had carried over from the West Indies at the instigation of the current governor, Sir Robert Brooke. Another part of the job was to help the soldiers start up allotments for growing vegetables and raising milch cows. This, as he wrote when invited to be the superintendent, he was very happy to do. Establishing gardens and acclimatising plants was just an extension of what he was doing already.

The man who had appointed Henry Porteous, Sir Robert Brooke, was a remarkably resourceful and capable military officer, who had tackled the governorship of the island with huge energy right from the day he had stepped on shore, May 12, 1788. Ably aided by Major Francis Robson of the Madras regiment, who had been appointed lieutenant-governor, his priority had been to reform the military establishment, which had been in a state of mutiny.

Not only did Brooke manage this, but he increased numbers, so that at times the garrison numbered over a thousand men—that is, if one included the soldiers from Company regiments who were recovering from wounds, or were just out from England and being drilled before going on to India. A parade ground was established, and gun emplacements set up on the cliffs that overlooked the anchorage, with accompanying signal stations. Potato plantations were extended; water was piped and drained; a new landing place was built. In 1792 it became illegal to import slaves into the island, and men who badly treated slaves who were already there were punished with substantial fines.

Governor Brooke's job became even more exciting in May 1795, after His Majesty's ship *Sceptre* called with a convoy of East Indiamen. A third rate of 64 guns, *Sceptre* had pursued a busy life since her launch in 1781, having been sent to the Indian Ocean just in time for the Battle of Trincomalee, an action that was briskly followed by the Battle of Cuddalore, where *Sceptre* captured the *Naïde,* a French frigate of thirty guns and 160 men, after surprising her in the night. Since then she had been in and out of St Helena with her richly laden charges, but in May 1795 her captain, William Essington, had important news, as well—that the political situation in the Cape of Good Hope had radically changed. French forces had invaded the Netherlands, turning the friendly Republic of the United Netherlands into the enemy Batavian Republic. Was Dutch-held Cape Town now fair game? When Brooke and Essington talked it over with John Pringle, who had been the Cape Town agent of the East India Company, Pringle agreed that an invasion was legally feasible. They could make the excuse, he said, that they were anticipating a French attack, and moving to forestall it.

St Helena, 1790, engraving by Thornton

Accordingly and forthwith, three hundred picked men were embarked on the *Sceptre,* and the East Indiamen in port—*General Goddard, Manship,* and a small fast packet called *Orpheus*—were unloaded to make room for still more. And, on June 1, 1795, the four-ship armada weighed anchor for the Cape, with Captain Essington acting as commodore, and Governor Brooke as the general.

Their high expectations were dashed the following morning, however, when they fell in with the Company storeship *Arniston,* just out from England, and learned from her captain that an expeditionary force, headed by Sir George Elphinstone and General Craig, was already on the way. Essington and Brooke prepared to return to St Helena, but moments later they were joined by the packet ship *Swallow,* just out from the Cape, and her captain revealed that a convoy of twenty richly and heavily laden

Dutch East Indiamen had just sailed from Cape Town, bound for Rotterdam.

The mental switch from invader to privateer was easy – the *Sceptre,* followed by the *Orpheus, General Goddard* and *Manship,* set out on the hunt, while the captain of the *Swallow,* equally hot for blood, kept the rear. A storm blew up, scattering the ships, but the *General Goddard* and the *Swallow* were still with the *Sceptre* on the afternoon of June 14, when seven sail were raised on the weather bow. Slowly, as the evening drew on, they closed in on the Dutchmen, with the *'Goddard* keeping her wind, and the *Swallow* and *Sceptre* steering across the fleet's course. Night fell with the ships all in sight of each other. Then, suddenly, action was taken. An hour after midnight, the *'Goddard* dashed through the Dutch fleet, splitting them up. Though fired at, she completed the flamboyant manoeuvre without firing a single shot.

As the Dutch Indiamen struggled to reassemble, it was merely a matter of shepherding them to the two other ships, which were coming down fast with all sails flying. At dawn the *Orpheus* and *Manship* heaved into sight, also under a cloud of canvas. The impressive display worked – after firing a few ineffectual shots, the Dutch commodore surrendered, convinced that he was faced with a superior force. Not a single life had been lost.

It was not the end of excitement for Governor Brooke. Just a few days after the rich prizes, herded by the *Sceptre* and the triumphant East Indiamen, left on their way to London, HMS *Sphynx* arrived, carrying a plea for help from Sir George Elphinstone and General Craig. Their invasion of the Cape of Good Hope was not going at all well, as they had not had enough men. Could Governor Brooke send some troops? Some guns—six-pounders, perhaps—would be most acceptable, too, along with some expert artillery men to work them. Sir George could also make use of some specie—for bribes, perhaps, or maybe to pay his men.

It was as good as done. The storeship *Arniston* was immediately requisitioned, and loaded with nine pieces of field ordnance, ten thousand pounds in bullion, ammunition, provisions, three companies of infantry, and one of artillery. And so, in due course, the Cape was taken, along with so many prisoners that the St Helena soldiers had to stay on in Cape Town, in the capacity of guards. Naturally, everyone was grateful. Governor Brooke received letters of high commendation from both the Honourable Court of Directors of the East India Company and Right Honourable Henry Dundas, the Secretary of War. Marquis Wellesley, the Governor-General of India, was so impressed that he decided to sent his brother, Henry, to St Helena to make a formal presentation. For this, he chose a fine ceremonial sword with a diamond-studded hilt that was part of the great treasure looted from the Tippoo Sultan's palace after the Battle of Seringapatam.

The twenty-six-year-old Honourable Henry, who had acted as his brother's secretary ever since the Marquis had become Governor-General two years earlier, called at Cape Town on the way to St Helena, arriving in October 1799. Lady Anne, wife of Andrew Barnard, Colonial Secretary, was delighted to welcome the noble young Irishman to the Castle, not just in her capacity as the official hostess of the absent Lord Macartney, but because the Wellesleys were friends. She enjoyed Henry's stay, and it seems that he must have, too. She was an avid listener, and young Wellesley had gripping stories to tell of the storming of Seringapatam, the death of Tippoo Sultan, "the Tiger of Mysore," and the wonderful riches that had been plundered from his palace.

Almost beyond belief was the description he gave her of the Tippoo's throne. Made of pure gold and pearls, it rested on a "Golden Leopard the spots of which was made by rubys emeralds etc – the eyes of diamonds – a gold Stair case was on each side of the Leopard by which the sultan ascended." The "fringe round the canopy was four inches deep & composed intirely of pearls," and overhead hung the great figure of a mythical bird—"the Huma a bird of lucky omen," a bird of paradise that was "believed to fly constantly in the air & never to touch the ground." This huge flying effigy was completely set with precious stones, while its beak held an enormous pearl, which Henry Wellesley was carrying to London to present to the Court of Directors. Indeed, he was so heavily loaded down with loot that it was easy to sort out a couple of gem-set rings to give to Lady Anne and her cousin.

Then, that gallant gesture over, Henry Wellesley sailed for St Helena on 24 October, escaping a destructive storm by mere days. The *Sceptre,* still a convoy escort but now commanded by Valentine Edwards, was not so lucky.

An hour after noon on November 5, 1799, Lady Anne Barnard was sitting at her drawing board in the cupola of the Castle when she heard all the ships in port firing their guns. She stood up in alarm, to be told it was just in commemoration of the anniversary of the Gunpowder Plot, though the *Sceptre* had struck her topmasts to ease the ship in the face of the strengthening gale. There was a heavy swell but the sun shone brightly, so her ladyship returned to her sketching.

Then panic hit—"at two o clock people run thro the room to look at the *Jupiter* Man of War and the *Sceptre* who had run foul of each other—the Sea was now become tremendous." Both of the cables that anchored the *Sceptre* had parted. As the people on the foreshore watched in horror, the grand old warship ran slowly and irrevocably onto the reef. At seven, she struck, and lay pinned with her beam to the breakers. Men ran out to the beach to light beacons, but too late. The *Sceptre* broke in two, turned bottom up, and collapsed into splintered wreckage.

"Heavy now pourd down the rain," Lady Anne recorded, while the fires flamed up sporadically, sending light flickering over planks and bodies covering the sea.

Loss of HMS Sceptre, *from* Gleanings in Africa *(1805)*

This meant that when the *Friendship* arrived at the Cape, Eleanor Reid found a town in mourning. Not only had there been a horrifying number of bodies to bury, but the commander-in-chief, Admiral Hugh Christian, had died. So there were no teas, dances, or dinners.

Eleanor was not even able to tour the famous Great Constantia vineyard, as the owner, Hendrik Cloete, was not there to escort her—as Lady Anne revealed in her journal, he had died of a surfeit of cucumbers. In the meantime, however, Eleanor had enjoyed a good time on the island of St Helena—and this is where her sea-letter continues.

At the end of October we made St. Helena, having been little more than eight weeks from Cork. A boat was dispatched from the ship to report our arrival and business to the governor, in the afternoon our boat returned with permission for the ship to anchor.

Our salute of nine guns was returned by the batteries on Ladder-hill. We found lying here, five sail of Indiamen waiting for convoy, some of which had been detained upwards of six weeks. As they were all full of passengers, their stores were almost all expended; in consequence of which, the private adventures, consisting of eatables and drinkables, such as hams, cheese, butter, porter, wine, &c. came to a good market.

The island at our coming into the road, and also from the anchoring place, appeared a barren rock; as only a few trees were seen in front of the governor's house facing the sea. Pursuing the prospect up St. Jems valley, where the town stands between two hills, if the island were subject to earthquakes, it might be feared that it would sometime or other be buried, by the high perpendicular rocks which overhang on each side. The only conspicuous buildings from this point of view, besides the government house, are the church and hospital.

In the evening that captain waited upon Governor Brooke, to whom he was known, and was received in the most friendly manner. Notwithstanding the island was rather short of provisions, three bullocks were supplied for the prisoners; and plenty of vegetables, which arrested the progress of the scurvy, which had begun to appear on board.

On the same day the Captain had the pleasure to see his old friend and shipmate, Mr. H. Porteous, the Company's botanist, who had accompanied him to the Coast of Guinea, when sent thither by the present governor in 1792. This gentleman insisted that I should proceed to his country residence, called Orange Grove, nearly at the extremity of the Island. His kind invitation was accepted, and next morning we went on shore.

I was mounted on a fine little pony, and proceeded up the zig-zag road, called Ladder-hill, whence we had a fine view of the shipping below; they appeared much diminished in size, from our being so high above them. The guns at this place pointed down immediately at the road.

Jamestown, from the sea, from Fowler's Views

We still ascended and passed the governor's residence, called the Plantation house, to the right, after which an immense high peaked mountain opened to our left, called High Knoll, on which it was intended to place cannon. We arrived at Mr. Porteous's house about four in the afternoon, and found his lady a most affable pleasant woman; she was born upon the island of European parents.

I was happy to have this change from being on shipboard, and in the morning was surprised by finding myself actually among the clouds; for soon after sun-rise they rolled down the hills in columns, like curling smoke, not spreading like a mist which obscures all around; at other times we saw detached columns descend, by the eddy winds, down the leeside of the hills, which had a grand and wonderful effect.

Plantation House, from Fowler's Views

We rode over several parts of the island, and were most hospitably received by the Lieutenant-governor and family; by Col. and Mrs. Robson, at Longwood; also by Mr. John Thompson, who accompanied my husband to Guinea with Mr. P. I feel much indebted for his great kindness during my stay at this place, and for the courtesies of some of Maj. Bassit's family.

At Orange Grove I spent nine days very happily in the society of Mrs. P., whom I left with regret. She wished me much to stay with them until the return of the ship in the voyage home; but this could not be, as my mind was made up to follow the destiny of my husband. Kind Providence had conducted us thus far to safety, and we were enabled to trust "Him" for the future.

While we remained here a ship arrived from Madras with dispatches, announcing the capture of Seringapatam, in carge of the Hon. Mr. Henry Wellesley, brother to Lord

Mornington (now Marquis Wellesley) then Governor-general of India.

Mr. W., on seeing Capt. R. expressed a great desire to go on board the *Friendship,* and see some of the unfortunate men who had been in the rebellion; he of course was invited on board, and went over the ship, visiting the prison, &c. In walking round the deck where some of the prisoners were sitting, he stopt suddenly before one of them, and called out, "that cannot be Sutton," who directly looked up, and replied, "yes, it is S— " "Good God," said Mr. W. "did I ever expect to see you in this situation? Pray how was it?"

Sutton still kept his sitting posture, desiring that no question might be put to him, as he should not answer any. Mr. W. turned from him, and taking the captain aside, said that this unfortunate young man had at one time a prospect of being eminent in the law, and had been a school-fellow of his; and if any pecuniary aid was wanting for his comfort on the voyage he should be happy to furnish it. The captain informed him, that there were eleven of the prisoners, including S—, who had a little stock of wine, and other comforts remaining, which had been laid in for them by their friends, previous to leaving Ireland; also, that he had some money of theirs in his hands, which would be advanced as it was required on coming into port. Shortly after this Mr. W., and several gentlemen who had accompanied him, left the ship; next day there was a quantity of vegetables, potatoes, &c. sent on board for the use of these poor men. The supply came by the government boat, but it was not known who was the donor; at all events it was most acceptable to the prisoners.

It had been reported to the governor, that some French ships were cruizing off the Cape; in consequence of which he advised our putting in there for intelligence. Capt. Amos Norcott of the 33d regiment, and Lieut. John Chetwood, who were at St. Helena, availed themselves of the opportunity to proceed with us.

On the evening of the 13th Nov. we sailed from this island; thence, until we reached the 27th degree of south latitude, we had what is called a strong trade wind. It was pleasing to reflect, that the crew and the prisoners were in the best health, which may be attributed to the refreshments, and to a plentiful supply of water; they always having been on full allowance of this most necessary article.

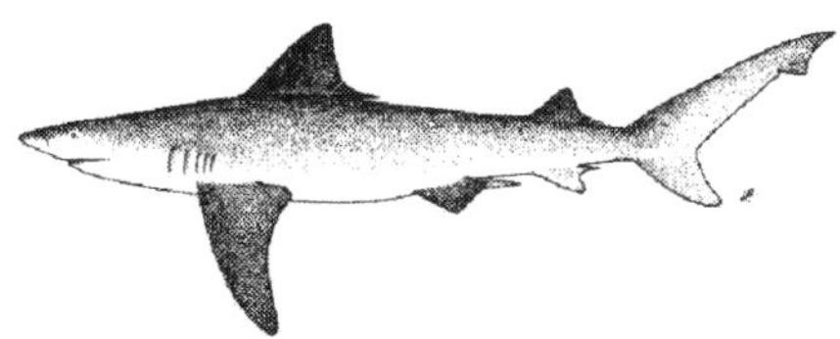

Between the south-east trade and the variable winds, we were again subject to calms. I was much surprised one morning to hear a most distressing cry upon deck; on enquiring of one of the servants what was the matter, he informed me that one of the seamen had his hand nearly bit off by a shark. I at first supposed he had been bathing in the sea; but upon farther inquiry learnt, that a shark had been caught in the night by a small hook and line. The line not being of sufficient strength to pull it upon deck: they had played with the animal in the water, in order to drown it. The shark, at length exhausted, was lying as dead on the surface of the sea: a rope was now passed round its body, and it was pulled into the ship; and while a sailor was employed disengaging the small hook from the jaw of the fish, the jaw closed upon his hand and could not be separated, the sufferer roaring lustily all the while, until a wedge of wood was thrust into the shark's mouth. Three fingers were horribly bit, and bled profusely; how ever no bad effects attended this casualty, as the seaman was able to do duty again in eight or ten days.

Another still more singular circumstance followed the taking of this animal. Every other day since leaving St. Helena, some of our best fowls had been found dead in the coops in the morning; but their periodical mortality could not be accounted for. As the captain never allowed these poultry to be used at his table, the steward gave them to the people, who tended the stock. On opening the shark, the head and part of the neck of a cock was found in its stomach; upon examining which, some verdigrease was observed adhering to the back part of the head. The cause of this appearance was next traced to be a pin stuck down into the neck, which had touched the spine and caused instant death. We now discovered, by the intervention of the shark, how our poultry had dropped off. One of the assistants to the poulterer being interrogated, confessed that the head-man (who was a Chinese) had been seen one night in the act; but the witnesses connived at it, knowing they would get them next day for their own use, and not being over scrupulous in what they eat. The delinquent was punished, and deprived of his office. As a farther check, whatever poultry was afterwards found dead was thrown overboard in the captain's presence.

Had any south-sea whalers been where we were, they most certainly would have had plenty of employment, as daily a number of whales were seen, many of which came very close to our ship and spouted the water very high. It was observed that when the huge animals wanted to go deep down, they turned their body perpendicular, *viz*, head downward, and the tail shewed itself entirely out of the water.

The addition to our society of Capt. Norcott and Lieut. Chetwood made the time pass pleasantly; they both had gone from India to St. Helena for the re-establishment of their health, and were now on their return, going with us to the Cape. The former was a well-informed man; had seen much of the world, and some service in the cause of his country. The latter, of a mild unassuming character, was at the same time a perfect gentleman.

Capt. N. was sometimes hard upon the Doctor; who, if he had possessed fine feelings, would often had been put to the blush; but that was impossible. One day, the captain asked the surgeon, if he had served in any other ship? He said, "yes, he had served in the West-Indies in a man of war." The name of the ship was demanded; he replied, it was the —, naming a sloop of war. "It was my old friend (pronouncing his name) who commanded her," said Captain N., "pray how did you like him?" This quite took the doctor aback, who was not prepared for a charge in quick time. The fact afterwards turned out to be, that he was only the surgeon's servant in the sloop; and all the medical education he had received, consisted in attending his master for about 18 months. The truth, however, was not then known on board, and he evaded the dilemma by saying, that he had been a supernumerary on board that ship, in which he went home to England on account of bad health.

We had had for some days past a cloudless sky, and at night all the luminaries of heaven sparkling in the native splendour. Those spaces, in the southern hemisphere, called the Magellan Clouds, appeared now almost over our heads. In the early part of the night they were three in number; two had a white appearance like the milky way, and the other appeared dark, almost resembling a perforation in the canopy of heaven; many strange stories were told respecting them, but too absurd to notice here.

We were now fast approaching the southern extremity of Africa; and had the satisfaction, on the morning of the 7th of December, to see the Table Mountain, the Sugar-loaf, and the Lion's rump. This place is so well known to seamen, and so remarkable, that in case of an erroneous reckoning, it cannot be mistaken for other land.

The ship anchored in Table Bay about noon. We were much concerned to see several wrecks lying on the shore, and most sorry to learn, that about three weeks previous, there had been a most tremendous gale of wind from the north-west quarter, in which the *Sceptre* of 64 guns had been driven on shore; when the captain, his son, and a number of the crew perished; there were also a Danish man of war, an American, and two other ships lost at the same time. This melancholy disaster, with the death of Admiral Christian, had filled all the British here with sincere regret.

I must confess, I was surprised and pleased with the view of Cape Town from the ship; with the white-washed houses, and green painted windows, it had a clean and handsome appearance.

On the vessel anchoring, the commodore's boat came on board, with an order from General Francis Dundas for the captain to proceed immediately on shore, with all the letters and papers he might have for the settlement. It appeared that they had had no intelligence direct from England for upwards of four months; in consequence of which, we were a most acceptable arrival, having the latest

East Indiaman and frigate at Table Bay, Sutherland (1824)

news from India by way of St. Helena, as well as from Europe.

On shore, my husband saw his old commander Capt. H. [Michael Hogan of the *Marquis Cornwallis*], who among many other enquiries asked, "How many of those Irish rebels he had with him, and how they had behaved on the voyage?"

Capt. R. replied, "that they had behaved so well, they had put it out of his power or that of his officers to lay a finger upon one of them : and that he was in hopes of landing them at their place of destination, without introducing the machinery of punishment." This answer appeared to surprise him not a little, and no doubt brought reflections to his mind respecting incidents during a former voyage, when they sailed together.

We were received as inmates in the family of Mr. Blackenburgh, a Dutch gentleman, known to my husband formerly, where we were comfortably situated. His sister-in-law, Miss Rouseau, spoke English : and thus her pleasing manners made it most agreeable for me to be again in female society. During our stay here, little parties were made, with arrangements for visiting the neighbourhood, and among other places, the famous vineyards of great and little Constantia. In going to the latter place, we passed many country-seats belonging to the Dutch and English gentry, and made a circuit round a *bush,* where the Lieut.-governor sometimes resided. Here we saw, in traversing the country, the red and white grapes, hanging in rich clusters from fine spreading vines, fastened to a kind of lattice-work projecting from the wall.

When we arrived at the great Constantia, the proprietor, Mr. Hendrik Cloete, jr., was from home. However we were more fortunate at Constantia the less; and were hospitably received by the host, his wife, and family. One of the sons spoke pretty good English, and appeared happy to communicate any information in answer to enquiries. We walked through the grounds, gardens, and vineyards; the trees in the orchards were loaded with the finest fruits, such as oranges, apples, pears, quinces, peaches, nectarines, almonds, &c. in abundance.

I was rather disappointed at first viewing the vineyards: I had expected we should have walked under the lattice-work supporting the grapes in all directions round us; but instead of this, when the vineyards were pointed out to me, I really thought it was a nursery ground, dwarf standards stunted by training, detached and planted in regular rows, appeared at first only like small gooseberry bushes. On inspection, however, we found the stem very thick, and some of the little branches so loaded with fruit that they weighted it down, and the clusters of grapes rested upon the ground. Probably, in this want of care, lies the proximate cause why the Cape wines have an earthy taste.

We were shewn the wine-press, and were informed that the stalks and all were thrown in, when the juice was to be compressed. One of our party took a branch of the vine, desiring our host's son only to taste the stalk, as we all did, and found it had a most unpleasant flavour. It was observed to him, that if the stalks were left out, the wine would be much better; he replied, that it would take too much time, and that it had always been their custom so to do.

I could not help contrasting this middle of December with that of last year, when I was with my much-esteemed parents, where we had nothing but frost and snow; and here it was the middle of summer, where all nature smiled. I could hardly think I was in the same world. We had a plentiful table set out for us, particularly in fruits. On our return to the house, my husband ordered some casks of their best wine, both red and white, to be sent to him. A small sum was given to some of the slaves; but it would have been considered an affront to have offered money to any of the family.

As we were going through the grounds, we were frequently cautioned not to leave the paths, as amongst the grass many dangerous snakes were known to be hid. A slave had lately been bit by one which caused his death; we saw none, but did not fail to attend to the advice. There were frequently seen amongst the vines, small land tortoises, apparently domesticated; for they did not shun any person when approaching them; we also saw a number of little fresh-water turtles in a brook; the largest did not exceed in size a small frog.

Several tortoises were sent on board and lived amongst the sheep in the long boat. I kept a little turtle of the above description alive for many months, in a tumbler of fresh water; it lived upon flies, which it would take out of the hand. It was a kind of thermometer, always lively and playing about in fair weather, and as constantly keeping at the bottom of the tumbler in dull rainy weather, only coming to the surface to respire once in 10 or 15 minutes.

On one of the party expressing surprise at several of the peach and other fruit-trees being damaged, and the fruit taken before it was ripe, we were informed that just before the gardens had been beset by a formidable set of plunderers from the mountains. We immediately concluded that these must have been some runaway slaves, or what are called *Bushmen*, but, so such thing, the incursion was made by baboons, great numbers of which inhabit the adjacent hills, and often come down and destroy ten times more than they eat, and are so strong and ferocious, that their largest dogs dare not attack them. We saw a specimen that had been shot and stuffed. It had a most frightful appearance; it was a female, and had a young one clinging to it when taken: the latter was preserved alive and sent to town.

As the gardeners dreaded the depredations of the baboons, so we were told, did the farmers the wolves [hyenas]; for if a horse, or cow, were by accident left out at night, they were sure to be destroyed before morning; and it was unsafe to send their slaves out at night on that account. After hearing many wonderful, and I suspect exaggerated stories of the wolves and other wild animals, I returned to Cape Town, much pleased with our excursion.

In consequence of the late disaster amongst the shipping, there was no gaiety here at this time. Mr. Hogan mentioned above, my husband's former commander, acted as agent for the ship. We dined twice with him and Mrs. H.

As we were the only English residing at Mr. B.'s we had a further display of some of the African Dutch manners. As for Blackenburgh himself, he was a perfect bruin, and considered his poor wife in no better light than a piece of household furniture; she was a good meek soul, and fond of her children; however, I could have but little converse with her, as she did not speak English; her sister, Miss Rousseau, occasionally interpreted between us. Generally after dinner some of their Dutch friends would drop in, when the pipes went to work; at these times I was glad to retreat. Mr. B. had a place in a public office, which kept him from home all day, and at breakfast he never appeared: — they kept a plentiful table, after the Dutch manner, with abundance of fine fruits and vegetables; the former, which wanted no dressing, I enjoyed. I cannot say much for the cooking; the fish and vegetables were generally swimming in oil, from the fat of sheep's tails; everything fried, appeared the same; the bread was light, but very sandy, which often-times gritted between the teeth.

The time drew nigh for our departure; and when the day of embarkation was fixed, I was much surprised by my friend, Miss R., telling me the evening before, in a positive tone, that we should not part so soon. I told her, that nothing but some unforeseen accident could detain us: — she took me to a back window, desiring me to look at the Table Mountain, which I did, and saw the white clouds curling over the brow of the hill, and extending to the right and left; she said, it was very common to see the table-cloth spread upon the Table hill; but when the Old Boy put his nightcap on the Devil's *Berg* before supper, it was a sure sign of a south-east gale coming on (this latter is a *peaked hill,* on the north side, and only separated from the other by a small ravine). The case was as these quaint local sayings described; and for three days no communication could be had with the ship: the wind was so high, that it made the sand fly in all directions, which may partly account for the bread being sandy, as these gales of wind are frequent in the summer season.

On the 24th December we embarked, in the afternoon. Our ship appeared like a Noah's ark, as my husband had sent on board eight horses, ten cows, three score sheep, with pigs and poultry in abundance; and as there was plenty of room on board, no inconvenience was felt. Next morning, being Christmas day, 1799, we left Table Bay, committing ourselves to the protecting care of that Providence who had hitherto preserved us.

On the second day, we spoke the *Sir Edward Hughes,* from Madras, having three other Indiamen in company; they had no news, but said they had met with very bad weather, off Lagullas Bank, for fourteen days past, and only made progress as the current impelled them against the wind.

For five or six days after this, we experienced very bad weather ourselves, notwithstanding the wind was fair, and the ship running at the rate of from 140 to 150 miles in the 24 hours, with only the foresail set. Still we suffered; for during that time nothing could be cooked as the high sea came rolling in at both sides of the ship, constantly filling the decks with water; as for myself, if the best dressed victuals had been placed before me, I could not have looked at it, being sadly sea-sick the whole time.

East Indiamen speaking, from Clipper Ship Era

During the gale, the captain lost three fine horses, and a great quantity of other live stock; the only apprehensions they had, were of the helm-ropes breaking, but a kind Providence took care of us.

The late gales appeared to be the last blast of the old year; for the first day of 1800 was ushered in by fine settled weather; that the new year might be propitious to the poor prisoners, the captain ordered the fetters to be taken off an additional number of the best behaved amongst them, promising the rest, that if their conduct merited well, as soon as land was seen on the coast of New Holland, every prisoner should then be released from his irons, but that all depended upon a proper subordinate behaviour. Several of them had been relieved from the weight of fetters shortly after we left Ireland, and continued so all the voyage, having conducted themselves with every propriety. It was fortunate both for themselves and us, that there were amongst them men of education and sense; who doubtless contributed to restrain the others from evil and violence; one [Rev. James Dixon] was said to be a Roman-Catholic clergyman, and we trusted that his influence was beneficial.

After setting things a little to rights, from the derangement caused by the late gales; being at sea, one evening the captain said, he should next day have some of his stores up which the shipped waves had reached to dry. I seldom interfered or spoke on such a subject; but, in this instance, could not help observing, that if they intended drying any thing tomorrow, they would most likely be disappointed, for it would be wet, telling them I judged from my barometer, which was the little turtle, which had kept at the bottom of the tumbler all the evening.

They laughed at my remarks; but so it turned out; as, for several days after, we had many squalls of wind and much rain. I was hence frequently asked about the weather, Whether it would be rain, or sunshine? This living barometer of mine did not always foretell the changes in the atmosphere exactly; but three times out of five it did so, when enquiry was made, but observing it: sometimes it happened never to be thought of, for days together; but it always had a few flies thrown in daily by one of the servants, for that was a kind of stock we had a most abundant supply of.

We were now in the neighbourhood of the islands called Amsterdam and St. Paul; but as the weather was unsettled, with squalls and rain, it was judged proper to pass to the south of them.

The gunner of our ship had been formerly in an Indiaman which called at these islands, where they found some men that had been left there by an American, to procure seal-skins. These men had been upon the islands five months, and had procured many skins; they had no desire to leave the place, saying they knew their own ship would call for them. In narrating their local adventures, they informed the Indiaman alluded to, that at first they had been much alarmed, supposing the place was haunted, hearing strange rumbling noises, but afterwards discovered it was occasioned by earthquakes, to which, from their frequency, they had become accustomed.

Island of St Paul, from Pinkerton's Travels *(1812)*

There are upon Amsterdam hot springs, running into a pond, in which these men cooked the eggs of the wild sea birds which they caught. The Indiaman gave them two bags of biscuits, a little spirits, some shoes, and other little necessaries; these recluses appeared reconciled to their situation, and were left as they wished.

Having still strong winds from the western quarter, the ship went on at a great rate each day, until we drew near Van Dieman's Land; but it so happened that the ship had gone upwards of 300 miles farther than the log measured, since leaving the Cape, which was found out by the moon's distance from the sun and stars.

This frequently caused altercations between the chief and second mates; the latter, who had been always employed in the West India trade, knew nothing of finding the ship's place by observation, and always treated such science as erroneous. It happened one night, that the captain and chief mate got what they called good sights of the moon and some stars; and their first calculation was confirmed next day by observing the sun and moon's distance, which enabled them to know the exact position of the ship: in consequence of which the chief mate, after dinner, asked the captain if they should prepare the anchors and cables, as it was expected the land would be seen next day.

The captain answered yes; but the second mate was so positive that his own reckoning was right, that he offered to lay any wager that the ship was 400 miles farther from the land than they supposed. The captain had often, on the voyage, tried to persuade him to have confidence in the lunar observations, but to no purpose. The anchors were, however, got ready, and people looking out from the masts' heads, before night, for the land; at the same time the ship was put under a reduced sail during the night.

After dark, we were surprised to see many luminous blazes or flashes in the water, a little under the surface, near the ship; it was not fish, for when the flash was emitted, it appeared stationary for a few seconds, and then disappeared. This was not confined to a single object, as at times eight or ten corruscations were seen in different directions at the same instant. As the substance causing these appearances was not seen, it cannot be farther described; they were termed in the logbook, Van Dieman's Water Lanthorns, from our vicinity to the land of that name; for next morning, 23d [January] at daylight, it was descried, very much to the disappointment of Mr. Macdonald, who said, it must be some new discovery, and not New Holland.

However he afterwards was convinced; for the captain observed in a *jocular* manner, that if it was the southern extremity of New Holland, a ship would very soon be discovered; for the last time he passed this place one was stationary off the south cape; he had scarcely done speaking, when the men on the yards, letting reefs out of the sails, called out that they saw a ship on the bow. The captain replied, "Very well;" but told Mr. Muirhead, what was taken for a ship, was only a perpendicular rock, and had been called the Eddystone, by Captain Cook, from its likeness to the lighthouse of that name in the British Channel.

As all sails were set, we soon approached the land, and passed a small island, which they called Swilly; it was covered with sea birds, particularly the *gannet*. As we drew near, each one on board was straining his eyes to behold new wonders on this strange land; some of the prisoners thought they were to be sent on shore, until convinced, that the ship was near 1000 miles from Port Jackson. Agreeable to promise, every man was now let out of irons, but carefully shut up at night, as usual, and only a certain number permitted upon deck, in their turn, in the course of the day.

Sydney Cove, from Historical Records of New South Wales

Three

New South Wales and Norfolk Island : January to May 1800

Sir Joseph Banks was not just behind the transfer of landscapes from one country to another—he was behind the mass relocation of people, too. In 1779, eight years after his return from the voyage of the *Endeavour,* he celebrated his first year as President of the Royal Society by proposing that the current glut of convicts should be sent to Botany Bay. There were plenty of recommendations for New South Wales, or so he claimed in a talk he gave to a parliamentary committee. Dredging up memories of botanizing there in May 1770, he assured them that there were no dangerous animals, that the natives were docile, the soil was fertile, and there was plenty of fish, grass, and fresh water.

The government really liked the idea. Men, women, and children were being sentenced in great numbers, often for offences as trivial as the theft of short lengths of cloth, petty crime having become a way of life for families who had been forced off farms and into the teeming cities. The problem was what to do with them. Transportation to the Americas was not possible any more, America having won its independence, and the few prisons had become so impossibly overcrowded that convicts were being herded into derelict ships that lay mouldering in the mud of the Thames. Accordingly, it was easily seen that sending the convicts to the other side of the world was an excellent way of clearing out the gaols, while the remoteness of the banishment would be a deterrent to future crime.

Sir Joseph's proposal took quite a while to work up through the corridors of power, however, and it was not until August 1786 that the Admiralty was ordered to organize a convoy of suitable convict ships, with a flagship, a storeship, and an escort. Captain Arthur Phillip (a personal friend of Banks) was put in charge, and the little fleet sailed out of Portsmouth on May 13, 1787. After a relatively uneventful voyage, the ships arrived at Botany Bay in January 1788—to find that Banks had been dangerously over-optimistic. The anchorage was too shallow for the ships to lie safely, and the land was too boggy to set up camp. A hasty reconnoitre was made for a better ground, and the fleet shifted to Port Jackson, ten miles further up the coast.

But, while the harbour there was magnificent, possibly the best in the world, the situation was not a huge improvement. The people refused to forage, as no one knew which native plants were edible and which were poisonous, so the scurvy that had begun at sea became rampant on land. Because the whole company was reliant on the provisions the fleet had carried, supplies became so low that livestock meant to breed for future herds had to be slaughtered for food. The storeship *Guardian*, which had been sent out from England with life-saving supplies, wrecked on an iceberg, and in 1790 the settlement's one large ship, HMS *Sirius*, also foundered.

That same year the Second Fleet arrived—with over seven hundred more mouths to feed, and with most of the prisoners in an appalling state of health, the system having been abused by the private contractors. Despite these immense difficulties and almost total isolation, Governor Arthur Phillip prevailed. There were still times when everyone was on short rations, but in 1792, when failing health forced him to leave for England, he was able to hand over a reasonably viable settlement to the lieutenant-governor, Major Francis Grose, who took charge until Phillip's successor, Captain John Hunter, arrived in 1795.

For Hunter, accepting the governorship must have been an act of courage, because he had unpleasant memories of the penal settlement. He had arrived in New South Wales with the First Fleet as captain of HMS *Sirius*, and within months had been sent to the Cape of Good Hope for desperately needed supplies, an expedition that involved a voyage around the world. Sent out a second time, he had had the misfortune of losing the *Sirius* on a reef at Norfolk Island.

Rescue eleven months later had been followed by a nightmare voyage back to England on the chartered *Waaksamheyd,* and then he had undergone the humiliating ritual of a court martial for the loss of his ship.

However, when compared to the administrative problems that awaited him in Sydney, all of this seemed relatively trivial.

The soldiers of the New South Wales Corps had been troublesome from the moment the company was formed, back in 1789. As service in the remote colony was considered an undeserved life sentence, the roster had been filled out with parolees from military prisons, officers on half pay, and men with no prospects at home. The post, however, had turned out to be very much more rewarding than anticipated. Once Phillip (a naval officer) was gone, Major Grose altered the arrangement to the advantage of the military. Not only did the soldiers get better rations than the convicts, but they were able to apply for 25-acre grants of land. With these free farms came convict labourers who were clothed and provisioned at the public expense, and the right to sell produce to the government store.

The profits that could be made were irresistible. While this was an age where anything to do with trade was considered beneath the notice of the lofty, many army officers became as venal as the despised shopkeepers back in Wapping. Because coinage was scarce, the common currency became spirits, or "rum," and the New South Wales Corps officers turned this to their advantage by buying up all the barrels of spirits as they arrived, thus cornering the market. When supplies of rum became low, ships were chartered to fetch more from Bengal, where arrack could be bought for just eight shillings a gallon. Once landed in Sydney, each gallon of the liquor would fetch as much as three pounds sterling, or its equivalent in labour or goods. Another way of bending the rules was to buy Spanish prizes that had been captured by London whalers off the coast of Peru, and bring them in with their holds packed with barrels of aguardiente and wine. With good reason, the New South Wales detachment became known as the "Rum Corps."

The self-appointed leader in this highly illegal business was Lieutenant John Macarthur, an ambitious entrepreneur who took full advantage of his friendship with the easygoing and amenable Major Grose. With his wife, Elizabeth, Macarthur established the leading station up the Parramatta River, starting out with a 100-acre grant of some of the best land available, and turning it into a profitable stud farm.

The departure of Grose in December 1794 made little difference, because the major's successor, William Paterson, proved to be equally tolerant of the military regime. An easygoing man who was a keen amateur botanist, Paterson was more interested in corresponding with his friend, Sir Joseph Banks, than in stemming the entrepreneurial ambitions of his officers. This paid off handsomely when Paterson returned to England, where he advised Banks about which plants should be sent out to the colony. First, he was elected a fellow of the Royal Society, and then, in 1799, he was sent back to assist John Hunter.

Rumours had been sifting back to London about the "sullied" reputation of the British army officers in New South Wales, and it was wrongly supposed in the corridors of power that William Paterson, being honest and reliable, could mend matters there. The problem was just not the blatant opportunism, but infighting among the officers, too, particularly between the navy men and the soldiers. Hunter had done his utmost to take the control out of the hands of the military, and restore it to the civil administration, but Macarthur had proved to be a ruthless enemy. Not only did he forward a barrage of signed complaints and criticisms to the secretary of state and the military commander-in-chief, but anonymous libels were sent at the same time, charging Hunter with the very excesses that the embattled governor was trying to curb. Even before Paterson arrived, the decision had been made to replace John Hunter with Philip Gidley King, the man who had established the small sister settlement on Norfolk Island.

King's commission as Governor of New South Wales was originally dated May 1798. There was a long delay, as the *Porpoise,* which was specially built for the colonial service, proved to be so utterly unseaworthy that she had to be condemned. Accordingly, even though he tried to speed up his return by sailing to Port Jackson on a whaleship (rather fittingly called *Speedy*), King did not step on shore until April 13, 1800—to find that Hunter was strangely reluctant to hand over the reins. John Hunter insisted that he would not step down until he was ready to leave, and, as he refused to sail on the *Friendship,* which had arrived in the meantime, this meant that he reckoned he should stay in control until the new colonial ship *Buffalo,* which was currently at the Cape of Good Hope, had returned to Port Jackson.

Why he declined to take passage on the *Friendship* is a mystery. Certainly, he trusted Reid, as he gave him copies of important despatches to deliver in London, and according to Eleanor's account, they were good friends. It may have been because Hunter's nephew, Captain William Kent, was in command of the *Buffalo.* Perhaps Hunter did not want to admit that Macarthur had won their private battle. Whatever the reason, it did not augur well for amicable relations between the outgoing governor and the man who had come to succeed him—as Eleanor quickly noticed.

Captain Reid had been in Sydney Town before, as first mate of the *Marquis Cornwallis,* but this time the experience was quite different. Not only did he have a wife, but his responsibilities were greater. Once the convicts were discharged, and all the paperwork involved complete, he had to sell the freight the Mangles brothers had sent out, along with what was left of his own adventure after the sales he had made at Cape Town and St Helena.

According to the manifest entered at Port Jackson, it was a very mixed cargo, including 35 barrels of oil, 100 kegs of paint, "1 case Hatts," 367 seal skins, a trunk of books, six casks of fishing tackle, six cases of window glass, two boxes of ladies' dresses, one trunk of men's clothing, and four trunks of haberdashery. There were three cases of looking glasses, seven cases of pictures, varnish, mustard, stationery, boots and shoes and carpenters' tools, four horses, eight cows, ten ewes, 1,000 gallons of spirits, and 480 gallons of wine. This last was probably what he had invested in at the little Constantia vineyard, while it is likely that the animals had been pre-ordered by landowning New South Wales Corps officers. Like the trade in rum and the private chartering of ships, investing in livestock was against Company rules, but the profit was irresistible: one of the horses Reid carried from Cape Town was most probably Washington, a "remarkable fine stallion" thoroughbred that was valued by its importer, John Macarthur, at £650.

While all of these goods would have been easily disposed of, being paid was much more difficult. Reid had to accept bills on London bankers and goldsmiths—which meant that he was forced to trust men who were "ticket of leave" men, or even still serving out their sentences. Despite all his care, both he and his first mate, Mr Muirhead, were soundly cheated by George Crossley, a lawyer who had been transported for perjury, debt, and forging a will, and who was now running a trading store. The Mangles brothers' loss was £1886 sterling on three bills of exchange—a large sum, particularly considering that the chances of getting it back were so small—while Mr Muirhead said goodbye to about £400. Though Crossley was tried and convicted, he was allowed to continue trading, and was pardoned the following year—a surprisingly common story in the saga of the penal settlement.

On his previous visit, Hugh Reid spent his leisure hours in a building near the barracks that was maintained as an informal coffee house, where ships' officers gathered to drink and gossip, and billiards could be played. Eleanor, obviously, could not set foot inside such a place, but finding alternative entertainment was not easy, Sydney being such a male-dominated town. Apart from touring the countryside, visiting or receiving visitors was the only social activity for women. The local houses were very small, too, meaning that there was no family with the space to take in lodgers, as there had been in St Helena and Cape Town. Accordingly, Eleanor had to live on board the anchored *Friendship*—which, as it happens, was no hardship at all. Once the front part of the poop—the cuddy—had been cleared out and furnished with a long dining table and chairs, occasional tables and lounges, her shipboard parlour was much more luxurious than any equivalent room on shore. It is certain, for instance, that none of the shore wives could have seated thirty-eight guests for dinner, as Eleanor did. On the other hand, they did not have Eleanor's problem of juggling the guest list so that mortal enemies were not eating at the same table.

Captain Reid had to take his own social precautions. Though he might sell thoroughbred horses, wine and spirits to John Macarthur, it must not go on record that he had entertained him on board, as the New South Wales

Corps officer was *persona non grata* with the Honourable East India Company. The HEIC had a Royal Charter, which conferred on the Company the exclusive right to control all trade to and from the colony, and yet Macarthur, in a consortium with other New South Wales Corps officers, had chartered cargoes and imported goods. He was the head of "the serpent that we are nursing at Botany Bay," as Sir Francis Baring, who was one of the Company directors, spluttered. This was a pity for Eleanor, as she would have had a great deal in common with Elizabeth Macarthur, who was stylish, elegant, well-educated and strong-minded, but John Macarthur's actions made it impossible to be seen with her socially.

Eleanor's presence did bring some benefits for Hugh. Without her, he would never have been invited to a social occasion at Government House, though of course he would go there on business. Because East Indiamen captains were merchant adventurers as well as master mariners, they were considered to be common traders—no matter how rich an East Indies commander might become, he was not acceptable in higher social circles until he could afford to buy a country estate and go in for politics. But, because Eleanor was there, Captain Reid was a welcome guest in the drawing room of Government House.

Though Governor John Hunter was a lifelong bachelor, he did have a hostess to preside in his parlour and at his dining table. This was the amiable Eliza Kent, wife of his nephew, Captain William Kent, who was currently away, in command of the colonial ship *Buffalo*. Eliza, even though she had small children, including a baby boy born the previous year, was pleased to welcome Mrs Reid to tea, where she introduced her to respectable ladies—such as

Government House, Sydney, from Naval Pioneers

Louisa Abbott, whose husband, Captain Edward Abbott, was an engineer with the sense not to involve himself in the rum trade. Another was Mary Johnson, wife of the chaplain of the settlement, Reverend Richard Johnson.

Obviously, Elizabeth Macarthur would not be included in any of Eliza Kent's parties. Nor would Elizabeth Paterson. Not only was Mrs Paterson one of Elizabeth Macarthur's close friends, but William Paterson had been writing a stream of letters to Sir Joseph Banks that were very critical of Governor Hunter, the man he was supposed to be helping. Eleanor Reid would have to meet Elizabeth Paterson in different rooms and on different occasions, finding her a comfortable little Scotch lady who was devoted to her husband, and also a great gossip—it would be from her that Eleanor learned about the state of social strife that ruled here. And, after the new governor, Philip Gidley King, arrived, Eleanor would meet King's sweet-natured wife, Anna, at the Patersons' place, though not at Hunter's Government House.

For Hugh and Eleanor Reid, there was not just the confused social situation to decipher, but the added complication that the convicts the *Friendship* brought to Port Jackson were strangely unwelcome. The colony was built on brawn, most of the convicts being used as labourers, and the Irishmen the *Friendship* landed were unlikely to provide the muscle that was needed. Not only were a few very old, but many were well educated professionals. And, as the secretary and day-to-day chronicler of the Colony, David Collins, remarked, it was morally difficult to set an apothecary, a lawyer, or a man of the cloth to menial labour, no matter what his crime had been—

> *On the 16th, the "Friendship" transport arrived from Ireland with convicts, who came in good health; notwithstanding which, they were not calculated to be of much advantage to the settlement; but little addition being gained by their arrival to the public strength. Several of them had been bred up in the habits of genteel life, or to professions in which they were unaccustomed to hard labour: such must become a dead weight upon the provision store; for, notwithstanding the abhorrence which must have been felt for their crimes, yet it was impossible to divest the mind of the common feelings of humanity, so far as to send a physician, the once-respectable sheriff of a county, a Roman Catholic priest, or a protestant clergyman and his family, to the grubbing hoe, or the timber carriage.*

As well as this, Irishmen were thought to be dangerous, and the literate ones particularly so. Up until the late 1790s, the few convicts who were educated professionals were easily absorbed, being useful as clerks and administrative assistants. However, it was considered impossible to trust the well-educated Irishmen with clerical positions—or even out in the open countryside. This turned out to be at least partly justified, as many were still imbued with revolutionary fervour, and ready to resume guerrilla warfare. Within months of their arrival, uprisings and rebellions were planned—by men who had come on the *Friendship*, as well as those who had arrived on the *Minerva* and the *Marquis Cornwallis* earlier. Patrick Galvin, who had been a captain with the United Irishmen forces, is an instance. He was flogged and sent to Norfolk Island for conspiracy, and was one of those who tried to pirate the brig *Harrington* in 1807.

Yet, as Eleanor's journal demonstrates, all the men had been carried to Port Jackson with no trouble at all.

Back on February 15, 1799, while the *Friendship* was still fitting out, John and James Mangles had written to their agent, James Duncan of Great Tower Hill, Blackheath, asking for twenty-five extra seamen to be shipped on the same terms as the regular crew—"As we are very anxious to give Capt Reid of our Ship Friendship all the protection possible to secure the Conveyance of the Convicts to Port Jackson, & thinking the choice of the guard essentially necessary for that purpose."

Duncan passed on the plea to the Duke of Portland, but it was impossible for the Home Secretary to grant the request. Not only did the East India Company have strict rules about the numbers of seamen on their ships, but Royal Navy captains were so desperate to fill out their crewlists that press gangs were ranging hotly in the docklands of London. Yet, because of his unpleasant experience on the *Marquis Cornwallis*, Captain Reid did not want to carry soldiers.

Eventually, an unusual remedy was found— 25 Lascars were sent on board, with a *serang,* or native officer, in charge. This was probably organised by Duncan in his capacity as a representative of the East India Company, though it was against Company rules. Indeed, it would have been easy, because shipping twenty-five Lascars on the outward-bound *Friendship* would have suited the Company very well indeed.

Lascars were Indian seamen who had been recruited in Bombay, Madras and Calcutta. Shipping them was usual resort for the homeward voyages, as the East Indiamen lost great numbers of men in the Indies—not just to death and desertion, but to the press gangs, too. So many seamen ran away or died of disease in the Bay of Bengal that navy officers on the East Indies station were even more rapacious than those in England, raiding the East Indies merchant ships while they were still dropping anchor. With their crews so drastically reduced, it was not possible for the captains of East Indiamen to weigh the anchor again unless more men were shipped, but the only men available were locals. The Indians might be fishermen who had never have left the Bay of Bengal before, but they learned their jobs well enough to get the ship home.

The problem, for them, was that England was not their home. Because, according to the Company's own rules, they could not be shipped as crew for the outward voyage, they were stranded in London, lodged in boarding houses that were supposed to be supervised by East India Company officials, but were often sinks of poverty and vice. It was bad publicity, and a blot on the HEIC image, and so the opportunity of getting some of them back to India was very welcome indeed.

It could have worked out badly. The Lascars did not have much English, and Gaelic was the first language of most, if not all, of the prisoners. A majority of the convicts were excitable rebels, while others were habitual criminals, and the situation could easily have boiled over. The *Luz St Ann,* which the *Friendship* had left behind at Cork, being very slow loading, was seized by the Irish convicts on July 29, while on her westing to Rio. Captain Stewart, his mate and the gunner had gone down to the orlop to supervise the cleaning and fumigation of the prison, and were surprised and confined. Their shouts for help acted as a signal to the convicts who were exercising on deck; as one, they rushed the guards. It was only because of the swift, decisive action of the ship's own crew that the uprising was quelled.

There was no such trouble on the *Friendship*. As Eleanor described, the prisoners were allowed to take the air on deck, watch and watch about, and those who had wine and other little luxuries were given access to them, yet no one took advantage. There is no record of punishment, and certainly no flogging. Like Captain Thomas Larkin of the *Warren Hastings,* nine years later, who objected when the soldiers he was carrying were routinely flogged by their officers, Hugh Reid did not like to see his quarterdeck turned into a slaughter house.

And his moderate attitude worked—when Reid was in Calcutta later that year, he met an old friend, Captain Robert William Eastwick, who was so intrigued when he heard that Reid had delivered convicts to Port Jackson on the way to Bengal that he wrote about it in his memoirs. His friend "had been chartered to convey these United

Irishmen (as they called themselves) to Botany Bay from Waterford, and declared that their demeanour on board had been very much to their credit, that during the whole passage he had no occasion to punish any one."

In a word, the Irish prisoners had behaved like gentlemen. This was a credit not just to the Irishmen themselves, but to the Lascars who looked after them. And perhaps the presence of Captain Reid's sympathetic, independent and strong-minded wife made a difference, too.

Which is where Eleanor's journal picks up again. It is February 1800, and the *Friendship* is on the way to Port Jackson with the prisoners still on board.

Notwithstanding our ship was reckoned a dull sailer, we had come upwards of three degrees per day, upon an average, since leaving the Cape, being 128 degrees of longitude in thirty-three days. In consequence of the wind, we could not come very near the shore the first day, but by the telescope we could see very tall trees rising upon the basis of the hills, and extending to the summits; some smoke was also observed in a small bay, which left no doubt of human beings inhabiting that neighbourhood. Many whales, seals, and porpoises shewed themselves in the course of the day; but the majority on board were too much occupied with the shore to notice them; only as I had stationed myself at the gallery window, I could not help looking at these marine inhabitants sporting in their own element.

During the night we had squally and unsettled weather, which continued for some time, and deprived us for six days of again seeing the land. When in the latitude of 40 degrees south, on account of the great and rough sea which came from the west, minutes were entered in the log-book, recording that it was thought some strait opened in that direction. On the 10th land was seen to the west, but at too great a distance to make any observations; but during the night several fires were observed, apparently very near the beach, and next day we were gratified by sailing very near the shore, between Wilson's Promontory and Cape How, where every part, as well hill as valley, appeared in verdure, with lofty trees interspersed, and as regular did these appear in some places, as if they had been planted by the hand of man.

All the telescopes were in requisition, and a good look-out kept, to discover if any natives were visible, but none could be seen; neither any smoke this day. From the favourable state of the wind, it was expected we should reach our port of destination in a few days. That every thing might be settled with the prisoners, prior to their disembarking, on the 11th they were called, one by one, to know how much money they had given to the chief mate, when their clothing was changed, in Ireland. Some little advances had been made to them while at the Cape, for fruit &c. All was right in their money account, and each man furnished with the amount he should receive when he quitted the ship. There were about thirty of these poor men who could not speak English.

On the 14th, we passed a high promontory, which is called Cape Dromedary, from its resemblance to that animal when viewed in a particular direction. All the hills, as far as the eye could reach, were covered with trees; some parts of the shore, next the sea, were bold and rocky, but no apparent danger for a ship, unless very near the land. At night fires were frequently seen near the sea, and smoke in the day, but no natives could be distinguished.

On the 15th, in the evening, we saw Cape Banks and Point Solander, which is very near the entrance of Botany Bay, which place Captain Cook first visited, and spoke so favourably of for a settlement; but it was found not to answer, for when Governor Phillip first came to form a colony (which is just twelve years ago) he found Port Jackson a much better seat for one in all respects. Some of the men were much surprised that we did not put into Botany Bay, as they had understood they were to be landed there, until convinced to the contrary.

All was anxiety in the evening of the 16th, and every thing prepared to enter the harbour. About twelve at night the ship was off the north and south heads, which form the entrance of the of the port, where we lay-to until morning. At length daylight appeared, and the wind being fair, we boldly entered the harbour; the captain being a good pilot, needed no other guide; in less than a quarter of an hour after, the ship (to use the sea-phrase) was completely land-locked.

We passed a dangerous rock (mid channel) called the Sow and Pigs; and saw a fine looking house, on our left, belonging to a Mr. Palmer, with several detached buildings, which gave it the appearance of an English farm. We also passed Garden Island, on the left, which had a fertile, luxuriant appearance, with a respectable looking house upon it. As we approached, we passed a barren rock, on the right, which is named Pinch-Gut island. This is small, and the most barren spot we had seen; it had a gibbet upon it, where a culprit had been executed for murder.

The surrounding country afforded a pleasant range of scenery, being diversified with hill and dale, with many inlets, forming little coves or bays. As we passed up towards Bennilong Point, the town of Sidney burst upon our sight. The ship anchored in the cove, about seven in the morning, and saluted the Governor with nine guns, which was the first intimation the settlement had of our arrival. Where we anchored, the distance of the shore on either side did not exceed fifty yards, which made it appear as if we were in a dock.

The Governor's house, on the left, towards the head of the cove, and the Lieutenant-governor's house on the right, with the barracks, and many other detached buildings, made the town altogether surpass our expectation. We found lying at this place the ship *Albion,* Captain Eber Bunker; the ship *Walker,* Captain John Nicholl; the *Betsey,* Captain D. Clark, all South seamen. The latter ship had come in with a Spanish prize, which she had captured near Lima, in South America. The *Minerva,* who sailed with us from Cork, had left this place for India three days prior to our arrival.

As soon as our ship was moored, the captain went on shore, to wait upon Governor Hunter, to whom he was known, from having been at this port as chief mate of the *Marquis Cornwallis,* in 1795. He also waited upon the Lieutenant-Governor, Colonel Patterson. The men could not be disembarked for three days, which time it would take to prepare accommodations for them: this was of little consequence, as they were healthy, and had plenty of water and provisions on board.

Sydney Cove, 1824

The next day we had an invitation to dine at the Government house, where we met an agreeable family party, comprising Mrs. Kent, niece to the Governor, whom I found friendly and well informed; also the Rev. Mr. Richard Johnson and lady; Captain and Mrs. Edward Abbott and Major George Johnston. After spending a pleasant day, we returned on board in the evening; and I must confess, that I thought our own apartments on board more comfortable and much safer than theirs on shore.

Next day we were invited to meet a large party at Colonel Paterson's, and were treated in a friendly and polite manner by himself and lady, from whom I received much information respecting this infant Colony; but was sorry to learn there was much party-spirit, with jarring and bickering among the free members of this small community, which was a bar to friendly intercourse between the adherents of the rival parties.

On the 21st, the prisoners were disembarked. Many of them left the ship with tears, and each boat-load cheered as they put off, which was rather a novel sight to many on shore, who had received harsh treatment on their passage out. The captain received a letter from the Governor, expressing his thanks and approbation for the kind treatment and good management during the passage, saying that such conduct would not be forgot in the dispatches to the Lords Commissioners of the Admiralty.

The captain spoke particularly to the Governor in respect of those prisoners who had seen better days, and who had conducted themselves so well on the voyage; he also made known the conduct of Mr. MacCullam, who had assisted the surgeon; from which favourable report he was immediately appointed to officiate as an assistant in a medical department, at an out-settlement called Town Gabby [Toongabbie, Parramatta], with a salary of fifty pounds per annum, and a free house.

As we were now left to ourselves, all prison-doors, bulk-heads, and armed gratings were taken down, after which the ship did not appear like the same.

Landing of the convicts, from Tench (1789)

We were now visited in return, on board, by the ladies and gentlemen of the settlement, and had many social, pleasant parties. It was arranged a few days after our arrival, that we should live entirely on board; indeed several ladies said they thought the accommodation which we had on board better than we could have on shore, especially as we had our servants and comforts about us. We judged this the best mode, as the access to and from the ship to the shore was safe and easy.

One Tuesday evening, the governor and his niece, Mrs. Kent, came on board to take tea in a friendly way; when he informed us that next day he had engaged a few friends to dine with him upon fish, it being [Ash] Wednesday; and if they were good Christians, they would be satisfied with it, for he had no doubt but a sufficiency would be procured with the sein; it all depended upon luck, and those who had any doubts would take something else, as a stand-by. The dinner was to be prepared down the harbour, near the entrance, under a large tree, with a rough table, and seats already fixed there for such parties.

We were included in this proposed expedition, and willingly accepted the invitation. On the morrow our friends, the governor and Mrs. Kent, called for me, and we proceeded down the harbour. I was introduced to a native chief, named Benallong [Bennelong]; his countenance and figure were most repulsive: his figure resembled a baboon more than one of the human species. He had been taken to England by Governor Phillip, and brought back by Governor Hunter; so that he had been a considerable time in civilized society, including the passage to Europe, the time he staid in England, and his last embarkation. Nevertheless by all this he had not profited, but appeared as much a savage as any of his countrymen that I saw.

We arrived about one o'clock at our station, and met a party of thirteen, including ourselves. The seamen went directly to work with the nets, and repeatedly drew them up empty; on which the governor desired them to try a lucky spot, where they before had met with success, and this time were not disappointed, for they got a draught of fine fish, which would have served fifty persons. They consisted of mullet, snappers, and several other kind of fish whose names I do not recollect.

Shortly after my husband joined us with some bread, cheese, bottled porter, and other viands. The cooks began their operations; and after half an hour's walk, we returned to an excellent dinner. The treat, being seasoned with the entertaining conversation rich in numerous anecdotes of our worthy host, made the day pass pleasantly. Several of the natives hovered about, but were not allowed to join our party without being properly clothed. This Bennilong was commissioned to tell them; and as clothing had been distributed to them a short time before, no excuse would do; however, plenty of fish ready cooked and others from the surplus quantity, were left for them on purpose. In the evening we returned to the anchorage, much gratified with the day's excursion.

I had often seen the natives at a distance paddling their little canoes down the cove, but none of them met my near view until the following incident. One forenoon I was rather surprised at hearing a strange humming noise under the cabin window; looking out I was more so, at beholding one of their canoes tied with a string to our rudder chains, with a native woman, and young infant in her lap. The canoe was nothing more than the bark of a tree, about seven or eight feet long by two feet wide, tied together at each end in a rough puckered manner.

The embers of some half-burnt wood were smoking before her as she sat cross-legged at her employment; she had a fishing-line in each hand over the side of her little boat, and was humming her wild notes, either to entice the fish or to quiet the infant. I saw her draw up a small fish with one of the lines; she immediately applied her teeth to the neck of it, which instantly ceased struggling. Taking it off the hook, she put it upon the embers, and blew them into a flame; before it was warm through she began to eat it, apparently with great relish; after which, she gave her child the breast, and continued her labours.

I threw down some biscuit, which she also eat; I then gave her a handkerchief, and some linen to cover her, which she took, and carelessly put on one side, repeating some jargon, which I did not understand. This poor creature might be about twenty-eight years of age, but it was difficult to judge from the sooty appearance of her skin; the child's appearance was about three months. The woman wore her hair matted and dirty; her features had been cast in the plainest of nature's moulds.

She afterwards became a frequent visitor astern of the ship, and never went away empty-handed; but I never saw the clothing upon her which had been given. She never ventured on board, although frequently entreated to come. She managed her canoe with great dexterity; with a paddle in each hand, about eighteen inches long, she could turn it in all directions, and make it go as fast as our boats with two men rowing in them. The canoe is so light, that when she came to the shore she pulled it up with the greatest ease a considerable way from the water. After she had landed, I frequently saw some of the native men come to share her little stock of fish, biscuits, and other acquisitions of industry and fortune.

The oysters are so plentiful here, that two boys sent from the ship in the course of an hour could bring on board several buckets full. They were about the size of our Melton, or Colchester oysters, of a delicious flavour; the beards of them, with a little of the oyster attached, made an excellent bait for fish.

One afternoon I was so fortunate in angling from the cabin windows, that, strange as it may appear, I caught as many fish as not only supplied the cabin-table, but furnished the whole crew with a meal next day. They were called snappers, and weighed from two and a half to three pounds each; so keen were they after the bait that evening, that the line was no sooner thrown out than they bit immediately. We never wanted fine fish while we remained here. The wallimy (otherwise called the light horseman, from the head resembling the cap of a trooper) is a most excellent fish for boiling, common specimens weighing from ten to fifteen pounds each.

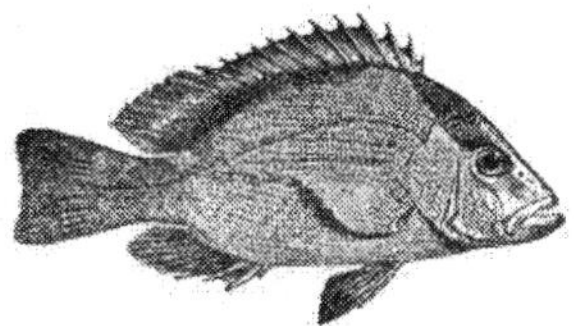

Fruit was in such abundance, particularly figs, that our people were almost surfeited with them. Baskets full of figs were frequently thrown into the pig-stye, in order that they might not be wasted. Culinary vegetables were also in great plenty. Butchers' meat, mutton, or pork, was high, at the rate of 2s.6d. per pound; as for beef, none was allowed to be killed. Poultry was dear in proportion. Butter, none in the market, except what came from Europe; it was a great treat when I had a little fresh butter presented to me by Mrs. Kent or Mrs. Patterson, made at their own dairies.

We frequently joined the oyster parties at different corners of the harbour, taking bottled porter, bread, and condiments with us. There was no ceremony observed on these occasions; the ladies were quite independent, each being furnished with a little hammer to knock off the upper shell; the oyster was then easily taken out with a small knife; after which, we regaled ourselves with bottled porter, sitting upon the clean projecting rocks.

At one of these parties, Mrs. K.'s little daughter had sat down upon a stone among the bushes; she presented screamed out, saying she had been bit on the ancle by something that ran under the stone; upon turning over the stone, we discovered numbers of large centipedes running about in all directions. We killed many of these disgusting reptiles; one of them measured about eight inches in length. So tenacious are they of life, that one which had been cut in two made it difficult to distinguish which was the head, as each part crawled about equally nimble. Mr. Harris, surgeon, put both parts into a small box, saying they would unite again; but whether they did or not I never learnt. The child sustained no injury from the fright.

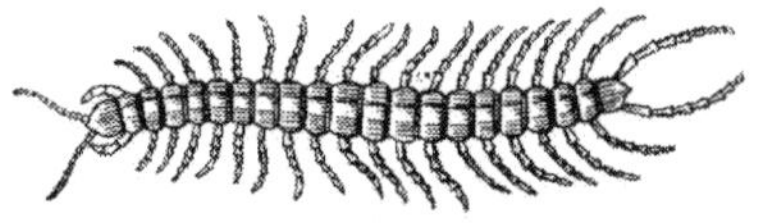

One morning early in March we had a visit from Capt. and Mrs. Abbott, with an invitation to take tea with them in the evening, in order to see a battle between two tribes of natives who had quarreled, and intended that their field of battle should be the Barrack-square, of which there was a good view of them from Capt. A.'s windows. I accompanied my husband to this gentleman's residence. At an early hour the natives began to assemble, and squatted themselves down, men, women, and children, as they arrived. I was anxious to observe all that passed, while I listened attentively to all the observations of the governor, who was present.

It was thought there would be no fight that evening, as the adverse tribe had not arrived; however, contrary to expectation, a single chief came in, advancing fearlessly, having a shield on one hand and a short club in the other. Presently the women and children got up, and retired to a little distance; when this single chieftain began an harangue, sometimes rising and sometimes lowering his voice; but he could not be understood by any of us. At length a native from the tribe who first arrived, advanced a certain interval towards him with a long spear, and a throwing-stick in his hand, and jabbered something for a few minutes; after which he appeared to be in great rage, throwing the spear with great force at the other, who caught it upon his shield, where it was perceived to break. This champion then stood for a time alone unsupported by any other; when presently another man advanced like the former, and after haranguing in the same manner, let fly his spear also, which rebounded, slanting off the shield.

This was done alternately by several men until dusk; at length two spears were thrown at him by different persons at the same time, one of which he warded off, but the other went through his thigh. One of the medical gentlemen present cut off the barbed part, and drew it back the same way it went in. Thus ended the combat, as the wounded man had given the offended party satisfaction. The quarrel was occasioned by one of their women having been taken away by this man. The governor observed, it was from motives of humanity he allowed them to settle disputes openly in this manner; as when left to themselves, natives of both sexes were sometimes found murdered in the woods, when the perpetrators could not be discovered. The wounded man was seen walking about next day, as if nothing had happened to him.

While we staid, two ships came into the harbour; one was the *Hunter*, Capt. Anderson, from Bengal [with 13,336 gallons of spirits and 727 gallons of wine]; the other a Spanish prize [*Euphemia*, Capt. Hugh Meehan, with 2,000 gallons of spirits and 17,337 gallons of wine], from the coast of Peru. Next day sailed the ship *Walker*, Capt. Nichol, to look after spermaceti whales.

The town of Sydney is small, with straggling detached wooden houses, extending about a mile north and south. The regular buildings then consisted only of the barracks, for the church had been maliciously set on fire sometime prior to our arrival; in consequence the chaplain, Mr. Johnson, was obliged to put up with a barn to perform divine service in; and we were informed that the clergyman at Paramatta, the Rev. Mr. Marsden, was as badly accommodated. One Sunday morning we heard an impressive and edifying discourse from a missionary minister, whom Mr. Johnson permitted to preach; he had just arrived in the Spanish prize from Otaheite, where she had touched, and was on his way by the first ship for England, for some more labourers in the same field. He said that their greatest enemies were some renegade Europeans, who had tried to thwart all their measures, but were ultimately frustrated.

Some bold, faithful pastors, disinterested men, sound in doctrine, and exemplary in conduct, might be of much use at this place. Religion seemed to be little regarded, particularly amongst persons in humble life. We observed evidences of much depravity; and some examples were obliged to be made, even amongst our own seamen, who had been enticed to pilfer from the ship. As to security on shore, locks and bars had no effect in keeping out the depredators there; for when they had a mind to plunder they opened a passage through the brick wall. Almost incredible were the stories we heard about the achievements of incorrigible thieves; and had we not been living on board, should most certainly have suffered much loss of property.

Early in April, we had an invitation from the governor to accompany him up to Rose Hill, at Parramatta, where he had built a new government house, and intended giving the first dinner in it to a few friends. On the morning fixed for this jaunt we prepared to start early, the distance being upwards of twenty miles. About six o'clock the governor's boat was alongside; but a painful duty now devolved upon our hospitable entertainer. Government stores had so often been robbed of late, that an example was determined upon. A convict had been detected in the act with some accomplices who had escaped. He was tried, found guilty, and sentenced to be hanged.

We saw all the preparation on shore, and the signal when the culprit was to be turned off was to be made from our ship, by hoisting a union jack at our flag staff. The fatal moment approached: the governor held his watch in his hand, and ordered the flag to be hoisted, but from some inattention to the person who had charge of it, the signal lines being jammed in the pully, the flag could only be hoisted half way up. The greatest agitation at this moment seized the governor, who running to the man, ordered it to be pulled down instantly. No time was lost in again preparing the tackle. At length the ensign run fluently to the top of the staff. It had been arranged, that should the provost martial see the jack hoisted half-mast high, the culprit was to be turned off; but if it rose to the top he was respited. It was at this critical moment the Governor's agitation was seen.

Mrs. K. and Mrs. A. were in the cabin with me. We were all very sad at the impending execution; but when our worthy and humane friend came below, and told us the man was respited, he had the most cordial thanks and smiles from us all; and I am sure he felt great satisfaction, in this act of mercy. We took an early breakfast on board, and set off quite happy.

To approach towards a just description of the beautiful varied scenery, of capes and coves, hills and valleys, as we passed up the river, is beyond my feeble abilities. The day was fine; we arrived at Paramatta about one, and walked up the town. The street is regular, and of a good width; the houses are detached, chiefly built of wood. As we walked up the street, a person came from his own door, and saluted the Governor. I was desired to notice him particularly, as it was the notorious George Barrington; he had lately been made high constable at this place and proved himself very useful in that station. He was tall and thin, of a gentlemanly appearance, but looked sickly.

I was rather disappointed with the new government house, finding it small, and much inferior to that at Sydney. As it was early in the day, an excursion was proposed to Town Gabley; and gigs were procured by the kindness of Capt. Piper, who commanded at this station. We had a picturesque ride over a pretty good road; we saw very little cultivated land, the soil being poor. They depend more upon the land about the Hawksbury river. Town Gabley had not more than forty houses when I saw it, and they were built of wood.

Parramatta, 1800

We saw here one of the individuals, MacCullam, who came out with us. He expressed his grateful thanks to my husband, for getting him the medical situation which he then filled; and that he was more comfortable than he had any reason to expect. We returned to Parramatta, dined, and proceeded by water to Sydney. We reached the ship at 10 at night, but the time appeared short; it was a fine moon-light evening, and several of the party enlivened us by singing some select songs, particularly Mrs. Kent who had a very fine voice; we had music, instrumental as well as vocal; a man in the boat played extremely well on the violin.

At the end of April a ship [whaleship *Speedy*] arrived from England, having on board Captain King, late governor of Norfolk Island, and his lady. Upon the resignation of the present governor, Capt. K. had been appointed his successor. We frequently met them at different parties. Mrs. K. appeared an amiable accomplished woman. Captain Kent also arrived in his Majesty's ship *Buffalo,* from the Cape of Good Hope; which additions to our confined circle of society made it more agreeable.

On the eve of our departure, my husband sent cards of invitation to the officers, civil and military, to partake of a farewell dinner on board the *Friendship*. Some individuals, either from party spirit or to avoid its collisions, politely declined the invitation; however, about thirty-eight ladies and gentlemen sat down to dinner. The Governor was saluted with nine guns when he came on board. A meeting of cordial friends brought with them the principles of harmony; and at the end of a pleasant evening, we parted with regret. Capt. K. afterwards gave a dinner to a smaller party, who could not conveniently join us on the former occasion.

During our stay, I was not idle in making a little collection of birds, quadrupeds, and other animals, and of the weapons and implements of the natives. The king bird and queen bird are of the parrot species, with a plumage of the most beautiful scarlet and green. The rose-bill parrots have their feathers still more variegated, combining a delicate yellow, purple, red, and green. Of the number collected, some were presents from friends, and some we purchased.

I had also a young docile kangaroo, received in barter for a bottle of spirits, which was preferred to one pound in money. It was rather larger than a hare, and grew fond of us; now sitting at our feet, and now with its nimble and active pranks, amused us by playing about the cabin; it ate fruit, vegetables, and bread from the hand, and answered to its name.

Early in May we prepared to leave this settlement, where we had been nearly three months; during which I have to acknowledge a constant display of friendship and kind attention. Although I never slept a single night out of the ship, still my intercourse with the ladies of the colony was as frequent as if I had resided on shore.

On the 4th of May the ship hauled out of Sydney Cove, and dropped down the harbour to a place called Bridley's Point, in readiness to proceed on our voyage to India. The captain was apprehensive that some of the convicts might be admitted clandestinely on board, and gave strict orders not to take any person from the settlement, as much trouble had been experienced on former voyages, by carrying on to Bengal some men who had been emancipated, the captain of the *Cornwallis* being obliged to give his bond to the government that they should not be left in Calcutta.

It was remarked, that no commander ever came here without being injured in some way or other; and so it proved with us. My husband had taken bills to the amount of two thousand pounds, from a person bearing the name of George Crosley, who by false vouchers made it appear that he was possessed of considerable property in England. This was a fiction; the bills were dishonoured, and none of the property ever recovered. Our chief mate, Mr. Muirhead, lost about £400 by the same individual.

On the 11th May we left the colony, intending to call at Norfolk Island for some additional stock; the inhabitants there giving live pigs for their weight in salt, of which we had a great quantity; they also exchange, on the same terms, Indian corn or maize. Next morning we were again out of sight of land, and circumscribed to ourselves, an isolated company on the mighty ocean. Our situation, however, was very different to what it had been on the voyage out. No poor prisoners to watch and secure.

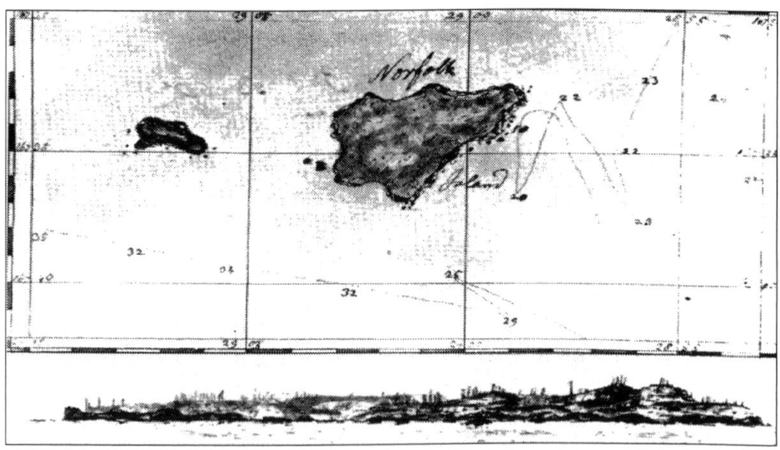

Map and drawing of Norfolk, Joseph Gilbert, 1774

On the morning of the 14th of May, we again saw land; it was called Howe's Island. We passed within a few miles of it; it seemed well wooded. Turtle abound here; also many species of fine fish. A high rock near it, called Ball's Pyramid, makes this land very conspicuous. On the eighth day, after leaving Port Jackson, we made Norfolk Island; passing between it and Phillip's Island, which is not above a league distant.

Prior to this, our boat had been sent on shore with the second mate. As the ship lay-to, drifting slowly through the channel, we had a fine view of the island: as we opened the valleys, many parts appeared under cultivation; fine streams of water were running down the rocks; the deep fall which terminates one large stream gives name to Cascade Bay. We saw a number of pigs upon Phillip's Island, which are the only inhabitants, unless when occasional visitors from the main island come to take them away, which is attended with no small trouble, so wild are these animals; they feed upon nutritive roots.

About noon the boat returned, with the commandant of the station, Capt. Braben [Brabyn]. A pleasant meeting took place between him and my husband; they had been shipmates in the *Cornwallis*. He dined with us, and gave orders for 20 pigs to be sent on board, with a proportion of Indian corn. We received while here upwards of fifty hogs, averaging in weight about 200 pounds each. This supply afforded our seamen a fresh meal three times a week until we arrived at Malacca: an equal weight of salt or maize was given in exchange.

Several persons entreated to be taken on board from this place, having been emancipated; but their wishes were not acceded to for the reasons given above. While laying-to, off Cascade Bay, some fine fish were caught. Towards five in the evening, our little business at this place being settled, we proceeded on our voyage. Next morning Mount Pitt, the part of the island which remained last in sight, was hid from our view by clouds.

Morning Dress for Feb.y 1799.

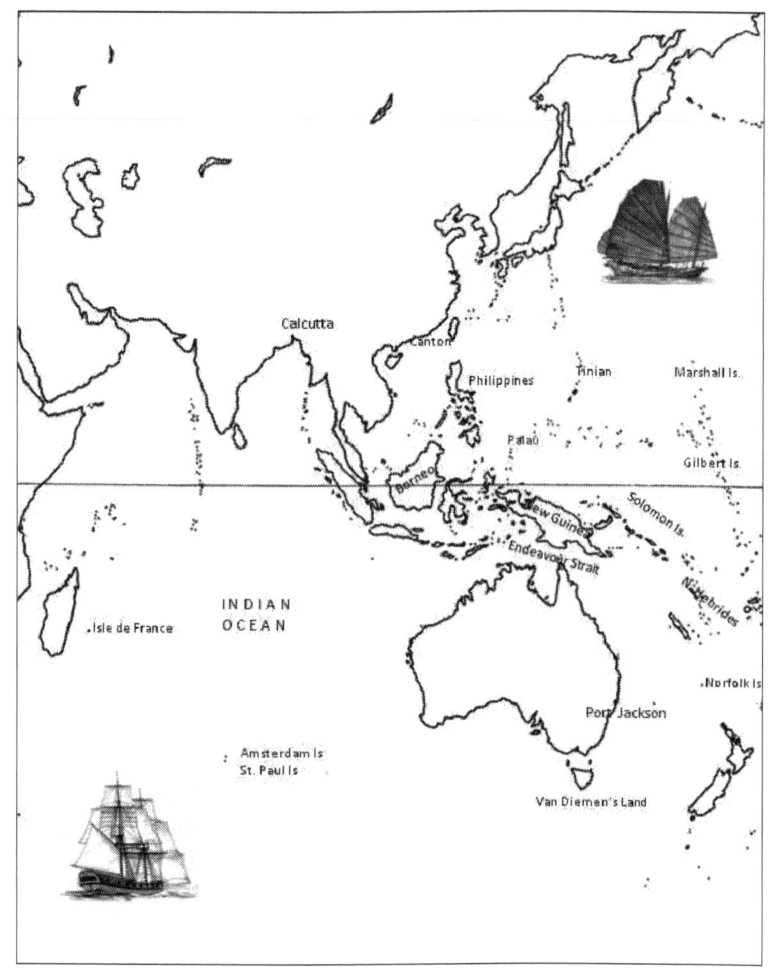

To the Spice Islands

Four

The Spice Islands : May to September 1800

Since May 5, 1788, when the First Fleet transport *Lady Penrhyn* weighed anchor for China, after discharging her convicts, captains like Hugh Reid had been steering from Port Jackson for the Orient. It was no small challenge in those early years—not only were the seas, reefs and islands largely uncharted, and the ships dependent on the seasonal winds, but the captains and their mates were usually navigating by the complicated process of working out longitude from lunars, this being the requirement of the Company, because the directors considered the new-fangled chronometers unreliable.

Consequently, unexpected routes had been taken, and unanticipated landfalls made. But, whatever the vagaries of the voyage, captains like Reid had given names to geographical features they fondly thought were newly discovered. They named promontories, islands, coves and coasts, mountains, harbours and reefs after politicians, dukes and duchesses, ship-owners and patrons; they named peaks after their ships, havens after places back home, and shoals after the seamen who had first sighted them. Captain John William Marshall of the transport *Scarborough,* which sailed from Port Jackson on May 6, 1788, named a string of equatorial isles, the Gilberts, after a fellow captain, Thomas Gilbert. The *Scarborough* was sailing in company with Gilbert's ship, the transport *Charlotte,* and the two captains were steering far to the northeast of Norfolk Island, in an effort to get a good slant to China. North of the newly named Gilbert Islands, they encountered yet another chain of atolls, which Gilbert named the Marshall Islands, presumably as a return compliment.

In August 1788, the *Charlotte* and the *Scarborough* dropped anchor at Tinian in the Marianas, an island that had been visited by another Englishman, Commodore George Anson, in May 1742. Anson had found Tinian by accident, and a very fortunate accident, too. When his expedition had set out from England in September 1740, with a mission to hunt and capture Spanish treasure galleons, he had commanded a fleet of eight ships. By the time Tinian was raised he was down to just his flagship, *Centurion*, and had lost over six hundred men from scurvy—as one of his officers phrased it, they dropped dead "like rotten sheep." After the *Centurion* dropped anchor at uninhabited Tinian a further 21 were buried, but the fruit that grew wild near the beach saved the rest.

Twenty-six years later, it was much the same with the *Charlotte* and the *Scarborough.* None of the First Fleet ships had been able to reprovision at New South Wales, as there were no recognisable fruits and vegetables to forage, and so there was scurvy on board before they even left Sydney Cove. Gilbert and Marshall were able to stock up with fruit and fill their water barrels at Tinian before a storm forced them to cut their anchor cables, and after that the voyage went reasonably smoothly. As the author of *Memoirs of Hydrography* laconically adds, "Macao roads were arrived at 7th September, 1788, without any further noteworthy occurrence taking place."

Captain Sever, commander of the first ship to sail from Port Jackson, *Lady Penrhyn,* sailed even further off-track, fleeing to Tahiti to save the lives of his scurvy-stricken crew. Along the way, one of the officers, Lieutenant Watt, sighted a couple of islands in the Kermadecs. A diplomatic soul, he named one of these Macauley, after his patron, London merchant George Mackenzie Macauley, and the other Curtis, after Sir William Curtis, who was one of the ship's owners. Captain Sever was not so deferential. After landing on Tongareva in the northern Cooks, he named it Penrhyn, after the ship. Then, like Marshall and Gilbert, he dropped anchor at Tinian, where the water barrels were filled before he, too, managed to get to Macao without further incident.

The captains of four more First Fleet vessels, *Alexander,*

Prince of Wales, Borrowdale, and the brig *Friendship,* intended to sail together for Batavia, Java, via Endeavour Strait (later renamed Torres Strait), between the northernmost tip of Australia and the southern coast of New Guinea. After they were scattered by bad weather, the captains of *Borrowdale* and *Prince of Wales* gave up and headed for Cape Horn on the breast of the westerly gales. The *Prince of Wales* was forced to put into Rio de Janeiro in distress on the way to England, as her captain was dead and many of the men were too sick to work, and it was the end of April before they were able to drop anchor at Deptford.

The *Alexander* and the brig *Friendship,* having managed to keep together, sailed doggedly northwest. Their course swung as far as Palau, east of the Philippines, which they reached on September 10, 1788. They were unable to make the natives understand that they were desperately in need of fresh fruit and coconuts, but at least they were able to pin down their location. After that, they struck south and made the Makassar Strait, raising the northeast coast of Borneo on 17 October. By this stage so many men were down with scurvy that it was impossible to work both ships, so, after moving everyone on board the *Alexander,* the brig *Friendship* was scuttled and sunk.

Slowly, the lone *Alexander* sailed for Java. By the time she arrived at Batavia, on November 19, 1788, only one seaman was fit to work aloft. Perhaps some small compensation for this truly horrible voyage was that they had named lots of promontories on the way, such as Cape Sydney, Cape Phillip, Cape Hunter, Cape Nepean, Cape Pitt and Cape Friendship. They also thought they had discovered a number of islands, one of which they named

New Georgia, after the king, and another after Shortland, the lieutenant who was in charge of the scattered fleet.

This naming tradition was continued two years later by Lieutenant Ball, commander of the penal settlement's brig, HMS *Supply*. In April 1790 he was sent to Batavia to order desperately needed provisions, and on May 19 he named two islands off Papua, one Tench, after a marine captain, and the other Prince William Henry, after the sailor prince who became King William IV. And the year after that, John Hunter, the man who was to become the second governor of New South Wales, had his turn at naming islands when he voyaged back to England on the rented Dutch snow *Waaksamheyd*. Discovering a collection of islets in 163° 18′ East, he named them Stewart's Islands, "as a mark of my respect for the honourable Keith Stewart" (a prominent parliamentarian), and another group, in longitude 159° 14′ East, was named after the First Lord of the Admiralty, Lord Howe, while some islands in the Carolines were named Phillip Islands, "after Arthur Phillip, the governor of New South Wales."

The track of the *Waaksamheyd* from the Carolines to Batavia was extraordinarily convoluted. The Dutch vessel crept down the eastern coast of Mindanao and zigzagged between the Celebes and the northeast coast of Borneo towards the Java Sea—and every league of the way, John Hunter checked his charts and books for clues about where they were, even though he was not the man in command of the ship. As the nineteenth century hydrographer Alexander George Findlay observed, navigators of that era "had to consult a considerable number of documents to gather the information they needed," and some of these documents were remarkable for their antiquity.

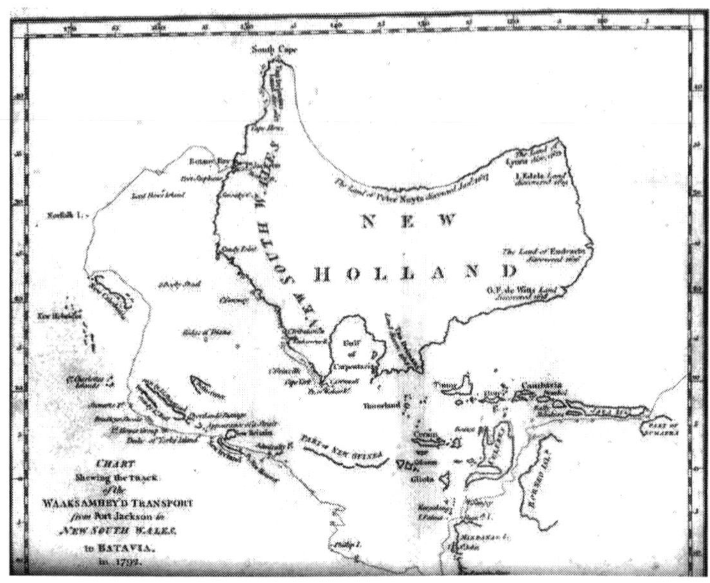

Route of the Waaksamheyd, *from Naval Pioneers*

Hunter's library included James Cook's account of the *Endeavour* expedition, and the voyages of Jean François Marie de Surville and Louis Philippe de Bougainville, all twenty years in the past. The reports of Lieutenants Shortland, in the *Alexander*, and Ball, in HMS *Supply*, were also closely studied, along with Shortland's charts. But the charts upon which he relied the most had been made back in 1767, by another epic christener of islands and straits, Captain Philip Carteret of the *Swallow*.

In 1766, when Samuel Wallis had been appointed to the command of the *Dolphin* on a discovery expedition, the Admiralty had commissioned Philip Carteret to take charge of the *Dolphin*'s consort, which, unfortunately, was a dog of a ship. Built back in 1745, the *Swallow* had been lying neglected in the Medway until 1763, when a survey found the ship to be gravely in need of repairs, which were carried out in a great hurry. Carteret described her in tones of disgust as "one of the worst if not the very worst of her kind; in his majesty's Navy." As soon as the two ships left Plymouth, on August 21, 1766, it grew obvious that she was such a dull sailer that progress was going to be very slow indeed. Samuel Wallis became so tired of reducing sail to let his consort catch up that it is probably no surprise that he left her behind when they finally arrived in the Pacific.

When Carteret found himself alone, it would have been logical for him to sail back to the Atlantic. Instead, however, he pressed on, heading for the western Pacific in a quest for the fabled Islands of Solomon, which had been found and then lost again by the Spanish explorer Alvaro Mendaña de Neira, back in 1568. He made history almost at once, discovering Pitcairn Island (which he named after one of the midshipmen) on the way. Then, probably to his own surprise, he did rediscover the Solomons, and, unlike Mendaña, he mapped them properly. After being attacked by natives, he carried on for the Philippines, charting the strait between New Britain and New Ireland that Hugh Reid was to sail thirty years later. He reached the Dutch colony of Makassar in December, only to be detained by the suspicious administrators. It was four months before he was allowed to weigh anchor for home. The poor, dull *Swallow* finally limped into Spithead on March 20, 1769, having been impelled around the world by nothing much more than the indomitable spirit, grit and courage of her captain, and despite the loss of twenty-five of her crew, mostly from scurvy.

East Indiaman Pitt, *1780, Edy*

Ironically, considering the terrible condition of his unsuitable ship, Philip Carteret made more discoveries than Wallis. And, while Wallis is famous for being the first European in Tahiti, Carteret left a legacy of valuable charts and observations for the men who were navigating from the Pacific into the reef-strewn waters of the Moluccan sea – men like Captain Hugh Reid.

The great swing through the newly discovered equatorial atolls of the Gilbert and Marshall Islands opened an important route to the rich abundance of China, one that was used often from then on. But of even greater interest to the Honourable East India Company was a route to China through the Spice Islands that had been discovered back in 1759, by Captain William Wilson, commander of the Company's largest ship at the time, the 50-gun *Pitt*.

Arriving so belatedly at Batavia from India that he had missed the last of the southwest monsoon that would have taken him through the South China Sea (between Malaya and Borneo) to Canton, Wilson headed east through the dangerous and little known waters of the Moluccas, calculating that once he reached the equator the northwest monsoon would carry him to the Pacific Ocean. After skirting New Guinea, he arrived in the Philippine Sea, where he sailed as far east as the Marshalls to get the wind abeam before bearing up for Canton. After he had filled his holds he returned by the same route, finally dropping anchor in London six months earlier than expected. For this remarkable feat, Captain Wilson received a gold medal valued at a hundred guineas. The Company, however, was even more excited by his new route.

Since 1678, when the first big shipment of tea had arrived in London, merchant-adventurers had been eyeing the enticing prospects of the islands to the west of the wilds of New Guinea, primarily Ternate and Tidore. From early history, cloves and nutmegs gathered there had fetched huge prices in Europe, and since then it had been found that the Chinese appreciated the value of spices, too. It had been a big problem that the Chinese *hoppo*s would accept only silver specie in exchange for tea, silks, and other Oriental treasures, because silver was becoming increasingly scarce, so cinnamon, cloves, nutmegs and pepper were an excellent alternative. The problem was that the Dutch were firmly in control of Ternate and Tidore, and the English government was determined to avoid conflict with that country. But, if an outpost in New Guinea could be established, it might be possible to trade for spices there.

The large, densely forested island was a daunting prospect, its mountainous interior shrouded in mysterious mists, its great inlets guarded by islets and reefs. The first Englishman to begin to chart its coast was the buccaneer-explorer, William Dampier, who sailed in the *Roebuck* from western Australia to Timor, and then, in September 1699, discovered an island off north-eastern New Guinea that he named Nova Britannia—New Britain—along with "a new passage between N. Guinea and Nova Britannia" that came to be called Dampier's Straits. The book of his travels, called *A Voyage to New Holland, &c in the Year 1699...* was published in 1703, but it was not until 1759, when Captain Wilson pioneered his new route through the Spice Islands, that the Company decided that the seas east of the Malayan peninsula should be explored further.

Alexander Dalrymple, one of the navigators in their service, was commissioned to do the job. He obediently cruised about in the schooner *Cuddalore* for the next two years and a half, in the process claiming an island called Balambangan, strategically sited in the South China Sea, between the northern tip of Borneo and the southern Philippines. This was done in the name of the Company, even though his instructions had been specific about choosing somewhere not quite so remote. The fact that Balambangan was small and barren was considered irrelevant, too, as Dalrymple envisaged it as a future trading emporium.

The Company eventually agreed, and in December 1773 an embryo entrepôt was set up there by John Herbert, who arrived in the ship *Britannia.* Like many of Dalrymple's brainwaves, however, the project was doomed. The local sultans were not happy about the idea of an English settlement in the South China Sea, and neither were the Dutch, who had been penning formal protests ever since Wilson had sailed through what they considered their territory. It is not surprising, then, that the settlement lasted less than two years, falling to a native uprising in February 1775, a fiasco that cost the East India Company nearly two hundred thousand pounds.

But, in the meantime, Herbert had been visited by a delegation from the heir-apparent of the Sultan of Mindanao. This train of nobles included a well-educated man named Ismail Tuan Hadjee, who was highly respected by the locals, having made the pilgrimage to Mecca. Being a political manipulator, Tuan Hadjee craftily revealed to Herbert that he had visited the north-eastern coast of New Guinea, and knew of nutmeg trees that grew outside the area of Dutch control. Herbert fell for the idea, and when Tuan Hadjee offered to guide an expedition there, his offer was immediately accepted. And, forthwith, an expedition was arranged.

Thomas Forrest, an ex-Navy man who was first mate of the *Britannia,* was put in charge—an excellent choice, because he got along well with sultans and princes, and spoke fluent Malay. Being familiar with the shoals and pirates of the waters where he would be sailing, he decided that his needs were best served by a native craft with a shallow draft, that would not be easily noticed.

Accordingly, he chose a 10-ton "Sooloo boat"—a *prahu* with a three-legged bamboo mainmast that was drawn back and forth with a wooden winch, and which carried a huge four-cornered sail. There were also small masts that could be stepped in the stern and bow, and which carried little lateens. It was remarkably well armed, with four swivel guns, two blunderbusses, ten muskets, and six pistols, "beside lances, bows and arrows." A European, Laurence Lound, was the gunner, David Baxter, an Englishman, was the mate, Tuan Hadjee was the pilot, and the helmsman was a Moslem priest. The rest of the crew was made up of native seamen and Tuan Hadjee's personal slaves, who helped to paddle. After naming his eccentric command *Tartar Galley,* and stowing Dalrymple's journal and Dampier's charts in a safe place inside his thatched cabin, Captain Forrest set off from Balambangan, firing a five-gun salute as he went.

Tartar Galley, *from Folkard*

It was November 9, 1774. Sailing through the "Sooloo" archipelago, he coasted about Waigeo Island, off the extreme western tip of New Guinea, where he gained the company of two *kora-kora*— outrigger craft with upturned ends like a crescent moon, which could be paddled very fast—that he named *Banguey* and *Borneo*.

In January 1775 this little fleet reached Dore Harbour, in the northwest of New Guinea, to land in a place that was a riot of colour and life, where the marshy lowlands teemed with crocodiles, snakes, leeches and mosquitoes, and the jungle flocked with gorgeous birds of paradise, hornbills, cockatoos, lorikeets and lories, in a myriad of rainbow colours.

Tartar Galley *at Dore Harbour, 1775*

Forrest also found that though Dore looked primitive, with longhouses built on stilts over the water, it was a bustling market place, where the Chinese came to trade for gold, pearls, tortoiseshell, live birds, feathers and slaves. Forrest, however, was only interested in nutmegs. He found some young trees with immature fruit, and even though Tuan Hadjee advised him that they were the wrong sort, the nuts being long instead of round, he dug up the saplings, and loaded them on the *Tartar Galley*.

That done, he set off back to Borneo, where he found the Company outpost in ruins. And, when he got to Calcutta, it was to find that the East India Company, smarting from the Balambangan fiasco, had lost interest in the nutmeg project, though they did allow him to write and publish his book. Meantime, though, Thomas Forrest's adventure had set off a series of events that changed the history of the spice trade, and affected the lives of thousands, including Hugh Reid.

Because he was voyaging under the aegis of Tuan Hadjee, Forrest had been received like a potentate. He drank tea with sultans, rajahs and princes, and gave them sugar candy, and in return they presented him with sago and rice, fowls, goats, and fruit. And those who could speak "good Malays" told him grim stories about the Dutch East India Company. If the English could help them to throw off the Dutch yoke, the Spice Islands would be theirs, they said.

Forrest blithely assured them that military help would be forthcoming. It was a rash promise, and completely counter to his instructions, yet he went even further, writing a letter to Sultan Jamaludin of the clove island, Tidore, in which he repeated his empty assurance that the

East India Company and the English government were anxious to enter into bonds of friendship and amity. Unfortunately, the letter fell into Dutch hands. Reprisal was swift. Sultan Jamaludin was seized and exiled to Batavia, and a puppet ruler put in his place. Hurt and furious, Jamaludin sent a message to his son, Prince Nuku, advising him to raise a crusade against the Dutch, and make allies of the English. And, regarding this request the equivalent to a solemn deathbed vow, Prince Nuku commenced a twenty-year campaign, one that involved constant envoys asking for the English assistance that Forrest had promised.

Some English backing did materialise . . . after a fashion. In 1785, the Governor of Bencoolen, Sumatra, sent Prince Nuku five barrels of gunpowder and twenty muskets in recognition of the prince's humanity in saving a boat's crew from the *Northumberland,* which had been cut out by pirates off the southwest coast of New Guinea. But most was undercover, as opportunistic country captains supplied Prince Nuku with arms in return for illicitly harvested spices. At the same time, like Captain Thomas Forrest, they pretended to have official backing by an administration in Bengal that was sympathetic to Prince Nuku's cause.

One of the most resourceful traders was a remarkable man by the name of Francis Light. Originally from Suffolk, Light had begun his career in the Royal Navy, but then he moved on to the much more lucrative business of commanding ships in the country trade.

Country ships were teak-built vessels from Indian shipyards, as large and as well-armed as regular East India Company ships, and even more elaborately decorated. These beautiful craft coasted between India and China and the intervening islands, but never sailed into the Atlantic, as the Honourable East India Company forbade them to venture west of the Cape of Good Hope.

The captains—mostly British—who strode the quarter-decks of country ships were a distinct and dashing species, and the European seamen who became their officers—Hugh Reid being an example—were equally flamboyant. Though their ventures were financed by Indian merchant houses, and their contracts were with the Honourable Company, the country ship captains were a power unto themselves. Once alone in sapphire seas, they made their own deals, grasped exotic opportunities, and smuggled when they could get away with it.

Captain Francis Light was perfectly suited for the country trade. Like Forrest, he spoke fluent Malay, had adapted well to the local cultures, and had excellent relations with the sultans. At one stage he made himself indebted to the Siamese ruler of Junk Ceylon (Phuket) by warning him of an imminent Burmese attack. He got on so well with the Sultan of Kedah that the prince offered him his own territory— Penang, a small, uninhabited island off the western coast of the Malayan peninsula—in return for a promise of military backing.

Captain Light passed on this generous proposal to the British in India, but, much to his irritation, it was rejected out of hand. Accordingly, when the sultan renewed his proposition later, Light agreed without bothering to tell the Company first. It was going to be hard for him to live up to his promise of military backing, as he had only fifteen artillerymen and thirty Lascars, commanded by a lieutenant and under the charge of a sergeant-major, but, being a country ship captain, he was a natural gambler. And so, on August 11, 1786, he took possession of Penang "in the name of his Majesty George III, and for the use of the Honourable East India Company," giving it the name of Prince of Wales Island.

Establishing a settlement should have been a daunting prospect, because of the jungle-ridden state of the island, but he solved it with typical flair. The only likely workers were itinerant Malay fishermen, but Light persuaded them to clear a large patch of ground by the simple means of loading his ship's cannon with silver coins, and firing them into the undergrowth. A township, called Georgetown, rose like magic, and teemed with inhabitants in record time, too, as Light enticed traders from the Dutch post at Malacca by making Penang a free port. He also allowed newcomers to claim as much land as they liked, a system that worked so well that by 1789 four hundred acres were under cultivation. Trade was mostly in tin ore and opium, but the planting of clove and nutmeg saplings was made a priority—a project that had the lively interest and active patronage of Sir Joseph Banks.

Francis Light died of malaria in October 1794, but the future of the port was assured by the arrival of Lieutenant-

Colonel Arthur Wellesley, who had the job of coordinating the island's defences against pirates. The island's only stockade was Fort Cornwallis, a star-shaped affair made out of palm-tree trunks, but the future first Duke of Wellington masterminded its conversion into a proper fortress.

Then he departed, leaving Penang to be administered by a series of civil servants, until in April 1800 the first Lieutenant-Governor, Sir George Leith, arrived to take charge—in time to greet the *Friendship* when the ship arrived, and shake the hand of Captain Hugh Reid, who was almost as seasoned a trader as Francis Light, and had experienced equally colourful adventures in the Java Sea.

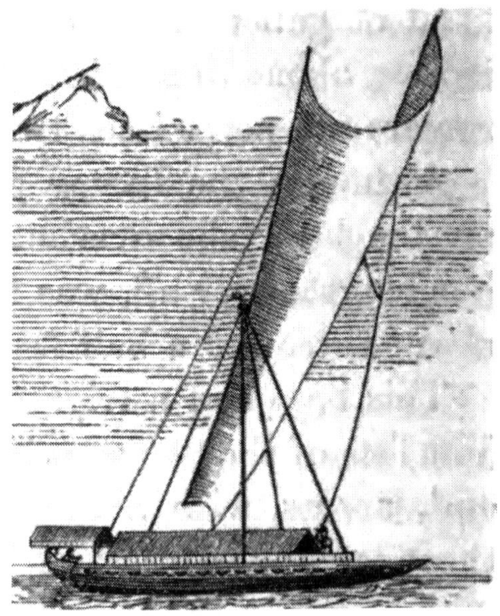

Prahu, from Folkard

Accidentally snaring a port at the gateway to the Orient encouraged the Company in London to get better charts of the waters east of the Malayan peninsula. Accordingly, in March 1790, the administrators in Bombay were instructed to have a proper hydrographical survey made. The man chosen to lead it was 31-year-old Lieutenant John McCluer, an officer of the Bombay Marine, which was the East India Company's fighting navy, and popularly known as the Bombay Buccaneers. In August 1790 he took charge of the fourteen-gun 150-ton sloop *Panther* and an escort named *Endeavour*, and took his departure with the usual salute of cannon.

McCluer first steered for Palau, part of an island group to the east of Mindanao. His mission, a delicate one, was to report the death of the high chief's son, Prince Lee Boo, who had died of smallpox in London, less than six months after Captain Henry Wilson of the East India Company had carried him there, back in 1784. This being January 1791, Lee Boo's father was not particularly distressed to hear it, as he had accepted the probability of Lee Boo's demise quite some time ago. Accordingly, John McCluer's welcome was a warm one.

After a month of being feted, he sailed the *Panther* to Canton. The decks were packed, because he was taking a tour party of Palauan men and women with him. The officers and crew of the *Endeavour* had been left behind, with orders to teach the natives how to cultivate the soil in the European fashion, but when McCluer returned four months later, it was to find that the *Endeavour*s had taken part in tribal wars, instead. So, after firing the ship's broadside to teach the natives about European firepower,

McCluer weighed anchor for New Guinea, to commence his proper job.

He took his route south through the Spice Islands, surreptitiously trading with rajahs on the way—an indiscretion that led to two of them being exiled to Batavia—and calling for supplies at Amboyna, where the Dutch accused him of spying. After extricating himself, McCluer steered along the southern coast of New Guinea, finding a deep, convoluted inlet that was given his own name.

While exploring this, he was accosted by about thirty *prahu* that were deeply laden with nutmegs and aromatic massoi bark. As he boasted after he arrived at Bencoolen in May 1792, not only were these the round "Banda" kind of nutmeg that fetched the highest prices in China, but the trees grew so plentifully on the southern coast of New Guinea that he could have filled his holds with them. He failed to mention to the Company what kind of money he made out of selling them, but it was definitely a lot.

One of the men he did confide in was a close friend and fellow officer in the Bombay Marine, Captain John Hayes, and Hayes, in his turn, discussed it with interested parties in Calcutta. Three Bengal merchants agreed that this was a great chance to break the Dutch monopoly, and a consortium was formed. Money was raised to purchase two country ships, *Duke of Clarence* and *Duchess*, and Hayes talked other Bombay Buccaneers into joining the venture.

To avoid the displeasure of the East India Company, the conspirators took leave from the Bombay Marine, so were voyaging on their own account. Accordingly, it was without great fanfare when, on February 6, 1793, they set out on an epic voyage to New Guinea.

Hayes intended to sail to McCluer Inlet through the Timor Sea, but was foiled by the northeast monsoon. Giving up after fruitlessly beating along the north coast of the continent that came to be known as Australia, he turned back and steered down the western coast, then southeast to Adventure Bay in Van Diemen's Land. There he dropped anchor, surveyed a large part of the coast, and gave names to topographical features in the time-honoured fashion, being completely unaware that others had named them before him.

Hayes then steered north via New Caledonia, where he took the southeast trades for New Guinea. His intention then was to sail along the southern coast, and reach McCluer Inlet from the east, but again he was foiled—not by the winds, this time, but by the serpentine reefs. Turning back, he headed for the northern coast of New Guinea instead. Because of this, and because his seamen were falling fast of scurvy, John Hayes gave up the idea of getting to McCluer Inlet. Instead, on September 18, 1793, he dropped anchor at Dore, on the opposite coast, the same cove where Thomas Forrest had landed the *Tartar Galley* twenty years earlier.

Hayes raised the British flag on the beach of what he called Restoration Bay, and claimed New Guinea—which he called New Albion—in the name of the King of England. Then he built a stockade, which he called Fort Coronation. Exploring the jungle even more energetically than Forrest, he found plenty of nutmegs of both the inferior long type and the more desirable round kind, and traded with the Papuans for cloves and massoi bark.

Dore Harbour as Hayes found it, 1793

Then he decided to head back to India, via Batavia in Java—with just one ship, the *Duke of Clarence*. The *Duchess* had to be left behind, being so battered from the long voyage that she was unseaworthy, but this did mean that a party, headed by Captain Thomas Watkin Court, stayed behind to look after Fort Coronation and keep an English foothold in the land.

The holds of the *Duke of Clarence* were packed with spices, tortoiseshell, beeswax and ambergris, and Hayes had the charts he had made throughout the voyage, along with a long and glowing report for the Governor-General of India, Sir John Shore, who had just succeeded Lord Cornwallis. So there seemed every reason for optimism. He arrived at Batavia in June 1794, to find ships of the Bombay Marine at anchor in the Dutch port, in company with some Honourable East India Company vessels. This meant a fine exchange of salutes, with nine guns fired for the commodore, and seven fired in return, but it also led to complications.

According to Hayes, Commodore Mitchell forbade him to sail to India. However, after he pleaded the urgency of reporting to Sir John Shore, Mitchell arranged passage to Bombay for the first and second officers of the *Duke of Clarence*, William Relph and William Risdon, so that they could deliver Hayes' charts and despatches.

Whether John Hayes was telling the whole truth is debatable, however. It is more likely that he seized the opportunity to forward his charts by other hands for commercial reasons. With Relph and Risdon given passage to India to submit the charts and documents and go through all the formalities, he was free to weigh anchor for Canton, where he sold the cargo at an immense profit.

Batavia, 1780

In October, when he was on the verge of sailing from Macao, Hayes very unexpectedly ran into John McCluer, who had just arrived in a six-oared boat. Bizarrely, when the *Panther* and *Endeavour* had returned to Palau in January 1793, McCluer had resigned his command and sent the two ships off without him, stopping behind in what he may have thought of as his island kingdom. It had taken him just fifteen months to see sense, and getting back to European society was a problem he had solved by rowing with a Malay crew to China.

The conversation between the two Bombay Buccaneers can only be imagined, but it certainly included glowing descriptions of the settlement Hayes had left behind at Restoration Bay. McCluer listened with such interest that he was tempted into returning to New Guinea. A brig named *Venus* was purchased in McCluer's name, but probably with Hayes' financial help, and in July 1794 the two friends separated, one headed for India to find out what the administration thought of his annexation of New Albion, and the other back to Palau to fetch his two wives, on the way to Restoration Harbour.

The outcome of both ventures was disappointing. In New Guinea, John McCluer found the settlement in deep distress. Fourteen men were sick, while several more were already buried, and the survivors were starving.

Not only had the rainy season brought fevers with it, but their stores had rotted. Shortly after Hayes had left, the stockade had been attacked by natives, and several of their Lascars and Sepoys had been seized and carried away to be sold as slaves. And the harbour was far less frequented than they had been led to believe, as McCluer was their first visitor. After a fruitless attempt to equip the *Duchess* for sea again, McCluer left in March 1795, expressing the hope that it would not be too long before Captain Hayes came back.

Hayes, in the *Duke of Clarence*, had arrived in Calcutta on December 5, 1794, to find an equally depressing situation. Sir John Shore and the government had already decided that the settlement in New Albion should be abandoned, and even reckoned that it should never have been started in the first place. If New Guinea really was so promising, they said, the Dutch would have been there for years. Not only did they dismiss Captain Hayes' claims for compensation for having made new discoveries, pointing out that Thomas Forrest had discovered that same area twenty years earlier, but they informed him that his period of leave had expired. He had to hand over the command of the *Duke of Clarence* to William Risdon, and return to duty with the Bombay Marine.

Captain Risdon was sent to New Guinea to pick up Court and his surviving men, and close down the settlement, but his arrival led to much more exciting events. No sooner had the *Duke of Clarence* dropped anchor at Restoration Harbour (now Dore Harbour again), than a *kora-kora* fleet arrived, flying great silken banners. And, with great ceremony, the ship was boarded by none other than the rebel prince of Tidore, Prince Nuku.

~

Ceremonial prahu, from Folkard

For the past twenty years, ever since his father had been incarcerated by the Dutch, Prince Nuku had been doggedly keeping to his pledge to seek an alliance with the English. Resourceful and determined, willing to stoop to subterfuge, he had become the most powerful noble in the Moluccas, with men from all the islands flocking to join his campaign.

Throughout, the British had been less than helpful. Though Prince Nuku pretended to the sultans that he had British backing, in reality he had gotten nowhere. His envoys, sent to Bencoolen in 1784 and to Calcutta in 1785, had been received with great courtesy, but there had been no promise of official support. By contrast, the country captains had not just treated him with honour and respect, but had brought him arms and ammunition, which they traded for his spices. Accordingly, the arrival of a country ship in any part of his domain—which included western New Guinea—was a matter of great interest to the prince.

Captains Risdon and Court welcomed him on board the *Duke of Clarence* with the usual punctilious civilities, but the conference went much further than that. While tea was drunk and sugar candy shared out, promises were made and the beginning of an important understanding reached. Prince Nuku invited Court and his officers to come with him on his *prahu* to his headquarters in West Ceram, while Risdon stayed in Dore Harbour to fix the *Duchess.*

Six weeks later, Risdon arrived with both ships, and after yet another conference he and Court carried a party of local leaders to Gebe, an island off Waigeo with a magnificent harbour. Shortly after they anchored, Prince Nuku and his fleet joined them, and over the next month their plans were finalised.

The *Duke of Clarence* sailed for Bengal, arriving in Calcutta in December 1795. "The ship *Duke of Clarence,* lately arrived at Calcutta from the Spice Islands, discovered by Captain Hayes, has brought a cargo of immense value," reported the *Madras Courier* on 23 December. "It consists of all the spices which are in the highest estimation throughout India, Persia, and Arabia, and which now being scarce in the markets of Europe, have risen in price beyond the precedent." The *Duke of Clarence* also carried an official party, including Prince Nuku's chief minister, Mohammed Arif Bila, who had a letter for the Governor-General.

In this letter, Prince Nuku described his long crusade against the Dutch, and made a strong case for an alliance with the Honourable East India Company. In return for the protection of the government of Bengal, he offered sole trading rights in the nutmegs, mace and cloves that had risen so greatly in value, because of the war.

The Council in Bengal was tempted, but Sir John Shore was a man who disliked making decisions. A precarious political situation had to be taken into account—in January that year the Netherlands, the homeland of the Dutch in the Java Sea, had been overrun and captured by French Revolutionary forces, and Holland was now a client state of France. It was bad enough that French cruisers roamed the Bay of Bengal, but now there was great danger that French forces would take over Dutch possessions in the East Indies, threatening India from both the east and the west. And there was the matter of Malacca to be taken into consideration, too. Once a Portuguese hub of maritime trade and commerce, Malacca had been turned into a military base by the Dutch. If the French commanded the port, they would have complete control of that seaway, and so it was crucial that English forces take over there—which they did, in a naval operation that had commenced in August, and was commanded by Admiral Peter Rainier.

The Council wanted the Dutch governor, Abraham Couperus, to remain as a puppet, but he had proudly refused to cooperate, so he was confined as a prisoner of war, and the city was currently occupied by the army. So, partly because of his cautious nature, and partly because of this complicated situation in Malacca, Sir John Shore refused to contemplate a formal alliance between Prince Nuku and the East India Company.

However, he sweetened the rebuttal by honouring Prince Nuku's ambassador with an elaborate farewell, accompanied by substantial presents—four brass carronades, sixteen iron three-pounder cannon, 1,000 rounds of ammunition, 200 muskets, 20,000 musket balls, and 200 barrels of gunpowder. The arms and ammunition were loaded on board three country ships—*Duke of Clarence,* Captain William Bellamy Risdon, *Sultan,* Captain Thomas Watkin Court, and *Phoenix*, Captain Samuel Stewart—and the fleet sailed down the Hooghly River, headed for the Spice Islands.

~

All three captains benefited greatly from delivering this bounty to Prince Nuku. For the next nine months the *Sultan, Phoenix* and *Duke of Clarence* sailed about the Spice Islands, illicitly trading arms for nutmegs, cloves and mace, and selling the spices in Bengal at great profit.

The big country ships became such a regular and reassuring sight in the Moluccan Sea that Prince Nuku benefited too, as the ranks of his rebel warriors swelled. Naturally, he gained in confidence. In September, it was reported that Prince Nuku had sworn a formal oath before a great congress in Halmahera that, with the support of the three English captains and their officers, he soon overwhelm the Dutch defence of Tidore.

In that same month of September, 1796, the *Marquis Cornwallis* was slowly steering up the Hooghly River, having taken on a pilot at the Balasore Roads. On the 17th Hugh Reid, the first officer, signed off the day's entry in the deck log for the last time. Having given his resignation to Captain Michael Hogan, he was about to leave the ship.

And the *Duke of Clarence,* with William Risdon still in command, was close by, also heading for Calcutta. On

October 17, the *Marquis Cornwallis* and the *Duke of Clarence* both dropped anchor off Fort William. By then Hugh Reid was on shore, having been replaced by an incoming officer by the name of John Roberts. He had choices. A convoy of East Indiamen was assembling at Diamond Harbour, on the Hooghly River, getting ready to leave for England, and as a well-regarded officer Reid would have had plenty of chances to ship on one of these. Being an old hand who had heard the gossip, though, he knew exactly where profit and adventure lay—and so he joined the country ship *Duke of Clarence,* taking the post of first lieutenant under Captain William Risdon.

On December 7, 1796, the *Duke of Clarence* sailed from Calcutta. Three months later, she was lying off the island of Bacan, to the south of Halmahera, in company with the other two country ships. Like the *Sultan* and the *Phoenix,* the *Duke of Clarence* was flying a great red silken flag at the stern, and a gold one at the bow. And, like the two other ships, she was surrounded by a clamorous horde of *kora-kora.* It was March 13, 1797, and Prince Nuku was ready for war.

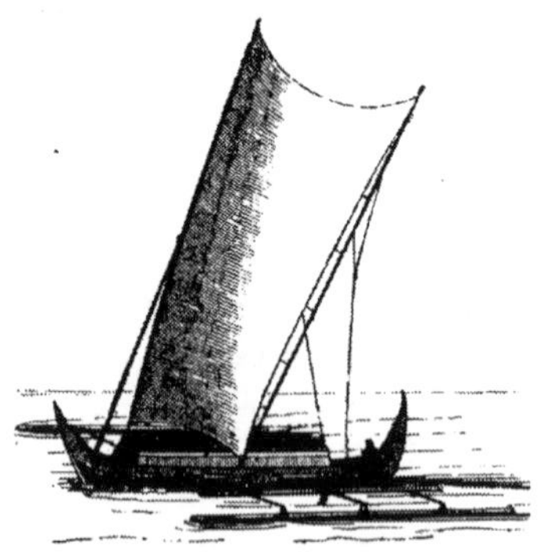

Kora-kora, from Folkard

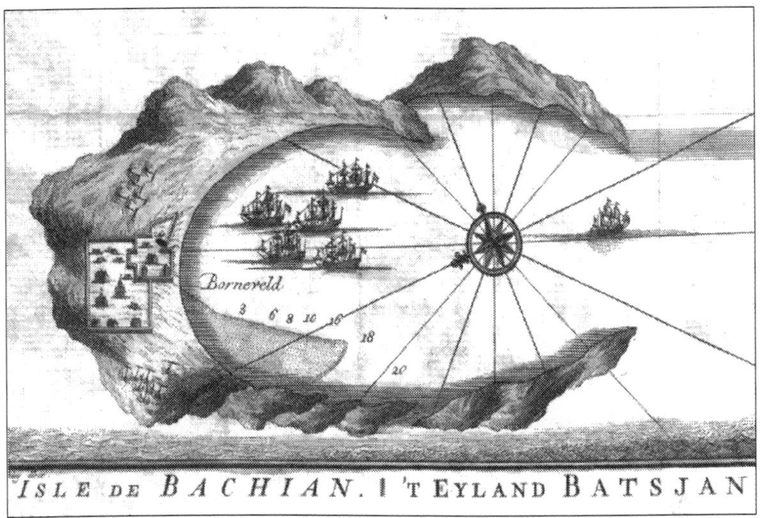

Bacan, c. 1750, detail from map by Bellin

There were fifty native vessels in the fleet, all geared up for battle, bare-chested warriors crowded the platforms, all with long *kris* or *parang* knives thrust into their sashes, for those who did not carry a weapon were not allowed to loot. Gongs beat, and gaudy banners blew, while light glittered on the barrels of muskets and swivel guns.

Ahead, the towering island interior was misted with cloud. The sun picked out the thatched roofs of dwellings and spice-drying houses, along with the minaret of the mosque. Coconut palms fluttered in the early breeze. The flag of the Dutch East India Company flew lazily above the walls of Benteng Barnevald, the ancient Portuguese fort, but there was no movement behind the snouts of cannon—not yet.

Fort Barnevald, Bacan

The siege was a leisurely process. Over the next three days desultory shots were exchanged, while the drums and gongs hammered out their incessant beat. Every man in the fleet carried his own water and provisions, and so there was no need for foraging parties to go on shore. Then, on March 16, the country ship captains held a conference. The fort was on the verge of surrender, or so they sensed, and it was known that many of the villagers were Christian, a legacy of the Portuguese occupation. Concerned that the so-called infidels would be slaughtered and enslaved, the English negotiated with Prince Nuku for permission to be the first to send a party on shore. He agreed, and that same day they landed.

Led by a uniformed officer with his ceremonial sword held vertically before his chin, a squad of musket-armed seamen marched under a flying banner to the fort. With equal formality the post-holder, Van Diest, walked down the steps to meet them. The officer demanded total surrender. Van Diest refused, and returned to the fort, and the Englishmen went back to the ship. But the next day, they were back—and the day after that.

It turned into a routine of more shots exchanged, more hammering on drums and gongs, and more delegations. After four days, Van Diest finally changed his mind. Grimly, he handed over his sword to the English officer. His courage was undoubted, however. When the officer from the country ship marched into the redoubt, it was to find that the fort had been defended by just five soldiers and a corporal.

With no more shots fired, the island was theirs. Anxious to cooperate, the local boatmen joined Prince Nuku's armada. Loaded down with the spoils of victory, the *Duke of Clarence,* the *Sultan* and the *Phoenix* followed Prince Nuku's *prahu* as he led the fleet of *kora-kora* to his major objective, his home island of Tidore. They arrived on April 12, 1797—to find the fort empty. The puppet sultan and the Dutch garrison had fled to Ternate on five *kora-kora.* The following night three of the *kora-kora* sneaked back into port, stolen by their Tidoran crew.

Prince Nuku's triumph was complete.

Leaving Prince Nuku on his rightful throne, the three country ships returned to the Bay of Bengal, calling at Penang on the way. Once in Calcutta, Hugh Reid signed off the ship, and walked down Strand Road to Esplanade Road and Dhurrumtollah Street, to invest his newfound wealth—a significant sum, each officer's share reputedly being as much as fifteen thousand pounds, plus whatever booty he had snared. His mood must have been ebullient. Not only was he rich in cash, but he was rich in colourful stories, too—anecdotes to engage and enthral Eleanor as they voyaged to his old hunting grounds in the Moluccan Sea. And it is at the start of this exotic stage of her adventure that Eleanor's shipboard journal continues.

For several days in succession, we were favoured with the finest weather. On the morning of the 24th of May, the boy at the mast-head called out, "Land a-head!" It proved to be a small elevated rock, with a few stunted trees; many tropical birds were about it. As it was not marked in any of our charts, the captain called it *Ephraims' Island,* after the boy who first saw it. To encourage vigilance, it was a standing rule on board, that the first discoverer of any new island, rock, or shoal, should have his name given to it.

The latitude of this rock was found to be, 22° 40′ south, and longitude 172° 30′ east. We were now but a short distance from the Friendly and Feju Islands, so celebrated in Capt. Cook's Voyages.

Next day the officers had good sights of the distance of the sun and moon, which made our longitude, at 12 o'clock .... 173° 54′ east

Adding the longitude of Dublin.......... } 6 6 west
Shews we are at the present moment..} 180
the antipodes of that city

Several jokes were interchanged about this circumstance. The carpenter, who was from the metropolis of Ireland, doing some little jobs upon the quarter deck, having listened to the conversation, quickly asked, "Where did they say Dublin was?"

He was told, in reply, "Directly under the ship's bottom."

Then said he, "I will send a token to my old sister," and fetching up a curious marked sixpence, he threw it over the side of the ship, exclaiming, "If old Judith sees this, she will know that Pat is not far off!" He was then appraised, that, although it was just noon with us, it was at the same instant exactly 12 o'clock at night in Dublin. He answered, "It matters not, for the sixpence, when it falls, will jingle upon the stones, and as the lamps shew a good light in Dublin, they can see to pick it up." We were amused by his apparent simplicity, while we gave him credit for knowing better.

Soon after this we came in sight of the islands, called the [New] Hebrides, in the vicinity of New Caledonia. In passing Annotam, Enomango, and Aurora, we saw much smoke from fires; but had no intercourse with the inhabitants of those islands, the weather being very bad, with heavy squalls of wind and rain.

Advancing on our passage to the 11th degree of south latitude, my husband was anxious to observe an island before dark, which had been discovered upon his former voyage in the *Cornwallis*, and named after that ship; but the exact situation could not then be ascertained. From the distance the ship had gone, it was supposed we had passed it soon after sun-set. The wind being fierce, the sea rough, and the night intensely dark, the ship was reduced under a low sail, and a good look-out kept, to give, if possible, timely notice of danger. The navigation of this unknown sea was so uncertain, that the ship proceeded only when it cleared up a little; as often as the squalls were seen coming, she was hove-to. This was alternately done through the slow hours of this trying night.

About four o'clock in the morning, just as an obscure squall cleared away, rocks and breakers were discovered close under the lee of the ship. All now was consternation; but, by the kind interposition of Providence, we were, at a moment of apparent destruction, preserved from collision with the rock. My husband is naturally gifted with presence of mind and coolness in the hour of danger. In this critical situation the helm and sails were properly managed, and, by the Almighty's goodness, we were saved from shipwreck.

I never can forget that night, when, looking out of the quarter gallery, I saw the furious waves dashing against the rocks with an awful noise, making all white with foam. The ship appeared to be nearly amongst the breakers; my feelings at the moment cannot be described. Meanwhile a great clamour and bustle continued upon deck; but as I saw the vessel gradually leave the white water at a distance, my mind felt a great relief, and my melting heart was impressed with gratitude to God for our preservation.

When daylight appeared, it was discovered that this was a dangerous reef of rocks lying off the same island which they had been looking out for during the night. The captain had every confidence in the mates; they were steady, sober, and good seamen; but as neither of them had been the voyage before, his anxiety was doubled whenever the ship was by contrary winds and counter currents driven out of the known track.

This afternoon we passed the island Edgecombe, about four leagues on our right; and saw, on the left, another large mountainous island, called Egmont or St. Cruz.

Continuing our course, about two in the morning, the mate of the watch reported that he saw, at a great distance, indications of an explosion, the same as if a ship had been blown up with gunpowder. As there are some low small islands in this track, the captain judged it proper to lay the ship to until day-light. On changing watch, at four in the morning, another vast illumination took place, a great distance to the west of us, tingeing the clouds in that quarter. It was not known what could cause these phenomina, until the captain, in looking over his old journal, observed there was an island called the Volcano, which he formerly passed without seeing any smoke or signs of eruption.

He now conjectured that the subterranean fire had again burst out. At day-light the black dense smoke was seen towering on high from the top of the island; as we approached all eyes were employed in observing this wonder in nature. The wind being light and favourable, it was decided that we should pass near it; and accordingly, at 10 at night, the ship, by computation, was about one league distant.

Explosions took place as we approached, with discharges of burning fragments into the air. The last eruption was followed by a longer interval than usual, and vivid admiration had began to be succeeded by a feeling of tranquillity, when, about 11 o'clock, the greatest horror and consternation seized every person on board. On a sudden the vessel laboured as if she had been amongst surf created by rocks, shaking in every part; and almost at the same instant, a tremendous eruption, accompanied with a correspondent noise, filled the air with fire, which cast such a light around, that all, looking to the moment when the ascending combustibles must fall, conceived our destruction was at hand. Most providentially for us, the wind blew the fiery fragments in the opposite direction; had it been otherwise, our vessel might have been consumed.

After this awful explosion, the streams of liquid fire descended the sides of the hill, and as they came in contact with the water, produced a hissing noise and a dense smoke, which curled from the bottom of the mountain. When our consternation had ceased, no time was lost in getting away from this scene of horror.

Volcano Island, from Forrest (1775)

The past had such an effect on all on board, as to banish sleep from every eye; the seamen stood continually gazing at the scene, when not called off to their duty. By two in the morning we were at a respectful distance. Meanwhile many small eruptions intervened. None occurred comparably to that which we had witnessed when nearest, until four in the morning, when another great explosion appeared, if possible, more terrible. The ship shook all over in the most violent manner, as if the land at the bottom of the ocean had been heaved by an earthquake; then followed the tremendous explosion, with the rush of liquid flames down the sides of the mountain as before. But our senses were now more collected, and being four leagues off, time and space allowed us to observe it.

At day-light we had still the island Egmont in sight. As the volcanic isle lies only about 10 or 12 leagues to the north of the above, in latitude 10 degrees south, and 166 degrees east longitude, it was supposed that it could not be above 10 or 12 miles in circumference; but from the great quantities of lava thrown out, it may be expected to increase in size. It appeared broad at the base, tapering upward like an inverted funnel, ragged at the top or edge of the crater.

In the afternoon we passed two small low islands on our right, named the Brothers; also on our left, covered with cocoanut trees. It was not thought probable that any inhabitants would be found on such a small spot, apparently not exceeding three miles in extent; but advertising to the possibility that there might be some, a boat was sent ashore to procure some cocoa-nuts, with strict orders that, if any natives were seen, not to land, but to return directly to the ship, which lay-to about a mile off. When the boat drew near the shore, we observed a number of natives amongst the trees skirting a part of the island, hidden from the sight of our people in the boat. We counted upwards of 30 of these naked savages; they were all armed with long spears, and what we took for bows and arrows. They frequently ran out of sight among the trees, and came to view again in a cunning manner.

The captain now was very apprehensive that we should lose some of our men; the only signal agreed upon for ordering their prompt return to the ship was hoisting our ensign, and at that time the ship's situation prevented them from seeing it. We observed the boat to lie a-back of the surf, and naturally concluded that they had seen the natives, and of course would not land.

We saw one of the islanders separate from the rest and approach the boat; he was unarmed, but had something in his hand which he held up, beckoning our people to the land; he then put down what he held in his hand, and retired amongst the trees, where we saw him join the others, who were still in ambush concealed from the boat's crew. Then two natives likewise unarmed approached the boat with some cocoa-nuts, which they held up; on this the boat appeared to pull up towards them. We were all very uneasy at observing this, as our party could not see the signal commanding their return. Presently all the savages left their ambush, and ran towards the boat.

Waaksamheyd *attacked by natives, from* Naval Pioneers

Luckily a gun had been got ready, and was now fired; the report of which drew the attention of the natives to the ship, which it gave notice to our people, who fortunately had not landed. The firing, however, did not intimidate the savages, for they came close to the surf, brandishing their spears, and discharged their arrows at the boat, which happily did no mischief; whereupon, to let them know our superiority, a gun was shotted and fired amongst the trees over their heads. As soon as this was done, they turned suddenly round to look at the trees, amongst which the shot had done some execution, and instantly retired from the beach.

When the boat returned, Mr. Henderson, who went in command of her, said, the natives appeared black and small in stature, having woolly heads like Africans; that they did not see more than two natives until the gun was fired, then, he said, they were seen coming from amongst the bushes, making a wild noise, and letting fly arrows at the boat. One man among them was painted red, as if by ochre. Thus ended our transient intercourse with these perfidious people; and happy were all that no disaster had occurred. From the hostility of the inhabitants, and some coral rocks in the vicinity, this was named Danger Island.

Having but little wind, our progress was slow; we were still in sight of the volcano. Saw to the south of us this afternoon Swallow Island, named by Capt. Carteret, who sailed in those seas in the year 1767; it appeared pretty high land, but too distant for accurate observation. Capt. Carteret found much hostility from the natives about these parts.

The weather now was very hot and sultry; the mercury sometimes standing as high as ninety degrees. We had much thunder, lightning, and rain; and several water-spouts passed near the ship. To us this phenomenon had the appearance of a long narrow smoky pillar let down from the clouds to the surface of the water, creating a white foam where the suction takes place, whirling round in a furious manner, but the vortex thus formed seems but a few yards in extent. Even to be involved in this is reckoned fatal to boats and small vessels; and the discharge of the column of water very dangerous to large ships, should it break upon their decks. The water first ascends to fill the cylinder. If a gun be fired near a water-spout, the vacuum caused by the explosion will disperse it. Several of our guns were made ready for this service, but were not needed.

Prior to leaving Port Jackson, Governor Hunter requested my husband, if he passed near Stewart's Islands, to ascertain whether they were inhabited, saying that he was at too great a distance when he first discovered and named them in 1791 to make any observation; hence, as they lay in the ship's track, they were looked out for.

On Thursday, the 5th of June, we saw and approached them; they appeared to be a small cluster of low islands. Three were counted from the deck, and five from the mast-head. We observed one more elevated than the rest, which was named *Mount Hunter*, in honour of the first discoverer.

We saw much smoke from different parts, and several canoes passing from one isle to another; about noon a number of canoes came toward the ship, each carrying from five to eight persons; these were unarmed, and came close to the ship staring at the masts and hull with the greatest surprise and wonder.

They appeared small muscular men, of sun-burnt complexion, having some sort of cloth round their waist; their hair was tied in a bunch behind. Signs were made to draw them close alongside, and little articles held out for them to accept; but for a considerable time they took no notice of these overtures; at length, a tall, fine looking old man, with a white beard, stood up in one of the canoes, and began talking very loud, often bending his body as if in the act of lifting something up; at the same time pointing to the shore, inviting us, as we thought, to land.

When he had done, some light things were dropped by the fishing-lines astern, which one canoe ventured to take; after which, several boats came round, to observe what was received. Presently a boat with five men paddled up to the main channel, and threw in two cocoa-nuts, and then paddled hastily away. At this stage, an accident happened, which put a stop to all farther intercourse. A canoe had hold of the line, to take something off, which the hook caught in the hand of the man who held the line; with a horrid yell he tore the hook out of the flesh, and all instantly quitted us; after which, no overture could induce them again to come near.

Their canoes appeared about twenty-five feet long, with out riggers fixed to one side to balance them. Many natives were seen on shore. We were very sorry that they had left us with bad impression, as we thought them to be a friendly good people. No doubt, were a communication established, ships might find many refreshments here, as abundance of coco-nut trees were seen from the *Friendship*. These islands lie in latitude 8°12′ south, and longitude about 163° east.

Vanuatu (New Hebrides) canoe (Ron Druett)

Next morning we saw Solomon's Island on our left. We soon after passed between that and Gower's Island, so named by Capt. Carteret. Gower's Island appeared small, and we soon lost sight of it, but Solomon's Island is of great extent, as we had it in view for three days, in which time the ship ran upwards of three hundred miles to the north-west; however there might be more islands than one, as several extensive openings were seen.

On the 9th of June, we descried the straits of Bougainville on our left, but entered a new passage between Anson's and Bougainville Islands, which was found safe. While we were proceeding toward St. George's Channel, so named by Capt. Carteret, who first sailed through it in 1767, six canoes came from Bougainville Island towards the ship, with about eight or ten men in each; they came alongside with confidence, and appeared to know something of traffic; readily exchanging bows, arrows, and spears, shells, necklaces, and ornaments from their arms and legs, for handkerchiefs, empty bottles, &c.

The Bougainville Islanders are small in stature, very dark, with frizzled hair. We observed a number of people on shore. While all the ship's crew were busy in traffic at the gangway, the steward being in the cabin, heard a noise at the rudder-chains, and looking out, saw a native very busy, taking the fore-lock from the shackle; he had swam from one of the canoes, and would not desist when called to. The steward had a kettle of boiling water in the cabin, which he took to the window, and with it threatened the fellow, who would not understand him; however, a little of the scalding water very soon made him desist, for he instantly jumped into the water, and kept at a respectful distance, swimming about until taken into a canoe.

After laying to for about an hour, the ship stood on her course. No persuasion could induce any of these natives to enter the ship, although a number of boats were still coming off, and followed us until we came near Anson's Island, when they all returned. We saw many natives, in groups, upon Anson's Island; but no boats came off from it; we supposed that they were not upon good terms with their neighbours. We found the weather very hot, but all the crew were in the best health; no doubt the fresh meals which the ship's stores furnished them, and plenty of water, greatly contributed thereto.

This day my poor kangaroo fell down the hatchway and broke its back; I had hoped to take it safe to England. Its innocent pranks, playing about the cabin and steerage, were often a source of amusement to the officers, who felt its loss as much as I did.

On the 10th June our track was to the left of several small islands; next morning we saw Cape St. George, the south-eastern extremity of New Ireland; we kept the coast on our right, at the distance of three or four miles: every part appeared to be covered with trees, of several species, some of which were tall and stately, particularly on the ridges of hill seated inland. The shore, on many points, was seen to be rocky. No natives were observed here.

About noon we descried Cape Orford, the eastern extremity of New Britain. From this to Cape St. George, the distance was supposed to be about forty miles, both being seen at the same time, forming the entrance to St. George's Channel, up which we proceeded, having the land on both sides of us, giving to the entrance of the strait the appearance of a large river. The weather was fine; we had a delightful view of both shores, with their fertile valleys, and gracefully sloping uplands, where, possibly in after ages, when the tenants of this wild shall become civilized, the plough may prepare yellow trophies for the sickle, and bleating flocks and lowing herds diversify the landscape with symbols of cultivation and weather, as in the beautiful hills and dales of Old Britain and Ireland.

As we approached the coast of New Britain, we saw several boats, but none approached near the ship until the evening, when a canoe, having an out-rigger, and eleven people on board, came within about a cable's length of us, where they lay gazing at the ship for some time; handkerchiefs were held up to draw them alongside, of which they took no notice. One of the men who stood up in the canoe, appeared tall, well made, and of a dark complexion. We for some time had thought that they had red and white turbans on their heads; but at length discovered that their hair, which was woolly and frizzled, was covered with a sort of red powder like ochre on one side, and with a kind of lime or chalk on the other; other individuals were seen with the hair all red, and others with it all white.

Nothing could entice them alongside. The canoe could paddle very fast; we did not suppose that any of our boats could overtake it if a trial had been made. As it drew near dark, they paddled round the ship very briskly, until coming to their first station, between the ship and the land, they stopped and blew something like smoke or dust from their hand lifted to the mouth, and let fly some arrows at the ship (which did not reach us) and quickly retired towards the shore. The audacity of these New Britons could easily have been checked by firing a shot over them; but the captain did not wish to intimidate them from again approaching a ship; and preferred a course of lenity to resentment for acts indicating their disposition to be hostile.

We made little progress in the night, having light winds; meanwhile we descried several fires in New Britain, but none in New Ireland, and concluded that the latter was but thinly inhabited. Next morning we saw the Duke of York's Island, lying nearly in the middle of the channel, which we thought should have been called the New Isle of Man, in correspondence with its relative situation. On the land of New Britain we noticed three remarkable hills, which have the shape of sugar loaves; one of which was much loftier than the other two; they had hence been called the *Mother and her Daughters* by Captain Carteret. They look as if they had been thrown up by a volcano, and we had no doubt but it had been so, for a little farther inland we observed smoke continually issuing from a hill which nearly resembles the cones just mentioned; several patches appeared like land under cultivation.

As we proceeded, a number of canoes was observed, coming from the Duke of York's Island. They came boldly on to the ship, singing, and playing upon an instrument of hollow reeds in the form of the Pandean pipes. They held out bunches of plantains and cocoa nuts. Many articles were exhibited to them for barter, but nothing pleased them so much as red and white cloth. The captain cautioned our people to barter fairly, and to take nothing without making a return. There were at one time upwards of 30 canoes about the ship. The seamen having got a plentiful supply of plantains and cocoa nuts, had finished bartering, when the captain shewed some narrow red and white buntin, with some of my old ribbons, at sight of which, all the natives in the different canoes appeared most anxious to possess these treasures, pointing to the shore, and by signs intimating a wish for us to stop until they returned with a fresh supply of fruit and other native produce.

Their boats glided to the land, and so anxious were the companies of natives to possess the pieces of buntin, that they were quarrelling as to which of them threw fruit, yams, &c. into the ports. However, all got some of our rags in exchange for a plentiful supply of yams, &c. They were satisfied, and so were we. They took old knives and pieces of iron hoops in exchange, but did not set any value upon them. Glaring colours of red and white cloth attracted them most, there were from five to twelve men in the different sized boats; they had spears, bows, and arrows with them, but appeared to have such confidence in us, that we conceived they were placed in their boats more in readiness to repel an attack from their hostile neighbours, than from any apprehension from us.

As there was a fine commanding breeze, the ship drifted slowly between the satellite isle of New Man and the Island of New Britain. Perhaps the Phoenicians, when they first discovered Britain, and had intercourse with our rudely painted forefathers, might think of the latter with mingled com-miseration, contempt, and dawning hope, as we did of these poor savage people.

The captain wishing to get clear of the channel before dark, made sail from the lessening coast of these fair dealing men. In passing the opposite territory of New Britain, we saw Port Hunter, where the *Waaksamheyd* had watered. Several openings led us to suppose, that where New Britain is placed there were more islands than one, particularly as some canoes went in at one opening and came out at another. We observed a number of people on a projecting point of land, holding up bunches of plantains, cocoa-nuts, and yams, but we, having a sufficiency, did not bring to; at the same time a number of canoes were following the ship from different parts. As we proceeded we still perceived patches in the ravines that appeared under cultivation.

Just as we cleared the Duke of York's Island, we were surprised to see a ship following us. We were nearly becalmed, but she having a fine breeze came near enough before dark for us to discover that it was the *Walker* south seaman, which sailed from Port Jackson about three weeks before us. They could not see our colours, the ship's head being towards them. As it was quickly dark, it was thought we should have no communication until morning; however, about eight in the evening, we heard the boats' oars towing their ship towards us, and presently voices of individuals in their crews conversing, the night being still—at length the captain of the *Walker* hailed us, saying, "What ship is that pray?" by which we knew that they did not know us.

"*L'Amitié*," was answered.

"From whence come you?" was the next question.

Hollandez nuova was replied.

"Who commands that ship," was then demanded.

"Capitaine Le Rouge."

We then plainly overheard them, conversing together, saying we were either French or Dutch. However, not to keep them longer in suspense, our captain called aloud in English, "How do you do, Capt. Nicholl?"

Their commander returned, "Who is that?"

"Don't you know the *Friendship*, Reid?" was rejoined.

Mutual civilities were then exchanged, and the captain of the *Walker* came on board us to supper, but quite altered in his looks since we saw him at Sydney. He was hardly able to come up the ship's side from weakness, in consequence of a severe wound which he had received in the breast about three weeks before, in an encounter with the savages of Egmont Island where he lost three of his people, and two more who had been wounded were not expected to live.

It appeared that after he left Port Jackson he intended to go to the northward, by the way of the Philippine Isles, and stretch over to the coast of America to look for sperm whales, but scurvy beginning to shew itself among his seamen, he was induced to call at Egmont Island, in order to procure as many cocoa-nuts, as possible; they could find no anchorage at the place where they touched, but seeing plenty of cocoa-nut trees on shore, and also a number of natives, they manned and armed one of their boats, the captain, accompanied by the chief mate, went in her, leaving the ship in charge of the doctor and a junior mate.

As they came near the shore numbers of the natives beckoned to them to land. Seeing the islanders appear friendly and unarmed, the captain and a party were induced to land, leaving the boat in charge of three men, desiring them to be very civil to the natives. The party on shore had but a few yards to walk to the coca-nut trees, but without advancing, pointed to them, shewing several trifles by way of barter; the natives then gave their visitors some nuts, but instead of offering to go up the trees for some, pointed to them, as much as to say, If you want them you may take them.

On this apparent invitation, two of the seamen ascended the trees, and soon cut down all the nuts on them. At this stage of the intercourse much muttering and signs of anger broke out amongst the natives; several, after betraying the most savage looks, suddenly disappeared. At this crisis the people were ordered down from the trees, and the whole party desired to keep close together for mutual support. Many of the inhabitants now shewed themselves, armed with spears and bows and arrows, and it was their manifest intention to cut the strangers off from the boat. The three men stationed in the boat had the greatest difficulty in keeping her from being pulled ashore by the savages, who had taken out several things by force, and were endeavouring to seize the muskets.

The concourse of natives increased in an alarming degree. At last the party joined the boat, but a number of the natives got hold of the painter, and would have hauled her ashore had not the man in the bow cut it. At his moment a flight of arrows was discharged amongst them, which wounded two men; the party now found themselves compelled to fire upon the savages; one man they saw drop, and others appeared to be wounded. Regardless of this, a number of the natives rushed into the water after the boat, charging with their spears, one of which wounded the captain, while, from distant assailants, arrows were flying so fast and thick as to wound every man in the boat (the mate excepted). Notwithstanding this dismaying obstacle to their retreat, the party providentially effected it.

As all were engaged as getting the boat as fast as possible from the shore, but few shots were fired; the horrid yells of some hundreds of these savages when they commenced hostilities were most appalling. There were now only three men able to handle an oar, fortunately they were not followed by canoes, or they must all have been immolated, so diminished was their power of resistance. To augment their consternation, they heard a gun from the ship, which was hid from their sight by a point of land. They at first concluded she had run aground, or had been overtaken by some other great disaster. However, on doubling the point, they were relieved from these apprehensions by seeing the ship some distance from the land, but at the same time observed a number of canoes paddling very fast from her towards the shore.

As soon as the captain, with his wounded companions, got alongside, and could be taken into the ship, they were informed, that shortly after they had left her to go on shore, a number of canoes approached her from the island. Portions of the crews paddling there, after some persuasion, came alongside, and subsequently on board, to the number of 18 or 20 individuals; no apprehensions were entertained respecting their intentions, until a goat was seized by a native and thrown overboard, when presently, as if a concerted signal had been given, they began throwing overboard everything they found loose about the decks, which the others, in the canoes, as readily picked up.

As the surgeon told the tale, the few Europeans on board were quite taken aback, for having seen the natives come alongside unarmed, they relied that their intentions were friendly, while they had no other disposition themselves than to cultivate an amicable correspondence in the absence of the captain. But now, in the midst of this return for courtesy, forbearance on our parts was out of the question; commencing reluctant war, the seamen thumped the trespassers with broomsticks, and anything they could get hold of, but nothing proved so effectual as the cook's scalding water, which he dealt out on their naked skins with such good effect, as made them jump directly overboard. They appeared quite at home in the water, and soon reached their boats; they were most anxious after live stock; the few fowls and ducks within the coops had stood a poor chance, if the plunderers had known how to get them out readily.

The surgeon observed that the most formidable quadruped which the savages had encountered on board, was a large Tom-cat, which was sitting quietly as usual near the main hatch; when Tom found himself seized by one of the natives in such a rough manner, he applied his weapons of defence so well, that the blood streamed from the arms of his assailer, who quitted his hold, glad to let his intended prize escape. Those in the ship then fired a gun, as well to intimidate the natives in the canoes, as to give a signal to the captain on shore. It was thought that the arrows were poisoned, as the three poor fellows who died suffered great agonies. The foregoing is founded on the reports of Capt. Nicholl and his surgeon of this distressing affair.

The *Walker* was thus rendered short of hands; two of ours volunteered to join her crew, which they were permitted to do, as we had more men on board than our complement.

As Captain Nicholl was unacquainted with the navigation of these seas, he expressed a wish to keep company with the *Friendship,* until we came to the Cape of Good Hope in New Guinea; with which Captain R. concurred. He generally spent the day on board our ship in fine weather.

We had reason to suppose that the New Britons were cannibals, from the following circumstances. About a week prior to the *Walker*'s falling in with us, while she was off that coast, several of the canoes came from the shore; in one of which was a lad about sixteen, who was fairer than the rest. He seemed anxious to get on board the ship, but was restrained by two savages; at length they were enticed alongside, when this boy sprung up the side in the greatest agitation, and wished to run below. He spoke a language which the *Walker's* company did not understand; but seeing a chart, which happened to be upon the capstan, he pointed towards Manilla and China.

This convinced Captain Nicholl that the boy had been once in civilized society, and determined him to retain the youth on board, if to stay were agreeable to himself.

Captain Nicholl then pointed to the canoes, which caused the poor boy to tremble all over; he then pointed down the hatchway the boy lost not a moment in descending below, where he remained until the canoes retired to the shore. This boy was brought on board of us one day, when it was discovered that he understood the Malay language. Three people of that country we had on board, to whom he gave the following narrative of himself.

He said he was born on the island Mindanio; that when very little, he was sent on board a small ship with one mast, of which a China man was captain; that they went to many islands, getting things in exchange for cloth, long knives, &c. That the ship one night got on rocks, and was soon full of water; that there were three China men besides the captain; there were about fifteen persons in all on board. They left the wreck and went in the boat, and were many days in want of water; they landed at a place which he did not know, but were quickly set upon by savages. Some of his companions ran into the woods, and were murdered, and afterwards eaten by these people. Two of the savages quarrelled about him; he thought one wanted to save, and the other intended to kill him. They struggled very much, and tore each other on the ground; many of the natives saw this, but did not meddle with them; he did not know whether one killed the other or not, for he was hurried on board a canoe, and taken to another place.

After this he had many changes of masters, and did all they required of him. When he was asked how long it was since he fell into their hands, he could not tell; but said, he was so high, putting his hand to his breast; which made us conjecture that his captivity might begin about five years before he was taken on board the *Walker*. He told many strange and incredible stories, respecting his savage masters. We had no doubt of their being cannibals, for he affirmed they at times had nothing else to eat but human flesh, of which hunger made him glad to partake; which was served out in very small portions.

When the ship was first discerned from the shore, he told his masters that if they permitted him to go on board, he would procure them many fine things, with which he would return. This induced them to comply with his request. In coming off in the canoe, he frequently trembled and shook very much, which was caused by the hope of escaping; they thought it was from fear, and asked him if the people on board would eat him. He said, "No, no, these people never eat man's flesh, and that it was only cold which made him tremble." The above heads [*sic*] of the boy's account were interpreted by our Malay seamen, one of whom was very intelligent, having been brought up with a Europe-born Dutchman at Batavia.

On the 14th June we cleared St. George's Channel, and next day passed, on our right, a large lofty island, named after Lord Sandwich. We had now frequent squalls, with rain, thunder, and lightning; a calm succeeded, which made it very tedious. We saw some large trees floating in the water, with abundance of fish about them.

One day, it being nearly calm, when Captain Nicholl was on board with us, a very strange fish was seen from the forecastle to pass under the ship's bottom; it was afterwards perceived astern, having a number of pilot fish about it, which readily took bait from a small hook. Three of them were caught, and put into a bucket of water, where they soon died; they were the most beautiful little fish I had ever seen at sea, being striped round with red and white, like a zebra: they measured about nine inches in length, and were delicious when cooked.

They are said to attend only the shark; but I rather think they hover about any large floating substance, as numbers were seen about the drift wood and trees. The monster gambolling amongst them was termed the Devil Fish, by Captain Nicholl's people; it was not afraid of the ship, and at times came very close.

It appeared to me like a very large overgrown skate, being nearly square; I reckoned it might occupy a space about the size of our main hatchway; they threw the fish-gig at it, which bounded off its back, breaking two of the prongs; it never came so near afterwards, and a breeze springing up, we saw no more of it.

On the morning of the 17th of June, the Admiralty Islands were seen. It was found that the ships had been driven by currents more north than they had expected; in consequence of which, they were, according to first appearances, embayed; but proceeding nearer the large island, which we named the Sovereign, it was observed that there was a considerable opening between the Sovereign and three smaller islands, which lay to the south of it. This induced our captain to ask Captain Nicholl if he would venture through. He replied, if our ship would take the lead, he would follow. The wind was fair for passing in that direction, and we proceeded accordingly.

Coming near, we observed a number of canoes approaching us full of men. Before entering the passage, we let them come alongside; which they did with every confidence, that made us suppose that they had had intercourse with ships before. Their canoes were large, and had a platform in the centre, with a fire upon it, and some bread-fruit and jack-fruit were roasting, which they gave us, exchanging it for any thing we offered them; but iron was their favorite. They thought we wanted eatables most, and handed up fish and cocoa-nuts, with the jack-fruit. They also presented calabashes of water, which made us suppose that some ship had been there in want of provisions and water.

If the natives had any arms, they were concealed under the platform, for we saw none. They appeared to be the most civil people we had ever met with in these parts; in consequence of which, the captain called the marine localities, Port Mangles and Friendship's Passage. It was thought there was some very good anchorage in the port, as the ships had from seven to twelve, and thirty fathoms, in passing through, with the land so near on both sides as to give the resemblance of a locked harbour.

On the island to the south of us many parts of the territory had the appearance of being under cultivation, with a sort of lattice-work in some places, as if designed to preserve fruit from the winged tribe. Many houses and inhabitants were seen on shore. To distinguish a remarkable hill, sloping gently down to a ravine that was cultivated, the captain, in compliment to the owners of the ship, called the former James' Mount, and the latter John's Valley. A projecting point of land was named Point Thomas; and a white coral bank lying off it, seen very plain under water, Reed's Bank. Another small opening was denominated Eleanor's Cove, and a little elevated spot Barclay's Peak. These names were all given to different parts of that island which is south of the Great Admiralty (or Sovereign) Island. Farther, some rocks, about five leagues to the west of this place, were called Muirhead's Reef, after the chief mate. We observed numbers of parrots and paroquets, flying about on the shore, amongst the trees.

As the *Walker* was about a mile astern of us, we were much surprised to hear firing of musketry from her, and to see the canoes leaving her in all directions. We did not learn the cause of this until next day, when it was reported that a crow-bar had been taken from one of the party, with which a canoe made off rapidly towards the shore. It was to bring the plunderers back that several muskets were fired at them; and, I am afraid, from what the surgeon said, that several were wounded, if not killed, in the canoe. We were extremely sorry to learn this, as it might be detrimental to other navigators passing this way. It had been much better to leave good impressions with these friendly islanders, who did not retaliate hostilities upon the *Walker*'s people. Having a favourable breeze during the night, next morning we were out of sight of land.

The captain wished to keep as near the old track as possible, as the least deviation in the night exposed the ships to danger. He also drew the line on Capt. Nicholl's charts, in case of separation; but as the *Walker* sailed much better than our ship, it was always in their power to keep company if they wished.

In our progress to the west, being so near the equator, we suffered much from excessive heat, particularly in the night, when we had little wind: the thermometer sometimes stood at ninety-five and one hundred. We had, however, plenty of water, the casks for the use of the prisoners on the passage out being furnished by the owners, were kept on board, when the other stores were returned at Sydney.

We saw islands and land to the south of us every day, from the 19th June until arriving off the New Guinea Cape. On the 24th we had much rain, with heavy squalls, accompanied with thunder and lightning. At day-light next morning, the *Walker* was not to be seen from our mast-head; it as supposed she had tacked in the night, to avoid a small low island, which our ship passed just at dusk.

In this track we passed many large trees and drifts: one tree which appeared very straight, was taken on board; but when the root had been sawed off, it was found very soft and full of worms; besides the smell was so offensive, that it was again thrown overboard. A species of cormorant were commonly perched upon these trees; which, when seen at a distance, made us at first imagine them to be canoes with people. Five or six of these birds were seen together upon one tree; they would fly away as soon as our boat approached; no doubt they were attracted by the fish that hovered about the wood.

We had the coast of New Guinea daily in sight on our left, but at too great a distance to make any observations; it appeared in many places very mountainous. On the 29th we passed the islands named, after their discoverer, Schouting's Islands; they lie off the coast, and have many low, dangerous coral reefs about them, which had been observed, with the advantage of a nearer view, by our captain, when previously in the *Cornwallis*.

On the morning of the 1st July we were again joined by the *Walker,* who had tacked, as before supposed. Captain Nicholl and his officers now delivered their letters to us, to forward by the first opportunity for England. He intended to separate from us that evening, and proceed to Dory Harbour; the high land of which was in sight; we accordingly parted, with mutual good wishes for the safety and prosperity of each other. Two days after this, having favourable winds, we came in sight of the Cape of Good Hope, the [north]-western extremity of New Guinea.

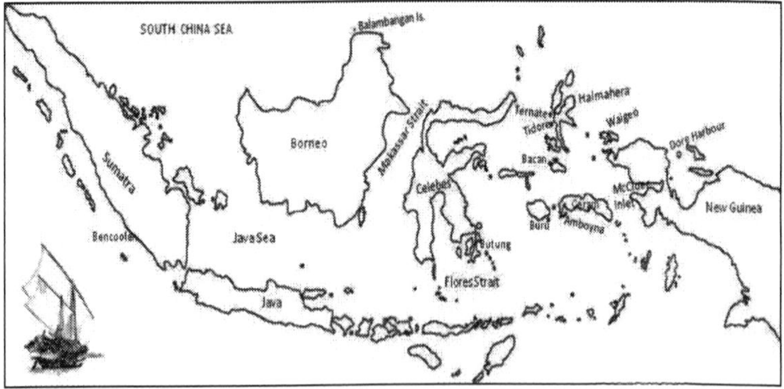

As something was amiss with the ship's rudder, which could not be rectified at sea, it was judged proper to put into some place for that purpose, and at the same time to fill the empty casks with fresh water to stiffen the ship, for old sailors say, that casks once filled with salt water never become sweet again. For this object the captain steered to make a port upon the island Golilo [Halmahera], which was well known to him formerly. In our way thither, we passed Dampier's Straits, having the coast of New Guinea (or Papua) on our left, and the island of Waggiou on our right; passing several islands whose names were not known. We then came in sight of Golilo, and in the evening anchored in a harbour called Osso.

The land hereabout was clothed with verdure to the water's edge. We had no communication with the shore that evening, but during the night were serenaded with many different and harmonious notes of the feathered tribe, as well as with the mixed under tones of many humming insects; the ship lying so near the shore, and the night being still, the least noise could be heard amongst the trees.

Next morning a proa [*prahu*] came alongside, with a chief and six paddlers. When he came on board, he immediately recognized the captain, and was most happy to see him, saying, everything in his power should be done to assist in getting the ship watered, &c. This person was an Imaum, or Mahometan priest: he might be about forty-five years of age; had a commanding countenance, which with his long white beard gave him a respectable appearance. He ordered some very fine pine-apples and plantains to be brought from the proa, with sago-bread, in the shape of little square cakes. The latter were not much relished, being of a dry nature; but the pine-apples were a great treat, having a most delicious flavour.

In the afternoon two large armed proas were seen coming into the harbour; but kept at a distance until we shewed English colours. When they directly entered, and came close to our ship. They were from Papua, or New Guinea. The chief men were Malays, but the others resembled the negroes, except that the hair or wool on the head was frizzled out like a large black wig, twice the size of the head; and a most ferocious look they had. These boats carried swivels, mounted behind a barricade, with loop-holes to fire through. They were trading vessels, but it was said they would plunder if a chance offered. We got some nutmegs, mace, and beautiful birds of paradise from them, in exchange for crockery, hatchets, and cloth; they very much wanted gunpowder, but that demand was not complied with. They had been at first afraid we were Dutch, which made them hesitate entering the harbour, until they saw our colours; observing, as they told us this, that the Dutch were their greatest enemies. The people on shore were glad when the proa went away, saying, if we had not been there they should have been plundered by them.

King bird of paradise, from Popular Science Monthly

I had often heard that the birds of paradise lived in the air, and could not approach the earth without certain death; that they had no feet, nor any terrestrial habits. However, those we procured from these people had not only feet, but claws like a parrot. The Malays informed us that these animals come to Papua at certain seasons, like birds of passage, and are snared.

We had three different kinds, the straw-coloured, the yellow, and the crimson; the latter are by far the handsomest; these are called the rajah or king birds: our specimens measured about nine inches in length, the body not thicker than a goldfinch, and the plumage of a most beautiful crimson, scarlet, and green colour. They had two quills projecting about seven inches from the tail; these quills appeared as if stripped of the feathers, until at the extreme end, which was curled up about the size of a small daisy, tinged with the most delicate colours imaginable. The yellow birds, although beautiful, were very inferior to the rajahs.

The nutmeg is very plentiful here, notwithstanding what is said to the contrary; the natives brought us the fruit upon branches, in all its stages, from the size of an olive to that of a peach upon the twig. The nut, when bursting the pulp or rind, and shewing the bright red mace over the shell, is exceedingly beautiful. I procured plenty in this state, and had them preserved in clarified syrup of sugar. The captain did not go into the woods this time, but I have heard him say that when here formerly as an officer, within an hour's walk from the shore he has counted upwards of an hundred trees bearing fruit.

There were several large proas, or corra-corras [*kora-kora*], which arrived from several parts of the same island to trade while we remained; they had plenty of spices, which they readily exchanged with us for cloth, &c.; but were particularly fond of some Scotch plaid. If we had had plenty of the same commodity on board, it would have turned to good account; indeed, the captain bartered all the merchandize he had for spices; and my small wardrobe of old apparel came in for a share. We found the Malays at this place very honest and fair dealing people. We were supplied with plenty of fruit, fish, and turtle, while we staid. They were afraid to take their trade to Amboyna, on account of pirate proas which infested those seas; and if any ship were so unfortunate as to get on shore, it was sure to be plundered, and the crew murdered by those vultures. This was the case with a ship under Danish colours, going through Dampier's Straits to China, the year before.

One night we were alarmed by the firing of two muskets from the forecastle of our ship; two proas were observed approaching, beating upon an instrument, and singing what was thought to be a war-song; notwithstanding they were challenged from the ship, they still advanced. Immediately on the muskets being fired, the captain went upon deck, and as he understood the Malays pretty well, soon found they were friends, and invited them alongside; when three chiefs came on board, and sent the proas away from the ship; one of them was an old friend of the captain's, named Twan-Allie [Tuan Hadjee]. His master, Sultan Newkoo [Prince Nuku], of Tidore, had dispatched him to collect tribute at the different ports of Messa, Weda, and Osso, which was paid in spices. It was very soon understood that he wanted some presents for his master, as also for himself. Captain R. gave him, in the presence of the other chiefs, a handsome pair of pistols, a sword, and a dirk, with four cannisters of gunpowder for the Sultan.

They wished the ship to go to Tidore, saying, that the Sultan had plenty of cloves and other spices, which he wished to part with. This, however, was out of the question, as we were not prepared for traffic.

It very much surprised the mates to find our captain so well known at this apparently wild place. But nothing will remain to excite wonder, when it is known that he assisted in reinstating the Sultan, just mentioned, as Chief of Tidore, an eminence which was his by birthright; but he had formerly been displaced by the Dutch, and a price put upon his head, in consequence of his having supplied an English ship with provisions, &c.

To revert to the origin of that transaction: in [1796], our captain received a lieutenant's commission, signed by Sir John Shore, and the other members of council at Calcutta, to act against the Dutch. The establishment he then belonged to fitted out several armed vessels, as well for trade as war; and the officers directing this force acted amongst these islands and people near two years, assisted by a number of war-proas well armed: they drove the Dutch from Tidore, and attacked Ternate three successive times, where a number of men were killed and wounded on both sides.

The Dutch at this time were almost starved out, and otherwise so harassed, that had any of our king's ships been present, these lords of the eastern seas would most gladly have delivered up the island; but they thought, and justly too, that the influence of the private ships were not sufficient to keep the hostile Malays in check. Some of the Dutch governors in these settlements exercise great cruelty and tyranny over these people, particularly if the natives be detected in trafficking with the English, the Batavian authorities having the power of life and death vested in themselves without any appeal. But, thank God, this abuse of sovereignty cannot be erected in any of our settlements with impunity.

Twan-Allie stated that the Sultan was very happy now at Tidore, and had not for some time been attacked from Ternate, the Dutch having no disposable force; but as he was upwards of seventy years of age, it was thought that his youngest brother, Rajah Mooda [Muda], from the island of Ceram, would be called to the government of Tidore. Our friend, Twan-Allie, continued on board all the time we remained here; notwithstanding his apparent strictness in keeping the institutes of the koran, he partook of our wine, and the common fare of the table, ham and pork excepted. He was too high a personage to trade, but made presents in hopes of a double return.

This is the custom with the Sultan and all his chief men in these parts. However, I must not say too much on this score, as I came off pretty well. He admired a topaz broach which I had; this was presented to him; in return he gave me three beautiful birds of paradise, two cockatoos, and two handsome luries [lories]; he was pleased with the exchange, and so was I.

We also received from this person about two ounces of seed pearls, and some fine tortoise-shell, in the rough state; for all which he got more than an equivalent. The Malays had also plenty of the edible bird's-nests, which are so much in demand amongst the Chinese, for making a luxurious soup: but as all our little merchandize was exhausted, we could purchase no more of their commodities.

The ship's rudder being now put to rights, preparations were made for our departure. The ship at this place was filled with parrots, cockatoos, and luries, belonging to the seamen and lascars; many of them equal in beauty to our Botany Bay birds, but not so hardy.

On the morning of the 18th July we left Osso, and proceeded on our voyage, passing between an island called Pulo Moor and Polut Potanny. Next day we saw the island Oby Major, and sailed between that and Pulo Gassas; then were observed the islands of Ceram and Booros, which we passed upon our left Amboyna is situated a little to the south of these islands, but being out of our track we did not see it.

On the 25th we saw the island of Bootan; at which place, when my husband was there in the *Cornwallis,* and in charge of a watering party [August 14, 1796], they would have been murdered, had not the treacherous design been discovered by one of the seamen, who understood the Malay language, he overhearing a conference between the Malays, who were all armed, and very numerous. He learnt that their first proposition was to massacre the boat's crew, and then attack the ship. But this was overruled by a chief, who observed, that if they could the next day entice the boat's crew to come again for water, that the ship's company would be more off their guard, and more easily overpowered.

A Malay, who spoke a little Dutch, enquired, in pursuit of this scheme, if the ship wanted any more water: it was answered that there was very little on board, and it would take three days to complete the watering. This reply induced them to allow the boat to proceed on board, not suspecting that their evil intentions were known. On the boat's return, the unpleasant discovery was communicated to the captain: the Malays were then instantly ordered out of the ship; and no time was lost in leaving a place where so much danger was to be apprehended. There were upwards of twenty war proas counted in the river, mounting from four to six guns, and capable of containing from thirty to forty men in each. Fortunately for the *Cornwallis*'s people, it was low water when she sailed, and most of the proas were aground.

Leaving Bootan on our right, we passed through the Straits of Saylair [Flores Strait], and next day saw a most dangerous shoal, called the Brill, upon which part of the wreck of a ship was visible, with three large pirate proas at anchor to leeward of it. The ship's head being turned towards them, they doubtless thought we were coming to reconnoitre: they instantly got under weigh, set their sails, and made off as fast as possible; after which we altered our course, and stood on, so as to clear the shoal. It being very fine weather, we passed within a few miles of the Brill; it appeared like a large white patch in the midst of the blue water, the white coral shewing the danger under the surface. The *Friendship* did not delay her progress by sending a boat to examine the wreck, as only some of the ribs or timbers were seen above water. At this time the high land of the island Celebes was in sight.

From July 27 until August 3, was occupied in passing through the dangerous Java Sea: and during this time we had seen the great island of Borneo on our right, of which the animal nearest in likeness to the human species is a native, namely, the Orn-Outang [Orang Utang], or man of the woods, according to the Malay language. There are also great quantities of gold dust procured at Borneo; but all ships trading with the inhabitants must be continually on the watch, and well armed, as one chief who barters the gold may employ another to way-lay the European party, and these, if overpowered, are sure to be murdered; too many instances of this have occurred to vessels trading amongst the Malays.

We had now reached the east entrance of Singapore Straits. On the 4th we were gratified by the sight of a ship coming out of them as we were entering; she proved to be the *Lowjee Family,* from Bombay, bound to China, with a cotton cargo. They informed us that many privateers were in the India Seas, and that some had been seen in the Straits; that the *Arniston,* Indiaman, had nearly been taken by one off Bencoolen. This information made our captain prepare for a defence, and put on as formidable an appearance as possible. The ship had but twelve guns mounted, but ports below for twenty-four: the vacant ports were filled with what the sailors called quakers, namely, wooden guns painted, which made her show at a distance as if she had upwards of thirty guns mounted.

It was very pleasant sailing through these Straits, having the land very near us both sides of us, covered with wood to the water's edge.

On the 6th of August, in the evening, we came to a place called Saint John's Island, where we anchored for the night. On the next morning a Malay boat came alongside, with three fine turtles, and a quantity of fish fresh caught, as well as some which had been dried in the sun. The captain purchased all they had with dollars, for the persons in the boat would take nothing else in regular barter. The turtle might weigh about two hundred to two hundred and fifty pounds each, and the three cost only five dollars and some spirits, the latter of which they seemed to prize highly.

We now left the straits of Singapore and entered the straits of Malacca, having the great Island of Sumatra on the left, and the very southernmost extremity of the continent of Asia, called the Peninsula of Malacca, on our right. Our only interruption, on passing these straits in the day, arose from very hard squalls, with much rain, thunder and lightning. These squalls generally lasted about an hour. We always anchored and furled the sails when the squall was approaching, and enjoyed a most agreeable change after it had ceased, as the thermometer would fall from ninety to eighty and seventy-five degrees.

I may here remark, that notwithstanding the difference of climate we had hitherto experienced, our seamen were all healthy, a circumstance perhaps which may be chiefly attributed to the large supply of fine pigs we got at Norfolk Island. This enabled them to have a fresh meal three times per week, and they were constantly at full allowance of water.

In the afternoon of the 9th, we had again the satisfaction of beholding a place where civilized inhabitants of our country lived; this was the fort of Malacca, which, with the city, had a very fine appearance as the ship entered the roads. We found lying here the ship *Commerce,* Capt. Lane, who with his purser, Mr. Edward Brightman, a young man of colour, came on board as soon as the ship anchored; he made many inquiries as to where we had procured the spices, &c. These questions the captain did not think proper to answer; but the purser, Mr Brightman, who understood the language of our lascars, was more successful, as they told him all they knew, and his ship was employed in the Malay trade.

The next morning the captain went on shore, to wait upon Col. Aldwell Taylor, the commandant at this place, who no sooner understood that I was on board, than he came off to invite me on shore. He would take no denial, and informed me that Mrs. Taylor had apartments at the castle quite at my service. There was here no alternative; I soon packed up a few necessaries, and accompanied my husband and the colonel on shore.

On landing I could make no immediate observations, being hurried into a palanquin, and shut up to avoid the heat of the sun. This mode of conveyance was indeed a great novelty to me, being the first of the kind I had seen; however, I was not so closely shut up as to preclude me from observing the shops and houses as we passed. They mostly appeared built of wood, having three, and some four stories, and reminded me of the Dutch houses at the Cape, the windows and doors being painted green, and having a similar external appearance. In the shops were plenty of sugar-canes, and all kinds of tropical fruits.

The entrance to the Dutch fort, 1811 – Wathen, Journal.

We soon approached, however, and entered the castle-gates, where I was received by Mrs. Taylor in the most polite and friendly way; her pleasing manners, affability, and ease, very soon convinced me I was welcome. There was another lady with her, a Mrs. Butler, a distant relation, whose husband was a merchant, and formerly commanded a ship in the country trade.

There was a small party engaged to dine at the castle that evening, where for the first time I saw and wondered at the eastern manners and style of living. The suite of apartments were lofty and spacious, and the table was covered with a profusion of delicate viands; after which, the finest fruits were served, the different names and properties of which were pointed out by our kind entertainer. Amongst these the mangosteen is, I think, without exception, the most delicious and finest flavoured fruit I ever tasted; it is about the size of an apple; the part to be eaten is enclosed in a thick dark brown rind, and when opened, it shews five or six white jelly-like fibres, resembling the small quarters of an orange.

The pine-apples were very large, and well flavoured; we had also mangoes and guavas, with the custard-apple; the latter, about the size of a large orange, with a rough grey coat outside; when ripe it appears to burst the skin, and exhibits a thick cream-coloured substance. It is eaten with a tea-spoon, and the hard black seeds, which it is mixed with, rejected. Many persons are extremely partial to this fruit, but I must confess it was no favourite of mine; we also had several kinds of oranges and lichees, originally transplanted from China. The latter is a very delicious fruit, a kind of pulp covered over a hard kernel, and a rough coat formed an exterior covering to the whole, about the size of a walnut. We also had the pumblenose [pomelo], or, as they are called in the West-Indies, chaddock; they are a fine cooling fruit, about the size of a cocoa-nut, and resemble the orange in colour: a still greater variety of others, the names of which I have forgotten.

After dinner the gentlemen joined the ladies at tea in the drawing-room; cards were then introduced, and the evening passed away most pleasantly. My long absence from female society acted as a charm upon my spirits, and made me meet it with a double relish.

I was informed at parting with Mrs. Taylor that a horse would be ready for my husband at daylight next morning, and that the colonel would drive me out in his curricle, to see the place before the sun rose too high, as it was only early in the morning that this could be accomplished. I thanked my polite hostess for her information and next morning was ready to attend.

We had a most delightful drive round the environs of the town. Passing the Chinese burial ground, and through the street where these people reside, I was surprised to observe a long chest, finely carved and ornamented, at each door of the Chinese houses. These the colonel told me were their coffins, and that as soon as a China-man saved money enough he then procured a coffin for himself, and generally slept upon the lid. He also informed me that a poor fellow had been lately murdered, while thus asleep upon his coffin, by a mad Malay, who had ran a-muck, or, in other words, had lost all his money and other property by gambling, and then given himself up in despair.

The Malays on such occasions often indulge in an intoxicating drug called bang, mixed with opium, and the operation of which causes raging madness. In this state they determine to stab, with their kresse [*kris*] or dagger (a weapon no Malay is without) every living creature that falls in their way, after first having sacrificed, if possible, the person who had gained their property.

The old invented story, however, about the upas-tree being possessed of a gum of a deadly poisonous nature, is nothing else than a scarecrow to keep European nations from smelling out the Dutch spices. It is well known that no grass will grow under the clove-tree, but the Malay kresse may be poisoned in various ways independently of this fictitious gum, the colonel told me that such scenes frequently occurred in the interior of the country; and when known to take place, a high price was offered to the first man who could dispatch the demon, for in this light they certainly deserve to be viewed; but we cannot marvel much at such atrocities taking place amongst these savage people, when, alas! but too many such instances occur amongst our own countrymen, after bad fortune at the gambling-table. There is but little difference (in my humble opinion) between him who shoots his friend in a duel, and afterwards destroys himself, and the mad Malay who runs a-muck, and always ends in self-destruction, if not overtaken.

Before we returned to the castle, the sun became so very warm as to render the shade not a little grateful. We breakfasted at a pleasant retreat on a hill within the boundary of the fort, and from whence we had a fine extensive view of the surrounding country; we commanded also a view of the shipping in the roads, and the lofty mountains on the island of Sumatra. Notwithstanding the proximity to the equator, being in lat. about two deg. north, the verdure and foliage are ever green.

Near the mount is an old church, which was built by the Portuguese upwards of two centuries ago, and might still be preserved at a small expense. Perhaps, however, the settlement may be given back to our Dutch friends, should a peace take place; in which case they should advance the needful for this purpose, but at present there is real danger, in walking across the slab floor, of the vaults underneath giving way. On these stones are many memorials of Europeans, formerly resident, and whose remains are interred here.

After breakfast we again descended to the castle, but on the way were detained to look at a reservoir of water, which contained many gold and silver fish, which eat from the hand.

I felt much indebted to Mrs. T. who took great pains to let me see every thing worth notice within the fort. It will be a matter of regret should they ever demolish the strong walls of this secure retreat; it was frequently, however, the subject of conversation, that orders were expected from home to blow up the works.

The commandant accompanied my husband off to the ship this afternoon; and amongst other things, very much admired a fine bull-dog we had on board, the very sight of which struck terror into the Malays; but he was docile and harmless, unless very much provoked.

I cannot help travelling back to Ireland for a short account of this faithful creature's adventures. He had belonged to an industrious blacksmith, who used to do jobs for the ship at the passage of Waterford; the owner had a garden that was not too well defended against depredators, in consequence of which a neighbour's cow entered, and was feasting away upon the cabbages. The blacksmith's son, a boy about fourteen years of age, seeing this, called the dog, who instantly seized her by the nose, and pinned the poor cow down, bellowing out so loud as to arouse all the neighbours, and amongst the rest her master. The dog was soon loosened from his hold, but left the blood streaming from the cow's mouth, the owner of which said the dog should not live; but the blacksmith, well knowing the threat would be put in execution, begged my husband (who happened to be present) to take the dog on board the ship, and save his life.

This was complied with, and a guinea given to his master, who shed tears, as well as his son, at parting with the animal; the dog, however, very soon became attached to the captain, who called him *Friends*, and was the same he now presented to Col. Taylor. The latter, highly pleased with the gift, declared that he need fear no mad Malay whilst *Friends* should be with him. The poor animal had been so long on ship board, that when he landed he seemed beside himself; he could not pass a bush without running round and about it several times; rolling on the grass was a great luxury to him: but on the way from the boat to the castle no Malay approached near; they all kept at a respectful distance, some were even running into their houses and shutting the doors.

These people have a most disgusting custom of chewing the beetle-nut with the chunam, which is a kind of paste prepared like lime from shells; and the better sort keep a slave in constant attendance, with a box, for this purpose. Their teeth are as black as jet, and their mouths and lips as if dyed with a deep red, in consequence of this filthy propensity. They are idle, and very treacherous in their dealings. The Chinese are the only industrious people here; a China-man is, indeed, generally a jack of all trades, and the colonel has several of them in his service as domestics, who act as cooks, gardeners, painters, shoemakers, and carpenters, all in turn. I was shewn a book of drawings, in which most of the fruits and shrubs of this place were coloured in the most correct and beautiful manner, by a China-man who was then at work in the garden. I think no person of the least observation could mistake a Malay for a China-man, let them dress as they will; and although they appear to have originally sprung from the same stock, they have the same flat cast of countenance, and the larger lineaments are closely similar, the Chinese having at the same time fairer complexions and smaller eyes than the Malays.

Some of the gentlemen riding out one morning, attended by the dog "Friends," were in a dangerous predicament, passing a large pool or tank of stagnated water, where several buffaloes were cooling themselves, with their heads just above the surface. At sight of the dog, they instantly rose, and pursued the party, leaving poor Friends to bring up the rear, who was reluctantly obliged to obey his master, and retreat also. These creatures are just like swine in the mire, their backs being covered with wet mud, from rolling in the dirty water, which is gratifying to them whenever they can indulge in such a luxury, but no doubt serves also to keep the stinging flies from biting them. They have no hair, only a few bristles on their skins, like those of a pig, but more thinly scattered over the surface of the body; they have a twisted rattan passed through the nostrils, in the shape of a ring, by which they are led when at work. When in a wild state, it is said that no animal, not even the tiger, will attack the buffalo, or if he do, is sure to give up the encounter first. There are numbers of tigers as well as crocodiles at this place, together with very large and venomous snakes, of which many stories were related by the inhabitants.

After spending five most pleasant days with our very kind and hospitable friends, we prepared to go on board, and parted with regret on both sides from several Dutch families, who visited at the castle while we were there, from Col. Taylor and his amiable partner, of whom all agreed in speaking in terms of the highest commendation.

On the 15th of August we sailed from Malacca with a fine breeze; no person on board had to regret touching here. The officers, seamen, and lascars, who were tired of the feathered tribe, sold their birds very well at this place; some fetched as high as ten and twelve dollars, each, particularly the luries from Gillolo. The lascars were then rich in money, as well as in many little comforts which the place so plentifully afforded.

East Indiamen, from Clipper Ship Era

In the evening we reached Cape Ricardo, where we were obliged to anchor and furl all the sails, in consequence of one of those storms of thunder, lightning, and rain, to which I before alluded as prevalent in these latitudes. There we remained all night and next day; passed through that dangerous channel which extends on both sides from the mount called Parcellar, on the Malay side, and some small rocky islands on the Sumatra side, called the Arrowes. Before dark we were reckoned clear of all danger, and the following day saw upon our right the islands called the Sambelongs. We were still, however, annoyed with heavy squalls, but were not, as before, under the necessity of anchoring, having, as the sailors expressed it, more sea room.

On the 17th we saw five sail of ships a-head : this number gave us more confidence than the sight of a single one would have done, and we therefore stood on towards them. One of these proved to be the *Arniston,* Capt. Campbell Majoribanks, bound to China : our captain went on board, and learnt from Mr. Jamieson [James Jameson, chief mate of the *Arniston*] the particulars of the attack made on it by a privateer at Bencoolen.

It appeared that the *Armiston* had just anchored, and the seamen were aloft furling sails; they had no suspicion of the strange ship that was approaching with American colours hoisted; but the privateer no sooner got within gun-shot, than she fired her broadside into the Indiaman. Not a moment was lost on the other side in getting the people down, when they slipped the cable and followed her; this was of little use, there was no equality between the sailing of the ships, and the privateer made off, no doubt finding herself mistaken in the superior force of the enemy, and the latter concluded that the privateer had taken them for a country ship, manned with lascars.

Capt. Majoribanks said that he had landed a detachment of seapoys at Penang, and advised our putting in there, having no doubt but they would be sent to Calcutta with us, and besides a protection, they being all armed, the business would pay the owners of the ships very well. In consequence of this information, it was determined upon to call at the above-mentioned place, it being also reported that the Bay of Bengal was infested with several privateers.

The next day we came in sight of Prince of Wales' Island, or Penang, and anchored in the harbour on the 20th of August, saluting Fort Cornwallis with nine guns, which number was returned. The ship had but just anchored, and the sails been secured with all possible expedition, when one of the Sumatra storms came on, with the most tremendous peals of thunder, lightning, and rain; but we were now so accustomed to these visitations, after a passage of thirteen weeks, and running upwards of eighty degrees of longitude within a short distance of the equator, that they had become little alarming to any on board.

After this, the captain landed, and repaired to the master attendant's office, when he was accompanied by Mr. John Baird to the government-house, and was introduced to Sir George Leith, the commandant.

The offer of the ship to take on the troops to Calcutta was accepted, provided the ship could stay four or five days, to enable them to prepare provisions, water, &c. It was mentioned that there was water enough on board for double the number of men to be conveyed to Calcutta;

however, they thought proper to detain us, saying, that as the troops were Hindoos they must fill their own water.

Mr. Baird, the master attendant, came on board, and very politely offered us apartments at his house during our stay, which were accepted, and I landed next morning, determined to make good use of my time while we remained. I was anxious to see all that was worth notice at this second Botany Bay, as it was termed by our host, Mr. B., who had much satire in his disposition and conversation, although in every respect a worthy and honourable character, and had commanded an Indiaman in the service of the Company many years previous to his appointment to this island.

Penang, 1814

We set off early next morning in gigs to view the waterfall; during our ride we passed for several miles between an avenue of the cocoa-nut and beetle-nut trees, and many huts or sheds occupied by that industrious race the Chinese, who have charge of the pepper plantations. The supported twig of the pepper plant appeared to me not unlike our hop plants, supported by poles; the pepper hangs in bunches like our currants when green.

We were highly regaled with the delightful fragrance of the aromatic shrubs, as we passed to the place under the hill, where we were obliged to dismount and follow our guide along a narrow winding path. In this spot the sun could not be observed at noon-day, so completely were its rays intercepted by the thick foliage of the lofty trees on each side. In many parts it was a thick impenetrable jungle, which had never been entered by man.

We heard the noise of the descending waters some time before we came near, a circumstance that roused the imagination, and prepared us for something magnificent. I had provided a pair of thick shoes, understanding that the walk was wet and heavy, particularly near the fall. Notwithstanding our fatigue, however, we were well repaid when we arrived at a certain point near the rocky bason, or natural reservoir, where this grand cascade descends with a roaring noise that entirely drowns the sound of the voice, and obliged us to reserve our admiration and opinions.

After we left the spot there was a haze all round the place, caused by the vapour of the falling stream, at the same time so cool as made it unsafe to sit long after our fatiguing walk. As we looked up through the open branch of the trees to the highest source of the dashing element,

Waterfall, Penang Botanical Gardens

it had a grand effect upon our minds. It was an imposing spectacle to behold the crystal stream impetuously rumbling over the rocky steep—

"Defying power of man its passage to stem
"Till with Ocean, the mother, it met."

The fall is said to be upwards of a hundred feet above where we stood. One of the party had brought a small mirror, which by turning one's back, and looking into the glass in a certain position, presented the alarming appearance of the waters falling upon our heads.

Having then rested, and feasted our eyes sufficiently, we thought of satisfying our appetite, which was acknowledged by all to be pretty keen. We only wanted the arrival of the captain, who, to our surprise, was still absent. We knew he could not miss the way, as there was no other path; however he soon joined us, and explained the cause of his delay.

Having staid behind to alter the stirrups of his saddle, and left the horse with the man who had charge of the gigs, he advanced alone up the path a considerable way, when he observed a snake coiled, and partly lying in the pathway. This induced him to retreat and make a noise, to frighten it out of his way, but the reptile kept its station; having, however, determined to make a bold push to pass it, if possible, and procured a large branch of a tree, he prepared to strike it while it lay shooting out its forked tongue at every respiration, and coming pretty nigh, he with all his force aimed a blow, which struck it near the head, and repeating the strokes, he made it quite defenceless, and passed on to us.

After our refreshment we returned, much gratified with the sight and scenery altogether. As we descended, we saw the snake writhing in agonies, being covered with ants, who were fastened upon it. One of the party soon put it out of its misery, and carried it on to town; we there found that it measured three feet nine inches, and was reckoned of the poisonous kind. There were a sort of leeches amongst the grass, which bit several of the gentlemen on the ancle above the shoe, and made the blood flow; but the bite was so small as not to be perceptible until the blood flowed from it.

We returned to George Town about four o'clock next morning; I was honoured by a visit from Lady Albinia Leith, with an invitation to dinner on the following day. She appeared about the age of twenty-five, with handsome features, but of a sickly appearance; she said that the settlement was scarcely tolerable, for want of society, and after chatting some time took her leave.

In the afternoon, Mr. Baird remarked that there were two of the greatest beauties brought for sale from the Queda [Kedah] shore that ever were seen, and that if I would accompany him after the sun was low he would be happy to shew them, as they were at present placed within his grounds at the water-side. No duty as yet, he added, had been fixed upon for their importation. Accordingly we went towards the jetty, where two of the most horrid monsters that ever met the eye were seen, covered with mud. They were, in fact, two young alligators, with their mouths tied up, and rattans twisted round their legs: one was about ten or eleven feet long, and the other about nine, but so disfigured with mud that we could see nothing of the colour of their bodies; thick scales appeared near their tails, but we had no opportunity of examining them a second time, as they regained their liberty: it was supposed by some that they had rolled down, as their feet were so secured they could not use them.

The next day we waited upon Sir George Leith and Lady L. at dinner, accompanied by our host, who was also invited. I was rather surprised at not meeting any other ladies at the government house, but was afterwards informed that Lady L. had but recently arrived, and had not formed much intimacy as yet with the ladies of the settlement. To me it was on this account less a relief to be entertained on shore, and less a disappointment that the company soon broke up.

On the 24th [August], the ship being ready, and the troops embarked, under the command of Lieut. L., of the Company's Bengal army, we prepared for sailing. There were only eighty seapoys, besides followers, but certainly they were the finest-looking native soldiers I had seen, the lowest in stature exceeded five feet nine inches. Another passenger joined us here, a Mr. F., purser in the navy.

Next morning the land-breeze enabled us to leave Penang; we sailed pleasantly for some distance along the shore of Queda, which is covered with wood and verdure, from the water's edge to the summit of the mountains. There were sent on board a number of boxes of a plant called Gamutta, intended for the botanic garden at Calcutta. This tree throws out black fibres from the large leaves near the top, like horse-hair, which is twisted and made into very strong ropes and cables; it is a species of the palm-tree. We had also a pair of large cassawaries, a present from Sir George Leith to Lord Mornington at

Calcutta. I purchased a pair of beautiful crown pigeons, which I intended for my friends in England.

In the afternoon we passed the islands of Latta, and came in sight of Pulo Boutou. Close in with this island a suspicious ship was discovered, under Danish colours; the crew were at work to disguise her, by placing black canvas over the quarter, to make the people on board us suppose she had a poop : this artifice did not escape notice, and preparation was accordingly made for an encounter.

A difference of opinion now took place between our captain and Lieut. L.; the former wished the sepoys to be kept out of sight until we were certain of the discovered sail being an enemy, and in that case for them not to appear until the musketry could take effect. At this time the stranger had made all sail towards us, and our ship had shortened sail to wait her approach the sooner, as the *Friendship* was not in a trim to run. The captain was firm in not letting the sepoys at present to be shewn; however we were soon relieved from anxiety, by the strange ship pulling down the steering sails and standing away from us. Now all concurred in one opinion, and that was not to follow her. We continued our course, and before dark she was out of sight. It was not doubted but that the strange ship was an enemy, and some expected that she would turn and attack us in the night.

We now passed on, with fine weather, between the Nicobar Islands and Junk-ceylon, until we came abreast of the Andaman Islands, when the weather became very unsettled, having constant gales, with heavy squalls of wind and much rain, which occasioned the loss of several sails that were blown from the yards, with much damage to the rigging. Owing to the thickness of the atmosphere, we had no observation of the sun for several days, so that the ship's situation could not be exactly ascertained; at the same time we were in shallow water, which rendered our state very alarming. We were compelled to carry a heavy press of sail, both day and night, to keep the ship off the Pegu shore.

In the afternoon of the 6th of September, our apprehensions were at length relieved, by seeing to the leeward of us that dangerous reef called the Alguada or Nagada, which disclosed to the officers our exact situation. These rocks lie near Diamond Island; we passed them at three or four miles distance, with thankful hearts to the Almighty for our preservation. The waves were dashing over the projecting reef in a frightful manner.

Before morning we had cleared Cape Negrals, the south-western extremity of Pegu [south Burma]. The weather still continued boisterous; but we now had plenty of sea-room, having entered the great Bay of Bengal. It was reckoned the breaking up of the south-west monsoon, which finishes at the autumnal equinox; the north-east monsoon succeeds, and continues until the vernal equinox. Seamen expect bad weather at the change of each monsoon, and prepare accordingly.

We were greatly alarmed one evening by Lieut. L. on a sudden remarking, in conversation, that he perceived the scent of something burning in the ship; almost at the same instant the mate of the watch called out to the steward below to know what it was that caused such a smell of fire. We were all in the greatest agitation at the moment, and poor Lieut. L., from weakness of nerves, fainted; but we were soon happily relieved from further apprehension, by its being discovered that the person who had lighted the binnacle lamp had left a cotton rag in it, which acted like a slow match, and kept smouldering. As soon as this was removed, all was quiet again.

When Mr. L. had recovered from the swoon, he acknowledged to me that it was a family failing; that his mother was the most nervous woman alive, and that he had often tried to conquer this affliction in himself. It was observed, that it was a pity he had chosen the army for a profession. He replied, that it was the only school to eradicate the disease; that when the privateer fired the broadside at the *Arniston,* in Bencoolen Roads, he was standing with Capt. M. at the gangway, not at all suspecting such a salutation, and that he never in his life had more command of himself, and readily assisted in preparing the ship for defence. He added, however, that he had been attacked in the same nervous way on board the *Arniston,* when she was struck with lightning. He was a mild, gentlemanly, well-informed young man.

We now drew near the Sand-heads, formed by the rapid streams poured out from the great river Ganges, with his hundred mouths; the river Hoogly, where Calcutta stands, being only a small branch.

Malacca Drawbridge (1808), E.H. Locker, from Pinkerton

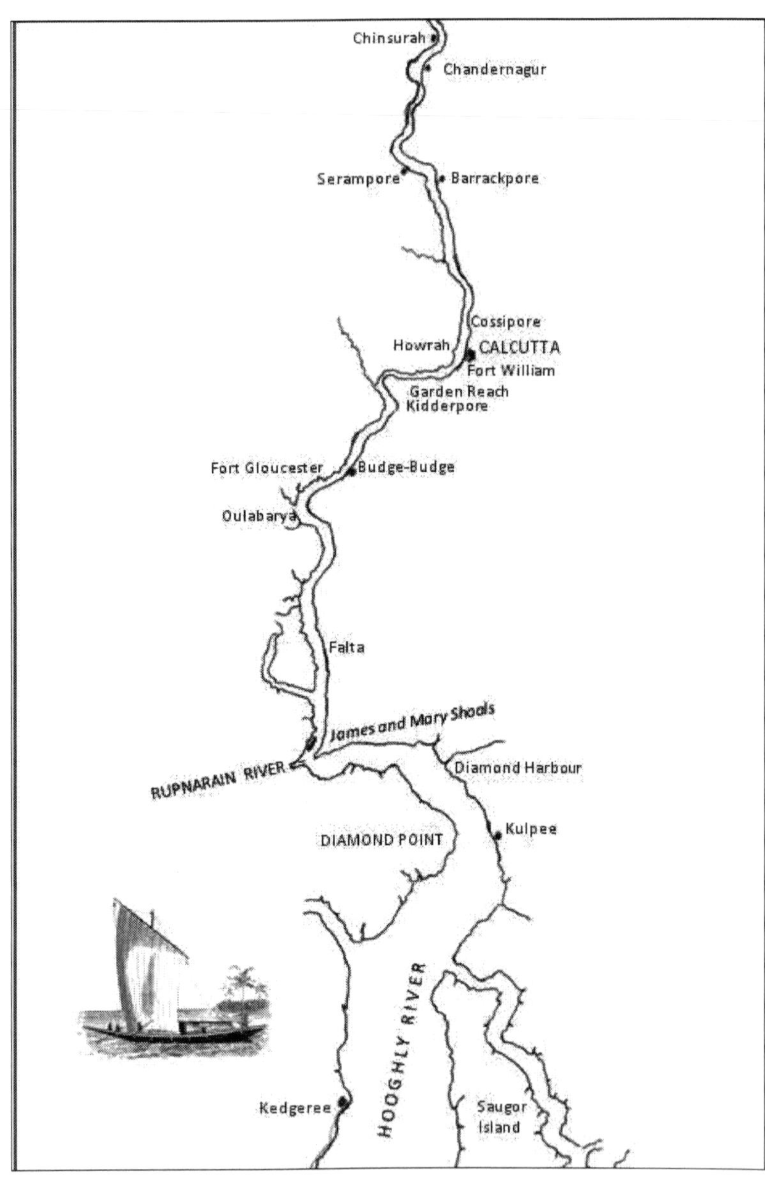
Chinsurah
Chandernagur
Serampore
Barrackpore
Cossipore
Howrah
CALCUTTA
Fort William
Garden Reach
Kidderpore
Fort Gloucester
Budge-Budge
Oulabarya
Falta
James and Mary Shoals
RUPNARAIN RIVER
Diamond Harbour
Kulpee
DIAMOND POINT
HOOGHLY RIVER
Kedgeree
Saugor
Island

Five

Calcutta : September to December 1800

Eleanor had survived storms, volcanoes, and waterspouts, and she had sailed through reef-strewn waters and faced the threat of attack. Yet the most dangerous stretch of her voyage lay ahead—the passage up the wreck-strewn Hooghly River, for which the ship needed a pilot.

The nail-biting business of guiding ships through the shoals and channels of the Hooghly had begun in 1669, when the factors in Bengal received orders from the Directors in London to employ small craft for a pilot service, which was "to be manned with intelligent seamen from the Indiamen, to take charge of the shipping up and down."

Two pinnaces, named *Madras* and *Diligence,* were duly commissioned, and six young men were recruited, to be paid at the rate of six English pounds a year for the most dangerous piloting service in the world. Of these only one, George Herron, survived the first three years, all the others succumbing to tigers, sharks, drowning, or some tropical disease.

Herron was noteworthy, too, for making the first chart—not that it was at all reliable, because the channels changed overnight. New bars and sandbanks materialized, and whole islands came into being—Saugor, which was a single island by the time the *Friendship* arrived in September 1800, was a group of three islets when first charted.

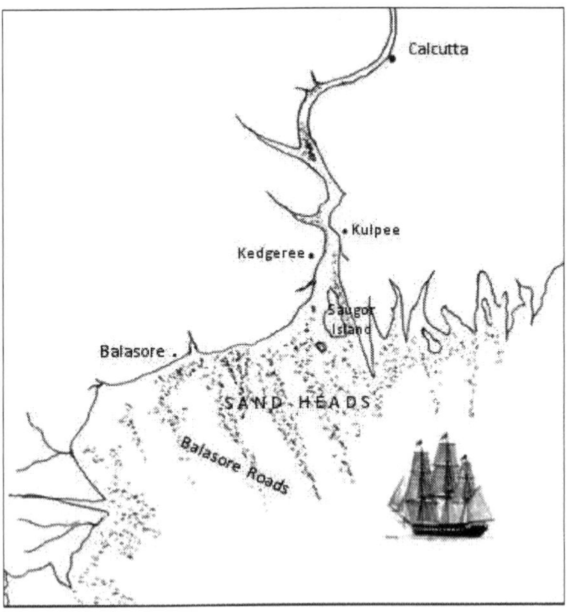

The stretch between the Sand Heads and Kedgeree was particularly "troublesome and dangerous," according to the pilots, but the entire river was notorious for "the three Bs" — bars, banks, and bores. All these were due to what a lady traveller, Jemima Kindersley, called "the prodigious force of the waters," which sluiced the riverbed, changing the shapes and depths of the first two Bs, bars and banks. A bore was a great wave that was impelled up the funnel of the river mouth by an unusually high tide, washing as far upriver as Calcutta.

For every good reason, the first commander of an East Indiaman to take a pilot on board and venture up the river — Captain Mariner of the 200-ton *Rebecca* — unloaded all the "treasure" in his holds before risking the passage, even though the doughty little *Diligence* was leading the way. That was in July 1672. One hundred and twenty-eight years later, despite constant sounding and charting, matters had not much improved.

Grounding on a bank that might have formed just the previous night could spell the end of a ship, because of the sticky, clinging nature of the mud, which held the helpless vessel fast while the tide sucked beneath her, until she fell over and sank. The James and Mary Shoal, named after an Indiaman that was engulfed there in 1694, was infamous as a quicksand that swallowed ships whole — a tragedy that was repeated often, because of the swivelling effect of the strong current flowing out from the Rupnarain River, which entered the Hooghly just at that point. Wreckage piled on wreckage, along with all hands on board, never to surface again.

Another hazard was added in February 1793, when Republican France declared war on England. Indiamen firing guns and blue lights for a pilot as they lay in the Balasore Roads were such easy prey that French privateers sailed out from their lair in the Isle de France (Mauritius), to lay in wait for them. And then, if a pilot schooner was captured, it could be used to lull even the most wary Indiaman captain into a false sense of security. On January 14, 1796, Robert Surcouf, the famous French privateer, seized the pilot schooner *Russell,* then used it to lure a second pilot boat, *Cartier,* into his clutches. Two weeks later, he used the captured *Cartier* to fool the captain of the rice ship *Diana,* and the day after that he seized the Indiaman *Triton,* again by hoisting French colours at the very last moment, before the English crew had a chance to understand that they were under enemy attack from what they had thought was their friendly pilot.

In March 1797, the East Indiaman *Osterly* was captured in the same fashion by *La Forte,* while on Christmas Eve, 1799, the East Indiaman *Eliza Ann* managed to fight off a French privateer only because the American merchant ship *Atlantic* came to her assistance. Though armed with just six-pounder guns, the feisty little American dashed up to the enemy, holding her fire until within pistol shot. Then she raked the Frenchman fore and aft, forcing him to limp off.

Less successful was Captain Rivington of the East Indiaman *Kent,* which was attacked at the Sand Heads on October 7, 1800, just days after the *Friendship* arrived. Again the privateer was Robert Surcouf, this time in command of the French sloop-of-war *Confiance.* Like the captain of the *Osterly,* Rivington thought that the *Confiance*

Confiance seizing Kent, by Gameray

was a pilot boat, and so he stood towards her, to be greeted by a broadside as the French colours were hoisted.

After ninety minutes of exchanging fire, the *Kent* missed stays while trying to bring her broadside cannon to bear on the enemy. Seizing his opportunity, the Frenchman grappled and boarded, and during the terrific hand-to-hand struggle that followed, Captain Rivington was killed. Fifty-five seamen were wounded in the battle, many of them mortally. Five of the passengers were killed as well, before the chief officer surrendered to save the lives of the rest.

So Eleanor Reid had every reason to be nervous as the *Friendship* lay off the Sand Heads in September 1800. The wait as Reid fired signals for a pilot must have been nerve-wracking—as her journal testifies, it was a stormy night, with the southwest monsoon blowing directly onto the shore, so that both gale and tide thrust the battered ship closer and closer to the shoals. The surf thundered on the beaches ahead, and each time the ship's leadsman brought up his sounding line, he screamed yet another warning.

When the pilot boat arrived, though referred to as the "pilot schooner," it turned out to be a rakish-looking brig, with square sails on its two masts. After rounding to, it lowered a boat that was driven by oars in the European manner, but with a Lascar crew. Another surprise—and a testament to the importance of his role—was that the pilot's arrival was a ceremonious one. Mr. Henderson, the *Friendship*'s boatswain, shrilled on his silver whistle as the pilot clambered up the side, and then saluted, just as he would if the commander of another ship were coming over the gangway. To suit, the man who arrived on board was wearing a uniform, generally composed of white breeches and a dark blue uniform jacket with crested brass buttons and blue silk lapels, but this last was often faded, and the entire rig was topped with a strangely informal hat, which was large, white and circular.

Undoubtedly, Mr Michael Parry was surprised as well as pleased to find the captain's wife on board—someone to relate spine-chilling tales to, as he guided the ship through the treacherous channels, past shores where jungle rioted and man-eaters lurked. At Diamond Harbour, forty miles above Saugor, the larger East Indiamen dropped anchor, either to lighten the ship so they could sail upriver without grounding, or to take on freight for the outward voyage. Clumsy-looking barges—*burrs*—surrounded them, either delivering freight or taking it away. Smaller were the *panswei*—called "paunchways" by the Europeans—that conveyed people from ship to shore, or gathered about the sides of the ships selling foodstuffs, spirits and exotic artefacts to the passengers and seamen. Broad cotton sails flew from the single masts of the country boats that were sailing downriver, while the others were paddled upstream with the easy power of men who lived most of their lives on water. The smaller canoes were steered by a man who stood at a long oar, but in the big country boats this steering paddle was replaced by an enormous rudder.

Ganges sailing boat, from Folkard

Just as exotic, but much more glamorous, were the budgerows, or pleasure boats, used by the rich for jaunts up and down the river. Beamy, flat-bottomed vessels that were steered with a great oar at the back, and paddled by teams at the front, they were often called "accommodation boats" by the Europeans, because each one carried a wooden bungalow. Jemima Kindersley, wife of an officer in the East India Company Bengal artillery, sailed up the river in a budgerow in 1764, writing, "the covered part generally divided into pretty good rooms, and an open veranda, carrying ten to twenty oars, and as many men, called dandys; the master, who steers, is called a serang."

The seamen had to be strong and active fellows. When the current was too strong to row, they jumped overboard and towed the boat by swimming or wading with ropes about their waists. During storms they also jumped overboard, but this time to hang onto the sides of the boat and keep it from turning turtle. Unsurprisingly, as Jemima went on to remark, they liked rowing best, and sang at their oars. Meantime, the passengers were borne in luxury. The windows were curtained with velvet or silk, and the rooms were nicely furnished with beds, chairs, settees and a dining table. On longer journeys the budgerow was accompanied by two or more boats, one being the river-borne kitchen, and the other carrying servants. Three times a day the boats lay at a mooring while food was cooked. Then the people on the budgerow wined and dined at leisure, while the seamen and servants ate rice on the beach.

Nearer Calcutta, the river became a crowded highway—much wider than the Thames at London Bridge but just as bustling, as Eliza Fay marvelled in May 1780. Eliza, who had come to Calcutta with her lawyer husband, was particularly taken with the snake-boats, which were long, narrow, crescent-shaped canoes with fearsome snake or dragon heads on their prows, paddled very quickly by teams of men. Wrote Eliza, these, "intermixed with the mercantile vessels and ships of war, render the whole a magnificent and beautiful moving picture." There were not just ships from Europe to watch, but dhows, baggalas, and pinisi schooners, too. Most numerous of all were the errand boys of the Hooghly River fleet, the small undecked boats that were both sculled and sailed, and were called *dingis*.

Dinghy, from Folkard

For all the observers of the time, sailing along the last reach of the river before the city was a revelation. On one side were the green lawns and thick woods of the Calcutta Botanical Garden, where the superintendant, Dr William Roxburgh—"the father of Indian botany"—had built a massive stone house for his growing family. On the other hand was Garden Reach, where deer and cattle grazed on lush grass and rested beneath great ornamental trees, and the abodes of the immensely rich were built. An intriguing combination of the architectures of the East and the West, these palaces were as formal as Georgian mansions, yet embellished with frivolous minarets and verandas. Beyond the bulk of Fort William, the spires of Calcutta rose into the misty sky, tall public buildings dominated by the dome of Government House. The banks became lined with stone steps called *ghauts,* and held a multitude of people—fruit sellers, pedlars, coolies and palanquin bearers, all frantic for trade from the people who came on shore.

Most passengers disembarked at Chandpaul Ghaut, the entry to Esplanade Row, the gateway to the part of the city where most of the one thousand or so European inhabitants lived. However, because she was the captain's wife, Eleanor would stay on board the *Friendship* as the pilot and her husband eased her to Old Fort Ghaut, off Lal Bazaar. For here, where European splendour met the maze of Indian Calcutta, stood the Customs House.

Chandpaul Ghaut, J.B. Fraser (1826)

Cossitollah Street, J.B. Fraser (1826)

Just a couple of blocks away was the street where Hugh would rent a house for them to live in while the *Friendship* was being unloaded, cleaned, repaired, re-caulked and re-coppered. This was Cossitollah Street, originally called that because it was where butchers were located, but now a hive of shops and industry, the address of coach-builders, landscape painters, surgeons and goldsmiths.

"Reader, should you ever 'do' the City of Palaces," advised a writer to the *Atlantic Monthly* in January 1858, "permit me to commend with especial emphasis to your consideration this same Cossitollah, as a representative street, wherein the European and Asiatic elements of the Calcutta panorama are mingled in the most picturesque proportions."

With the bazaar at the northern end, and European Calcutta to the south, it was a colourful merging of two cultures. And it was a commercial centre, too. Despite its beguiling mix of Eastern and Palladian architecture, it was primarily a place where merchants like Captain Reid haggled over cargoes and commissions.

He certainly haggled over the rent he paid for the house on Cossitollah—unless the landlord owed him a great favour. According to Eleanor, it cost him eighty rupees a month, yet in August 1780 Eliza Fay confided in a letter to her friends that her house "costs only 200 rupees per month, because it is not in a part of the town much esteemed."

That Reid got such a good deal could have been because the house was unfurnished. Mrs Kindersley wrote, "Furniture is exorbitantly dear, and so very difficult to procure, that one seldom sees a room where all the chairs and couches are of one sort; people of the first consequence are forced to pick them up as they come, either from the captains of Europe ships, or from China."

Hugh Reid, being the captain of a "Europe ship," did not have this problem, as he carried his own furniture. The *Friendship* had to be completely emptied of everything portable, and so his dresser, Eleanor's wardrobe, their washstand, his tables, his desk, and his chairs were carried into the house on Cossitollah Street.

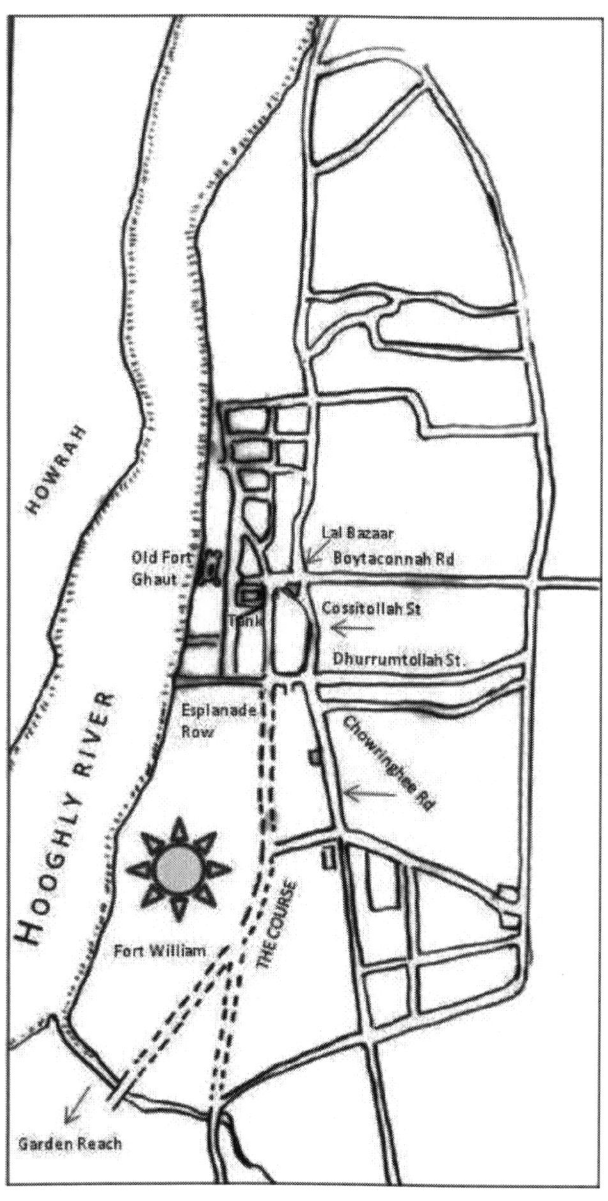
HOWRAH
Old Fort Ghaut
Lal Bazaar
Boytaconnah Rd
Tank
Cossitollah St
Dhurrumtollah St.
Esplanade Row
Chowringhee Rd
HOOGHLY RIVER
THE COURSE
Fort William
Garden Reach

If there was too much furniture for the living part of the house to hold, the overflow could be stored underneath, in the Calcutta equivalent of a basement. Hugh and Eleanor may even have slept on their shipboard divans, though Mrs Kindersley also testified that beds, "or, as they are always called, cotts," were cheap—"the woodwork, which is exceedingly slight, is made to take to pieces; the furniture is either gauze or muslin, made to put on all at once; and people sleep on a thin mattress or quilt; one sheet, and two or three pillows, complete the bedding." What she did not mention—though Eleanor does—was the absolute need for a mosquito net.

"The houses are large and spacious, with every arrangement for coolness and comfort," wrote a correspondent to a New York literary journal, *The Crayon,* in 1855; "they stand apart from each other, each in its own compound, protected by a high wall from the noise and dust of the street." The living quarters were all on the second level, the area below being devoted to storage, which also helped to make the house relatively cool and airy.

As Mrs Kindersley described, "in all the good houses the apartments are upstairs, and all on one floor; the rooms are large and very lofty; most of the houses are built with a *varendar* [veranda], which is a terrace on a level with the rooms in the front, and sometimes in the back part of the house, supported by pillars below, and a roof above supported likewise by pillars, with rails round to lean on. The *varendars* give a handsome appearance to the houses on the outside, and are of great use, keeping out the sun by day, and in the evenings are cool and pleasant to sit in." Also for coolness, the house windows were latticed with cane, instead of being paned in glass.

Memsahib with her servants

One of the first adjustments that European wives had to make when setting up house in Calcutta was to learn how to manage the servants. On board ship there were two stewards, one for the officers and one for the captain, and one cook, with his mate. Here in India, Eleanor was forced to employ a dozen. Jemima Kindersley blamed it on the caste system, writing, "The division of Indians into casts is a cause of great inconveniences and expence to the English, as it obliges them to hire three times the number of servants which would otherwise be necessary; for none of them, even on the greatest emergency, will perform the most trifling office which does not belong to their particular cast."

Mrs Eliza Fay, on the other hand, blamed it on laziness. "I just now asked a man to place a small table near me," she related in July 1780. Instead of obeying, he "began to bawl" for the bearers to come and help. "Why don't you do it yourself?" asked Eliza. Because he was Bengali, the steward replied—"I no strong like English."

"I am happy to say that our house is a very comfortable one, but we are surrounded by a set of thieves," Eliza wrote in August. This was because the servants, having asked for very little pay, supplemented their income with kickbacks and over-spending. "My *Khansaman* (or house-steward) brought in a charge of a gallon of milk and thirteen eggs for making scarcely a pint and a half of custard. This was so barefaced a cheat that I refused to allow it"—upon which he promptly demanded double wages. Then Eliza lost her "*Compradore* (or market man)," because, as he claimed, "poor servants have no profit by staying with me." They relied on making at least a rupee a day out of kickbacks, or so she learned.

Calcutta dinner party, Charles D'Oyly (1820)

Another lesson was that the climate ruled the daily routine. Everyone rose early for breakfast, and carried out as much business as possible before the next meal, which was dinner, held at two in the afternoon.

This was surprisingly substantial, considering the heat. Eliza Fay described a dinner menu that included "soup, roast fowl, curry and rice, mutton pie, a fore-quarter of lamb, a rice pudding, tarts, very good cheese, fresh churned butter, fine bread," accompanied by Madeira. "After dinner everyone retires to sleep," wrote Jemima Kindersley; "it is a second night; every servant has gone to his own habitation; and all is silence."

As Eliza Fay observed, between four and five in the afternoon the streets of Calcutta were "almost as empty of Europeans as if it were midnight." When evening drew nigh, everyone bathed (daily bathing being one of India's novelties), dressed, and sallied out to snatch a breath of fresh air.

A few headed out to the river to board their budgerows, but most of the Europeans and affluent Indians rode out to Calcutta's promenade, the Course. Young officers rode alongside open carriages, exchanging flirtatious smiles and bows with pink-complexioned girls fresh out from England. "For an hour, until it has grown quite dark, it is an animated, entertaining, showy scene," wrote the correspondent to *The Crayon*.

Dark heralded the hour when formal visits were made. "They are generally very short, as perhaps each lady has half a dozen to make and a party waiting for her besides," wrote Eliza Fay.

"Gentlemen also call to offer their respects, and if asked to put down their hat, it is considered as an invitation to supper," she went on, adding roguishly, "Many a hat have I see vainly dangling in its owner's hand for half an hour."

Those who were invited to stay were given tea to drink, though ale was also popular. Card tables were set up or some kind of musical soirée staged until supper was served at ten. Like dinner, this was a lavish affair, as Europeans in Calcutta liked to eat well, the old hands being connoisseurs of hot curries.

So Eleanor had a great deal to adjust to, and a great deal to observe—in the peculiar parlance of British India, she was a "griffin," or an inexperienced newcomer. Being naturally inquisitive, she was fascinated by the lives and manners of the natives she met, though often repelled by customs that were just too foreign to understand.

She had also many friends to make, Calcutta being famous as a sociable city where perfect strangers stopped to chat in the street. Among her new acquaintances would be notable characters, a major figure being Dr William Roxburgh, the Superintendant of the Botanical Garden, and one of Sir Joseph Banks's protégés. His sixteen-year-old daughter Mary (from his first marriage, to Marie Bonté) was already renowned as a beauty, and his current wife, Mary Huttenmann, was interesting, too, being the India-born daughter of German-Danish missionaries. Then there was Richard (Dick) Thomas Burney, headmaster of the Kiddepore School for the natural daughters of Indian Army officers, a local notable who was the half-brother of the famous writer, Fanny Burney, and had two brothers who had sailed with Captain James Cook.

But first Eleanor had to become acquainted with the voluble Mr. Michael Parry of the Bengal Pilot Service, for this is where her journal recommences.

On the morning of the 10th [September] we got ground at fifty fathoms, and before night the soundings gradually decreased as we approached to ten fathoms. The weather continued very bad, while the ship was repeatedly tacking to keep off the dangerous reefs, and firing guns, and burning blue lights during the night.

The next day we were not more successful, but continued beating about. Towards evening the ship was in shallow water, having only seven fathoms; the flood setting in, impelling her fast towards the reefs, compelled us to anchor. This we did most opportunely; for when it was low water we were but a short distance from a quick-sand, left alternately dry, and alternately washed by the waves rolling over it furiously. Our condition may be conceived by those who have been exposed to similar dangers.

The ship was anchored on a lee-shore, in a hard gale of wind, during a dark and howling night, with heavy squalls and much rain; the captain, mates, and seamen were constantly putting mats and ropes round the cables, to prevent their being chaffed at the hawse-holes. Meanwhile, the ship frequently pitching a sea over the forecastle, the hatches were battened down, to keep the water from getting below.

Occupied by these labours and precautions, we rode within half a mile of this dangerous sand, on which, had we been driven, there was little likelihood of any person on board being saved; the few who might escape the numerous sharks and alligators, had they reached the shore, would most probably have fallen a prey to tigers.

Kind Providence permitted the ship to ride in safety during this awful night, and next day we had the satisfaction of seeing a pilot vessel at anchor in the channel, behind the sand-bank. This proved to be Mr. Parry's schooner. The proprietor came on board himself, and took charge of us, desiring his pilot vessel to lead on.

He kindly brought some Bengal sheep, poultry, and vegetables. He informed us that many ships had been taken by French privateers off this Sand-heads lately, and amongst others, a pilot vessel which they used as a decoy. In consequence of this, the pilots were very cautious in approaching any ships.

We proceeded, and crossed the eastern sea-reef, and anchored in the eastern channel during the night. We were fortunate in getting Mr. Parry; he was a worthy good man, and knew his business well; he had sent all the junior pilots to town, in different vessels, and as his limited time was out, he intended taking the ship up to Calcutta himself; he said that the distance to town from the point where he came on board was upwards of two-hundred miles.

There is perhaps no part in the world where professional pilots suffer more anxiety than those of this station; so perpetually are they exercised by the shifting of the sands. Sometimes a hard gale of wind, or rapid tide, will wash away a sand, and deposit it as a shelving bank in another place; the pilot having a clear channel one month, may find himself obliged to take a fresh survey, in conducting a ship through the same passage the next month; still, notwithstanding every device of circumspection many ships are annually lost. At day-break a wreck of one was seen on Saugur sand, which had struck there a short time before. The persons employed in this service have every encouragement; for when they arrive at the situation of branch pilot, their emoluments are upwards of twelve hundred pounds per annum. They rise by seniority, but the occasional attainment of accelerated promotion as a reward for distinguished conduction leaves a field for emulation. There are about twelve vessels employed, each having a branch pilot on board, besides about ten juniors, who are termed masters, mates, boatswains, leadsmen, and volunteers. There are generally two vessels looking out at a time; which number is kept up by reliefs, or augmented, if necessary.

Next morning we proceeded towards Saugor Island. All eyes were directed to the shore, thinking we should at least see a dozen tigers guarding the beach, but not one appeared. Our pilot informed us, that a fine young man, who was third mate of a Danish ship, had been lately devoured by one of these dreadful animals. He went on shore with a party to cut wood; having in an hour collected a sufficient load from drift timber lying on the beach, Mr. Parry cautioned them not to approach the jungle. Being armed, however, they thought they might with safety enter the woods, where this young man was seized by a tiger. The horrid roar of the beast frightened the others so much that they were prevented using their muskets, each man running to the boat as fast as he could. When their panic had subsided some wanted to return, but this was overruled, when they reflected that their companion must ere then have been destroyed; and the party returned on board the Dane with the sad tale. The pilot concluded by saying, that scarcely a season passes but some Europeans are taken away by tigers, in consequence of fool-hardiness; while many natives are devoured amidst the perils of their necessary avocations. Saugor Island appeared an impenetrable forest, with much jungle wood and shrubs; the only clear part was at the Sandy beach.

Ganges, from Schouten's travels (1708)

We now crossed over to Kedgeree, and saw a neat-looking house, which belonged to the post-master. Some ships were lying off this station. We were visited by the dawk [*dak*], or post-boat, for the conveyance of letters to town. Several country boats came alongside with plantains, pine-apples, oranges, pumelnoses, bread, eggs, &c. which met a ready sale amongst our people, who had plenty of money from the sale of birds, &c. There appeared a number of straggling villages on the Kedgeree side, which looked like little thatched sheds, or mud cabins. We now passed up the river Hoogly, and anchored for the night off Hawkes' Channel, so named from the *Hawk* Indiaman passing up that way to avoid an enemy's frigate, during the American war.

Next morning we observed a number of beautiful deer grazing near our anchorage. This surprised us, as the place abounded with the tigers; Mr. P. told us he had seen upwards of thirty in a herd near the same place. A gun loaded with grape-shot was fired at them; they instantly bounded into the jungle. Several alligators were seen this morning, and one was pointed out to me, but I could only observe a black floating log, which had it not sunk, and again rose to the surface of the water, I should not have imagined it to possess life; they generally kept close to the bank of the river. Mr. Parry told us, that the best swimmer would have no chance, if he had the misfortune to fall overboard, as the river abounded with sharks as well as alligators. A dead fowl, which was thrown overboard this morning, was instantly dragged under water.

About nine o'clock we proceeded up the river, the deepest water being near the eastern shore. We had a near view of the jungle and underwood, but saw no living animal other than birds. Notwithstanding the great heat which prevails at this season, the boughs of the trees are clothed with a beautiful evergreen; as the old leaves drop off, they are replaced by a succession of new ones, so quick and abundant is vegetation in this country. The beauties of the scenery presented to our eyes, might have been augmented by the rains that had just subsided; the dry season was just commencing. At this time the stream runs almost constantly towards the sea, in consequence of the great rains that had fallen, the effect of which, in causing the freshes [freshets], or constant accession to the ordinary volume of water, lasts for some time.

It was not expected we should reach town before the next spring tides; however, as the wind was favourable, we soon passed Culpee, which appeared a poor village. We next approached Diamond Harbour, where several Indiamen were lying taking in cargoes for Europe. We saw a number of square buildings, occupied as the saltpetre warehouse; the hospital, and the harbour-master's house, appeared to be respectable edifices.

In ascending the stream, we came to an opening on our left, which is the entrance into a great river, called the Roupnaran, into which the rapidity of the tide had nearly forced the ship; but by the dexterity of the pilot we avoided this cross impulse. We had next to pass a shifting sand, called the James and Mary's, on which a ship of that name, many years ago, was totally lost, with all the crew; the force of the tide was such when she grounded that it turned her suddenly over, and completely round, carrying away her masts, after which she rolled upon the sand like a cask, and then disappeared in deep water. Scarcely a season passes in which ships are not lost on this dangerous quicksand. By a favorable breeze we were wafted clear of this danger. The views on both sides of this fine river now began to grow interesting, particularly as we approached a village called Fultah, which before the war belonged to the Dutch East-India Company. Some of the houses seen through the openings of the plaintain and cocoa-nut trees, from being white-washed, were more picturesque than those nearer the sea. Hundreds of fine cattle were peacefully grazing on the banks of the river, which, with the paddy or rice fields at a little distance, gave us the idea of a land blest with plenty.

Whenever we anchored, numbers of native boats, called apunchways, came alongside, with abundance of milk, butter, bread, eggs, fruits, and vegetables. Their approach was allowed until it was discovered that several of our people were intoxicated, and that something stronger than milk had been conveyed on board; farther intercourse with these boats was in consequence forbidden.

In our progress we saw on the left bank a large village, called Willoborough, at which was a cattle-market. A number of country boats were lying at this place, some laden with heaps of hay and straw, like floating stacks, and others with bricks and large earthern jars, all for the Calcutta market.

After we had got beyond this place, a fanatic came alongside, with a very reverend devout aspect; his beard, white as wool, reached down his breast, which contrasted with his dark complexion, gave him rather a striking appearance. This sage personage was called Peor Serang; on inquiry into his office, I was told it was through his prayers the ship had come safe. Our Lascars seemed delighted to see him, and rewarded him liberally.

We next passed, on our left, a place called Fort Gloucester, and a village on our right called Budge-Budge, where stood an old ruin originally built of brick. Both banks of the river were now covered with little villages, and much cattle feeding near the brink. At a place called the powder mills is a large distillery and a respectable looking dwelling house. The wind failing, we were obliged to anchor at a place called Sangerale.

Shortly after we were agreeably surprised by a handsome accommodation boat coming alongside, with a letter from Messrs. Hudson, Bacon, and Co. ship builders, saying that the boat and people were at our service, and that should any assistance be wanted they would with pleasure send it from town. This was not all; for a plentiful supply of fresh butter, bread, fruit, &c. was sent, with a fine round of corned beef, which would have done honor to an English table. This civility from a stranger was very gratifying to our feelings, as the only knowledge they had of us was by a letter from Malacca. However it was a good earnest of Indian hospitality, of which we had afterwards frequent experience. This boat was kept by the ship, and sent on shore for the little things wanted, until we arrived off the town of Calcutta.

All my pleasant thoughts were dispersed this evening, by seeing several human bodies floating down the river with the tide, and crows fasting upon the carcases. I could not at first conjecture what they were, but was informed by the pilot that those sights were so common as to excite no attention in the residents here; that he had often witnessed the horror with which a stranger from Europe was struck at first beholding them. We were told it was only the poorer class of Hindoos who throw their dead into the river, as those who could afford to purchase wood practised burning. Previous to committing the body to the sacred stream they swathe it in a piece of calico, and cause prayers to be said over it by their Bramins. At this season of the year there is very little flood tide, so that the bodies are not floated up: but indeed this rarely happens in any season, as they are food for the numerous sharks; or if cast ashore, they are devoured by wild dogs, jackalls, kites, vultures, &c. with which this country abounds. We happened to cast our eyes to a place in the mud, not far off, where lay a human body surrounded by crows. These were kept at a distance by three pariahs, or wild dogs, who were tearing the flesh; the sight made me shudder, and the recollection of it disturbed my repose, or deformed my dreams, during the night.

Calcutta from Garden Reach, from A Picturesque Voyage, *1810*

The next morning we got under weigh and proceeded towards Garden reach. The finest prospect burst upon our view as we rounded a point at the bottom of the reach; we beheld a number of elegant detached mansions, surrounded by every indication of affluence and elegance; they are seated in the midst of beautiful meadows and pleasure grounds, where the grass is like velvet to the water's edge. The appearance of this delightful spot far exceeded my expectation; it only wanted the variety of hill and dale to make it fairy land.

The tide now rushed down with such force, that we were obliged to come once more to an anchor a little below the Botanic Garden, which was on our left; and as the Captain wished to inform Doctor Roxburgh, the Company's botanist, that he had in charge the plants sent from Penang, the sun being low, I was induced to land, and take a walk in the fine gardens. We were most kindly received by the Doctor, who shewed us every thing worth notice. Mrs. R. [Mary Huttenmann Roxburgh] did not speak English like a native; I understood she was a native of Germany. She was extremely civil, and requested that I would spend a few days with her as soon as we were a little settled in town.

While passing through the different beautiful walks, I was surprised to see numbers of jackalls and foxes running about, as if they were domesticated, and asked the reason: the Doctor said that when the sun was down they always came from their lurking places; that they were so numerous in the country, it was impossible to keep them under. We then returned on board, after promising to make frequent visits to Doctor and Mrs. R. who gave us a general invitation.

Next morning the wind was adverse, and the freshes running so strong that the ship could not move. The river here was covered with vessels of all descriptions; many brigs and sloops, with large clumsy barges called burrs, were going down to the Indiamen with cargoes and provisions : there were also most beautiful pleasure vessels named budgerows, pinnaces, and snake boats, in constant motion. This scene was interesting.

Towards noon a breeze sprung up, which enabled the ship to proceed, when we soon came in sight of the flag staff of Fort William, passed quickly up towards it, and saluted it with nine guns. This compliment was returned from the saluting battery. The city of Calcutta was now in sight, with its stately buildings, appearing like so many palaces, particularly those about Chowringa. This, with the numerous masts of the shipping, lying off the town, which produced a grand effect, engaged all our attention and admiration.

Old Fort Ghaut, from A Picturesque Voyage, *1810*

None on board were more pleased at our arrival than the Sepoys; they had been absent some years at Bencoolen. They were all landed in the evening; the Captain then went on shore to report the ship, and to hire a house while the ship remained. We came to anchor off the Banks Hall, where the master-attendant has an office, near what is called the old fort, but which retains no vestiges of a fortification as far as we could observe from the anchorage. On the opposite side of the river a number of handsome looking villas adorn Howrah, or Saulkea; this suburb is situated abreast of Calcutta. Conspicuous amongst the buildings is the large one called the Female Orphan School.

When my husband returned I found he had procured a house in a street called Cossitollah, at eighty rupees per month, unfurnished.

Just before breakfast this morning, Mr. Muirhead informed me that a person had come from the shore with a present of fruit, &c. saying that he had got the house matted, and all ready for our reception, and that a couple of palanquins and bearers were waiting for us, at the ghant, or landing place. As my husband had gone on shore very early, and I could not think of quitting the ship before his return, I desired to see the person who had come off. He advanced to the cabin door, took off his shoes, and made three salams with great apparent humility; he was dressed in fine white muslin, thrown loosely over his body and shoulders, over this he had a beautiful Cashmere shawl. His complexion was not very dark, and his person was upon the whole rather prepossessing; he appeared to be about twenty-five years of age; he had two attendants. I inquired if he spoke English: he replied, "not great much."

I soon however understood by his broken sentences that his name was Kissen Chunda Bose; that the Captain, then mate, had employed him as sircar [steward], and that he wished me to speak in his behalf now, which I promised to do.

At that instant the Captain came on board and informed me that all was ready on shore, and that it would be advisable to land before the sun got too high. We accordingly left the ship and proceeded to the spot where the palanquins were waiting; we seated ourselves in them, and as we passed along the winding streets new scenes opened to our view. Every part was thronged with natives, of whom I shall not attempt a description until I have been some time resident among them.

We soon gained our appointed station in Cossitollah Street, where I was glad to rest, for in the narrow streets I found the heat very oppressive; the house was large and convenient, having on the first floor, which was the upper story, four good bed rooms, a spacious hall, with a veranda in front; apartments of the same size below, occupied by the ship's stores, and a large piece of ground, called the compound, at the back, for the live stock, &c. A winding staircase led up to the flat roof terrace all round, to which we sometimes resorted after our evening's ride for the benefit of the cool air.

We found ourselves obliged to submit to the custom of the country, in keeping up the following establishment: a Durwan [*darwan*], or porter, at the gate; a Sircar and two assistants for the ship; a Bobagee [*babarchi*], or cook, and his assistant; a Beastie [*bhisti*], or water carrier; a Mater [*mehtar*], or linkboy, and a sweeper, for the house; a set of bearers for one palanquin, seven. In addition to these we had the servants from the ship, and an ayah, or female attendant, for myself. All these, we were informed, were absolutely necessary in this place, we were therefore obliged to conform.

The same evening, my husband drove me round the circular road, Chouringa, and the course, to which all the fashionables of Calcutta resort morning and evening; the course is regularly watered in the dry season, which renders it by far the most agreeable place for an airing. I thought at first that all the Europeans here looked sickly and pallid, but this impression wore off after a short time.

I was introduced to several very respectable women, amongst whom were Mrs. K., now Lady M. K. with whom I frequently took a morning drive; I found her pleasing, and well informed; she kindly explained every thing which appeared a novelty to me. She resided with her sister, Mrs. J., whose husband was a merchant, and from whom we received friendly attentions. We were under the necessity of limiting our morning's exercise to an hour or two, for after seven o'clock the sun became so powerful that we were glad to return as quickly as possible to the house, and to remain there until evening, unless obliged to pay morning visits, which was generally done at the expense of a bad head-ache.

One morning the sircar told me we should have good fortune, for three argalls [*hargila,* giant storks], or adjutants, had rested upon our house-top all night. They had no doubt been attracted by the rats, which were generally caught in a trap, and thrown out at night. The quantity these gigantic birds will devour is astonishing. One morning, nine large rats had been caught, which one by one were thrown to an adjutant, who picked them up and swallowed them as a pigeon would peas; after which a leg of Bengal mutton, from which only a slice or two had been cut, was thrown out, which he picked up in a dexterous manner, and bolted down his throat.

The crows however, in this country, are the most daring of the feathered tribe; I have seen them come in at the windows of the dining room, and take cold meat off the table. So expert are they in thieving, that a watch is obliged to be set to prevent a surprise; a fine little English terrier, which we had was often annoyed by these depredators, as well as by the kites. When meat was sent out for the dog a battle generally ensued between her and the crows; while she was occupied in chasing one another came to plunder, the kites at the same time darting down from the house top, snatched up in their talons the bones of contention; those were in their turn attacked by their own tribe, and obliged to surrender the spoil in the air to others, who in their turn found themselves unable to resist some new competition.

I must confess I thought this country full of plagues, arising equally from the air, the water, and the land; for, without great precautions, Europeans could not exist, nor are they neglected by the opulent natives. The air is full of devouring animals, from the majestic adjutant to the small musquito, from whose tormenting attacks nothing but a gauze completely round your bed will preserve you. On land objects of terror and annoyance are innumerable, from the royal tiger to the ant; the latter you are obliged to keep from the bed by a trench of water, the foot of each bed-post being placed in a large brass or stone cup of water, to prevent their ascending among the bed-clothes.

The destroyers in the river I have already mentioned; many human beings are devoured by the ravenous sharks. One melancholy instance occurred to Mr. Henderson, the boatswain of our ship, while we were here, who by some accident fell from a small boat called a dingay, which was lying alongside the ship : he sunk to rise no more. Much blood was seen to discolour the water astern of the ship immediately after the accident; as this could not be occasioned by the fall, we concluded that he was immediately seized by some monster. The loss of this worthy man and good seaman was severely felt by the captain and officers.

When our live stock was collecting for the voyage, the poultry was sadly destroyed by jackalls, who came over the walls of the compound, although it exceeded seven feet in height. A trap, made of a wine chest, open at one end, was set for them. The first night a very large jackall was caught; it was shot in the trap, but none of the servants would touch it, and we were obliged to get scavengers to take it away.

Its legs appeared short in proportion to its body; it was covered with bites and scars, and has but little hair: it had a strong offensive smell. A covering was made for the poultry of mats and gram [pea] sticks, but still they were molested by these animals, and I have no doubt that if a dozen had been killed on one night, as many more would have appeared the next, rending the air with their dreadful howlings.

Snake charmer, Rev. W. Unwick, 1891

One forenoon some natives came to the gate with large round baskets, asking leave to exhibit the snake dance; when I permitted them to proceed, a man opened one of the baskets, where I observed a large snake about eleven feet long coiled up, which when irritated, sprung out, darted his forked tongue upon the man, who caught it near the head, and flung it from his several times; at length he let him bite his forehead, and the blood started from the wound.

This appeared to me very surprising, but I afterwards understood they have a method of extracting the poison from the fangs when the animal is first caught.

They also exhibited smaller snakes, one called the *cobra di capello,* the most dangerous of the serpent tribe; they appeared perfectly under command, and when the baskets were again opened they instantly crept in and coiled themselves up. The native music, the *tom-tom* and pipe, was played during this exhibition. At their departure I gave the men a rupee, with which they were well satisfied, and went away, making me many salams.

Early in October, we accompanied Capt. B— B—, by invitation to the botanic garden where we dined with a very agreeable party, and spent a pleasant day. The doctor's daughter, Miss Mary Roxburgh, was an accomplished beautiful girl, lately arrived from England, who afterwards married Mr. Henry Stone, a civilian. We also met Dr. Gillhunt, who proposed sending some children home with us.

In our walks through the gardens, the wonderful banyan-tree most attracted my notice, whose pendent branches had taken root in several places, and supported the immense weight of the spreading canopy above. If I were botanist enough, I should attempt to describe many other plants, but my treacherous memory could not retain one-hundredth part of those the doctor was so kind as to point out. In the evening we crossed over from the gardens and came up by land. The ride through Fort William is beautiful; had it not been for the number of cannon and

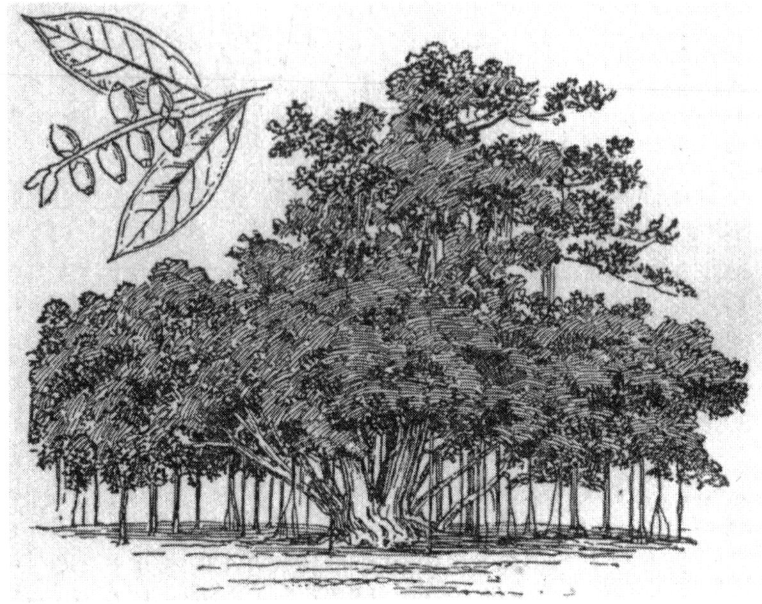

Banyan Tree (1922)

troops I should have thought it was some gentleman's enclosure; every thing appeared in excellent order, and deer and sheep were grazing on the banks and trenches.

We were told that Lord Mornington intended to have a superb palace built to the south of the city, facing the fort, which no doubt, when finished, will be a great ornament to Calcutta. St. John's church is an elegant light building, and well adapted to the climate.

We had often been invited to visit the school at Kidderpore. It is an institution for the natural daughters of officers of the army, who are unable to maintain them.

Indian girls' school, from Girls' Own Paper (1884)

By allowing a small sum from their monthly pay, they may have them placed in the school, where they are clothed and well educated; they are allowed to remain there as long as their friends think proper. We were much gratified with the regularity and order observed. Mr. Richard Burney, the head-master, is a most worthy man, and, as well as the mistress, is much respected. It happened to be the dancing evening, when the children are allowed to stand up with gentlemen invited by the school-mistress. During this time tea was served to the visitors, who generally retired at an early hour in the evening. The scholars are young ladies of colour, but many of them form very good connexions, in spite of the endeavours of the present governor-general to prevent marriage between them and young men in the service.

Although it is said that this city contains upwards of half a million of inhabitants, I question if one twentieth part of that number occupy brick dwellings. So little serves the natives for shelter, that a few rupees are sufficient to purchase materials to erect a house for a large family; these huts, however, composed of mats and grass sticks, occasion much misery in the fires, which are but too frequent here.

During our stay a fire happened, which in a few hours deprived upwards of ten thousand poor creatures of shelter, and several of life. It is said that this suffering is often purposely inflicted by wretches who deal in the materials. About a week after the fire, we drove past the place, and were surprised to find the ground nearly covered with new huts. The wants of these people, particularly the Hindoos, are few. A piece of cloth loosely thrown over the body, and another rolled round the head as a turban, constitutes their wardrobe. Their food consists of rice and vegetables, which they make into curries : this simple fare, with water, is all the luxury they require.

I had an opportunity of witnessing that deplorable fanaticism for which they are so celebrated. This was the time of their grand festival, for regaining their castes, and other ceremonies. I was surprised by the Sircar one day asking me to allow the Materanny [*mehtarani*] (the woman who swept the house) to regain her caste. I told him I had no objection, and that she might perform any ceremonies she pleased, provided her place was supplied. Three days after this, the woman presented herself, having cords passed through the flesh covering the ribs. There were a number of frantic looking men before and behind, some of whom held the cords while she danced backwards and forwards, drawing them through the wounded part at every movement, at the same time laughing and singing to the noise of their uncouth music. I was so much disgusted by the exhibition that I dismissed her.

This however was nothing compared to the ceremony of swinging, which I afterwards saw at a place called the "Bita Connah" [Boytaconnah Road]. This is a wide road, in which three posts were placed at angles across the top, where they met a long beam, which rested upon a pivot; this could be swung round at pleasure, by means of ropes managed by those below. To the extreme ends of the pole, or beam, were affixed by ropes several iron hooks, which were thrust into the naked back under the shoulders of the devotee, who is then raised into the air and swung round many times; in the meanwhile he throws down flowers, and other things to the gazing and admiring multitude, with the greatest apparent indifference. This was performed by many men and women while we remained.

We returned home, disgusted and distressed at the superstition and ignorance of these poor people; the streets were crowded with them, and wherever we turned our eyes, some spectacle of fanaticism presented itself. Some having cords passed in through their sides, in the way I have described, others had a long iron spit through the tongue, left to remain there for a certain time by way of expiation; but I shall not attempt a description of all the acts prompted by this atrocious enthusiasm. The horrid noise of their tom-toms, and other barbarous instruments playing before the processions and idols in the street, made it a great relief to our party to get out of the crowd and retire home.

We had invitations to several "nautches," or grand entertainments given by Rajahs and rich natives, in honor of their idols. We attended one of these, which fully satisfied our curiosity. I think the name of the chief who entertained his friends at this nautch was Rajah Nup Kessein. When we entered his house, we were struck by the blaze of light and the number of guards, &c. in attendance. In the principal hall the first objects that attracted our notice were their three deities, Bramah, Vishnu, and Sheevah; they were large gilded wooden figures, most frightfully formed.

We were told that these people admit no converts to their idolatrous worship, for none but those born Hindoos, and strictly adhering to their laws and ceremonies, will be retained amongst them; the slightest deviation is sufficient to render them outcasts. We were received with politeness by the Rajah and sprinkled with rose water. After we were seated sweetmeats were handed round, and the dancing and singing girls began their performance; but the whole exhibition appeared to us most stupid and inanimate. The tricks of jugglers, sword eaters, &c. formed part of the evening's entertainment. We left this scene at 10 o'clock, and were all very glad to return home.

Early in November a budgerow was engaged for an excursion to Chandernagore, a French settlement about forty miles above Calcutta. As we were to sleep in the budgerow, cots and curtains were provided, as well as table-linen, earthenware, and all necessaries for the trip. On the 6th we embarked, and proceeded with the flood tide as high as Cossipour, during which time we had a fine view of the fertile land on both sides the river; but it is too flat to be interesting.

As we passed along we saw several fires at the edge of the water, and were told that human bodies were burning. This I could scarcely believe until we anchored close to the shore, where a poor woman was making great lamentation; and when our boatmen enquired the cause, she told them she was going to burn the body of her daughter, who had died that morning. She had been performing some part of the funeral ceremony at the water side, before setting fire to the pile, which was only a few yards off.

Casting a body into the Ganges, from Girls' Own Paper (1884)

Some of our party wished to examine it, but were told if they did, they would interrupt the ceremony, and distress the relatives. The pile was presently set in a blaze, and in the course of an hour the whole was consumed to ashes. The smoke which the wind occasional wafted towards us, had a most disagreeable smell. This is certainly the best mode of disposing of their dead; if they committed them to the Hoogley, they would be torn and mangled by sharks and birds of prey; and were they to bury them, they would be dug up by jackalls and wild dogs. To prevent this, the burial grounds of the Europeans are surrounded by a high wall.

Next day we passed Barrackpore, where the Governor-general has a country house, opposite to which is a Danish settlement called Serampore, where a society of English missionaries from Bristol have an establishment and a printing press; they are most useful in instructing the natives, and are much esteemed for their meek Christian deportment.

We then passed Chinsurah, a Dutch settlement on the same side the river, a little above which we beheld a sight shocking to humanity. An old woman had been brought by her relatives to the brink of the river at low water to die; she was stretched on a sort of cradle in the scorching sun, and appeared delirious, crying out in a most piteous manner; some inhuman wretches belonging to her were looking on at a distance with apparent indifference. This is another effect of their brutalizing superstition; it is the privilege of certain castes to be carried, when life is despaired of, to lie on the banks of their sacred Ganges; and if the tide rises high enough to float them away before the breath is out of the body, their souls are believed to be secure of happiness.

In the afternoon we reached Chandernagore, where we landed, and had an excellent dinner at a French tavern. There was little to be seen here worth notice, except spacious empty houses; for the greater part of the inhabitants had left the place on account of the war. We returned to the budgerow, and next day retraced our course to Calcutta, where we arrived the following evening.

Towards the end of November, we dined with Mr. Charles Law at Howrah, where I was introduced to his sister [in law] Miss Loftie, who was to proceed with us to England. I found her very agreeable in her manners.

At table was a young gentleman who had been in the *Kent* Indiaman at the time of her capture. In reply to some questions about that unfortunate affair, he surprised us by saying that if the sailors and soldiers on board had only been armed with knives and forks they might have cut the enemy, who boarded them, to pieces; but from his account it appeared that all was confusion after the death of the captain. The prisoners had come to Calcutta on board an Arab ship, where they were put by the enemy.

We expected that Mr. Robert Morris, the purser of the *Kent,* would come home with us, as my husband offered him a free passage; but his affairs prevented his leaving India so soon. When the gentlemen joined us after dinner, I was surprised to observe many spots of blood upon the stockings of the young man; I soon understood that the musquitos had been feasting upon his legs under the table during dinner, and indeed I did not escape their merciless stings myself. He had not taken the precaution of having a bag made for each leg, which is often necessary. New comers are generally much annoyed with these plagues, and instances have been known of the loss of limbs, and even of life, from the effect of the bites of these little insects.

We had to cross the river to Calcutta, and were obliged to retire earlier than usual. It would have been fortunate, however, if we had been half an hour later, for just as the boat put off from the shore we heard a great noise fast approaching us; this was what is called the bore. Our boatmen appeared in great consternation; my husband desired them to land us again immediately, but they disregarded his orders, and pulled with all their might into the middle of the stream: this, as we afterwards understood, was the best way to avoid the danger.

The night was very dark, which increased the awful aspect of the immense white foaming waves, as it advanced with vast rapidity, rolling over the sand, causing the boat, although one of large dimensions, to tumble and toss about in the most violent manner, and nearly filling her with water; this, however, appeared to us of little consequence, we were truly thankful for the preservation of our lives. These bores do much damage on the river, causing the loss of many lives and much property.

On the first of December the ship left town, to complete her lading at Saugor. When the live stock was going off, the head Sircar, who was of the Bramin or priest cast, begged to have one of the kids, which was entirely black. I asked his reason for selecting that; he said intended sacrificing it to his God, and that at the same time he would pray that we might have a fortunate voyage. I told him he should have no kid from me for any such idolatrous purpose, and enquired what sort of a god or gods he worshipped; he replied that his god was my god also. I told him I did not believe in his deity Brahma; he said that might be, but that I believe in the great Supreme of all, who inhabited the heavens, and created the sun, moon, and stars, with this world; who had also created Brahma, Vishnu, and Sheevah, inferior gods, to rule on earth, and superintend the affairs of mankind.

I asked which of his gods required poor human creatures to sacrifice themselves in the Ganges to sharks, which I understood was their practice every year at a certain time. He said it was very true that it was so, and happy were the souls that were so taken from the body; that the god Varoona, who presided over the sea and all waters, immediately transported their spirits to the Supreme. I also asked him which of his gods required a woman to burn herself upon the funeral pile of her husband? He answered that such sacrifices were not enjoined by any law in their sacred books; that it was a voluntary act, that the soul of such a woman would be for ever happy; but that if she was pregnant at the time of her husband's death, she was not allowed to burn herself. He confessed, however, that the wife, who did not sacrifice herself, would be degraded and despised by her family.

I told him that I trusted the time was not far distant when his gods would cease to find worshippers, and yield to the pure influence of Christianity. He informed me that their sacred books, which were in the care of the heads of his caste (the Bramins), were written by the Supreme himself; that in them it is declared that no earthly king, or people, can be admitted proselytes to the religion of the Hindoos, nor be incorporated with them; but he acknowledged, however, that it is foretold in their sacred records, that at one period of time all mankind will profess one religion, and worship the Supreme God in the same manner; and that then the spirits of all will be taken from the earth, which will be consumed and vanish like smoke. He confessed that this universal religion could not be that of the Hindoos, but some other.

I often conversed with this man, who told me many strange things respecting their customs. He said his caste never ate any thing that had animal life; that their food consisted entirely of rice, vegetables, fruits, and milk, a kind of pastry, and sweetmeats made of honey, ghee, &c.; some of the inferior castes are allowed to eat fish, and some kinds of flesh made into curries with vegetables, but those are much more respected who abstain from such food. They respect all religions which enjoin the worship of the Supreme Being, and are commanded to give food and water to their greatest enemies. How very different is the mild deportment of these people to that of the Mahometans, who propagated the tenets of the Koran by the force of arms. The latter are the most numerous class here, and hate the poor Hindoos as much as they do the Christians; they are only kept in subjection by the great power of the English; they however respect our laws, which are administered to all impartially.

But I have made a long digression. To return to the kid which I refused to give the Sircar; he had still so great a desire to have it, that he said if I would give it to him he would beg my acceptance of a Bengal cow and calf, to take to the ship, provided I would faithfully promise not to suffer either to be killed. I gave way to his entreaties, and gave him the favorite kid; the next morning a fine young cow and her calf were standing in the compound for me.

I now became uneasy about the ship, as my husband had been absent with her four days, and it was reported a ship had run aground on a sand near Fultah; in the interval, however, I was gratified by receiving letters from my beloved parents in England, conveying good news of them and all branches of the family.

The next day my husband returned to Calcutta, saying the ship had reached Saugor, and only waited to be dispatched; in consequence of which all was bustle and preparation for our embarkation.

Indian temples, from Nordhoff

Six

Homeward Bound

While Eleanor had been following the strange ways of European daily life in Calcutta, her husband had not been idle. Indeed, it was probably only in the evenings that he was able to dress up in the uniform of the commander of an East India extra ship, and accompany Eleanor to the promenade on the Course. The rest of the time he was not just organising the cargo, the provisions, and his own private venture, but he was very busy with the ship.

Once the *Friendship* was securely moored opposite the Customs House, the first job was to pump the water out of her bilges. Then, after the cargo had been discharged, the holds were cleaned by the simple but arduous process of letting in Hooghly River water, then pumping it out again, repeating the process until the holds and ballast were well rinsed. Additionally, there was the hot, sweaty work of taking down the topgallant masts and topmasts, along with all their yards, gear and rigging. So it is probably not surprising that one of the men—Joe Maxwell—ran away after just four days, followed briskly by the rest of the European seamen.

This left Reid without a crew, as the Lascars who had come with him had all been sent home, according to his arrangement with the Mangles' agent back in London. John Muirhead, the chief mate, was staunch, and so was the second officer, John Macdonald, but the third mate, Mr Linton, followed the European seamen into the alleys of Calcutta, and so did the gunner. Hugh Reid was reduced to just two mates, his boatswain, and the Irish carpenter, Pat Lewellyn, to supervise the gangs that were readying the ship for the homeward voyage.

Those gangs were made up of natives—"25 lascars employed from the shore in Consequence of the Europeans having Deserted," Reid wrote in the ship's logbook on 28 September. They swarmed over the ship's hull, stripping, repairing, re-caulking, and re-coppering, under the eyes of the shipwrights of Hudson, Bacon and Company. On Friday, October 10, "The Orlop Deck was watered in the Presence of one of the port Officers," Reid recorded; this was presumably to make sure that the deck planks were watertight, so nothing would leak down onto the cargo.

Then, after being signed off as seaworthy, the *Friendship* was ready to receive a freight of saltpetre and sugar, "on Acct. of the Hon'ble Company."

First, dunnage—packing material—was laid down on the floors of the holds. This was thin bamboo, which was spread to a depth of several inches, with more bamboo stacked up the sides of the ship. Once packed down, the bottom layer was then covered with at least three layers of matting before it was ready for the Lascar stevedores to start heaving down the 168-pound sacks. Because of the risk of contamination—or even explosion, in the case of fire—the saltpetre was stacked in the after hold, away from the sugar, which went down into the main hold, where the notoriously vile fumes given off when the sugar "steamed" would not trouble the passengers.

Each bag, whether of saltpetre or sugar, was laid flat with the ends and corners tugged up, to make the first layers as level as possible. Once the holds were half full, a gang moved along the top of the cargo, beating down the bags so that as much as possible could be stowed on top. And so it continued, layer after layer, until the start of November, when at last both holds were packed as high as the beams. Then matting was spread on top of it all, by coolies who crawled between the rafters as they worked.

It was now time to load the orlop, the deck where Irishmen had once been imprisoned, and where the Hindu Sepoys had lived on the passage from Penang to Calcutta. This was where Reid was going to stow his private cargo, the venture that was going to help make the voyage profitable.

More dunnage was laid on the floor of the orlop, and covered with three layers of matting. Then twenty bales of cloth were packed on top, along with twenty-three cases of indigo. Both were worth a lot in Europe, particularly the indigo, which fetched such high prices that it was known as Blue Gold. Even the cases holding the dye would sell for a lot of money, being beautifully manufactured of teak, lined with thin oil cloth, and with tightly fitting lids, often ornately patterned with delicate chisel-work.

Disaster struck as casks of drinking water were being loaded in the forehold. Henderson, the boatswain, was drowned alongside the ship—"in a state of intoxication," as Captain Reid noted, going onto to write, "every means were used to find him but to no purpose." This meant that he had to replace yet another man, and a particularly valuable one, too, whose place would be hard to fill. As Eleanor (who did not know Henderson was drunk at the time) recorded, "The loss of this worthy man and good seaman was severely felt by the captain and officers." In the event, Henderson was replaced by a man who testified he was English, and who went by the name of William Plenquy.

East India Company regulations stipulated that extra ships had to be manned by twenty Europeans, including the commander, officers, petty officers, and servants, and Hugh Reid was going to be hard-pushed to comply with this. Indeed, though he was lucky enough to ship a new third mate, James Mitchell (who had come into Calcutta as fourth mate on the *Henry Dundas*), he had to resort to sneaking him into the crewlist twice, the second time as the ship's gunner.

He did find a gunner's mate, a Dane with the very English name (perhaps alias) of Richard Brown, but, where he should have recruited seven more European seamen, he could only find five—Jacob Baker, who was also Danish, and four Englishmen—Charles Smith, John Wilson, William Owens, and Walter Chrisholm. To make sure the *Friendship* was fully manned, Reid shipped a gang of thirty Lascars, led by a *serang* called Barragatolla, with a *tindal*, or boatswain, who was named Gallannossan.

The doctor he found, Charles Dumerque, should really have been a passenger, as he was an assistant surgeon with the Company, going home on furlough. Dumerque was fortunate—not only was he getting a salary of five pounds a month, instead of paying for cabin space, but he was allowed to carry two tons of private trade. To make the situation even more unusual, he had the privilege of dining in the cuddy with the captain and his wife, just as if he were a paying passenger.

While Hugh Reid was remarkably resourceful in completing his crew list, and had an unusually dashing history, commanders of East Indiamen were often colourful figures, particularly those who had spent many adventurous years in eastern seas. In London clubs and coffee houses, as well as in Calcutta, their pasts and personalities were discussed with the same energy and attention as the strategies of admirals and generals. This was not because their seamanship might be in question, but because everyone knew that the quality of the long voyage ahead depended largely on the captain's nature. Once at sea, the commander was god on the quarterdeck, completely in charge of the little world around him, and his passengers were just as much his subjects as his crew.

Captain James Ludovic Grant of the *Brunswick*, 1804, was so quick-tempered that one time, "in the anxiety of the moment" —as Midshipman Addison put it— he kicked the pilot overboard, leaving the ship at the mercy of the currents. Other captains were so fired up at the prospect of rich prizes that they would call the ship to quarters, load their cannon, and sail in pursuit of suspicious sails, despite the frantic protests of nervous passengers. Some were nervous wrecks themselves, Lady Anne Barnard observing on board the *Sir Edward Hughes* in February 1797 that the complexion of the commander, the very experienced James Urmston, "varies from yellow to Orange and from Orange to black as matters go ill or well." Oddly, Urmston soothed himself by cultivating little gardens in frames on the roof of the poop.

Captain Charles Chisholme quarrelled with all of his passengers on the 1778 voyage of the *Gatton*, with the result that no one was speaking to him by the time they arrived in Calcutta. On the regular East Indiaman *Baring*, in 1811, one of the more high and mighty passengers, Lady Maria Nugent, kept a journal in which she diligently logged the "violent and distressing outrages" committed by Captain Henry Templar. A young army officer was so insulted by one of Templar's outbursts that he challenged him to a duel, to be held at the first opportunity. Boats were rowed to the beach when the ship arrived off Saugor Island, and the combatants took their stance, assisted by their seconds. Both pistols missed, but honour had been preserved. Hands were shaken, formal apologies made, and the party returned to the ship without being troubled by tigers.

Duels were not at all uncommon, gentlemen of that time being apt to take great umbrage at surprisingly small slights. In 1779, Mrs Eliza Fay and her companions on the

Madras-bound merchant ship *Nathalia* became highly agitated when the captain ordered the ship about so that he could go on shore to settle a quarrel with one of the passengers, as there was no one else on board who could navigate. Captain Jonathan Court, of the East India regular ship *Prince of Wales,* lost an arm in a duel with a passenger during the 1762 voyage; that he survived to take command of the same ship four more times was a credit to his surgeon, Dr Valentine Humble. Less fortunate than Court was Captain Thomas Rumbold Taylor of the *Glory,* who, on March 4, 1804, was killed in a duel with one of his passengers, Major William Davison. The army officer had behaved so badly to another passenger, a young lady, that Captain Taylor had been forced to put him under arrest, and once released in Madras, Davison had demanded satisfaction.

Women could create so much trouble on board that it is little wonder Eleanor was relieved when she found that Miss Eliza Loftie, who was going to take passage on the *Friendship,* was "very agreeable in her manners." Ladies did not even have to be single to pose problems—in 1797 Lady Anne Barnard recorded that the first mate of the *Sir Edward Hughes,* Timothy Goldsmith, fell violently in love with a Mrs Saul, who was travelling to join her husband, "and hopes earnestly to hear of Saul's death when we arrive at the Cape."

Lady Anne's ten-year-old stepson, Hervey, imitated the gentlemen by falling in love with another passenger, Miss Mary Mein. His perceived rival was the purser, William John Eastfield, who was only joking when he "courted" Hervey's light of love, but put on a convincing act—"No no Mr. Purser," cried Hervey, according to his stepmother;

"she is not your mark, mind your beef and mutton Sir and your Pigs and your split pease. Miss Mein has promised to keep herself for me." Then, after Hervey deduced that he had yet another rival, a passenger by the name of Major Bayne, he challenged him to a duel. The lad was quite confident that he would win, having "already shot two Cock Sparrows." The major was not amused.

That a ten-year-old could make such a nuisance of himself did not augur well for Eleanor and Hugh Reid, who were to carry eight children to England. There were two Fulton girls, Eliza and Hannah, aged nine and seven, probably the daughters of Francis Fulton, who was an assistant in the Attorney-General's office. Two more girls, four-year-old twins Elinor and Henrietta Gillhunt, were the daughters of Dr Gillhunt, and it is likely that their passage was arranged during the Reids' visit to the Calcutta Botanical Garden. Miss Ann Horsley, aged seven, and her brother John, aged six, were possibly the children of Francis Horsley, the Sugar Inspector, who worked with Hugh Reid during the loading of the ship. Finally, as Eleanor recorded, there were the two Hudson boys, John, aged seven, and Nathaniel, aged six, who were the sons of one of the partners in the shipbuilding firm, Hudson, Bacon and Company.

These very young children were not travelling with their parents. Instead, they were being sent home under the Reids' care. The leave-taking, for both the parents and the small boys and girls, must have been heart-rending, but that was the way of European Calcutta. "There are few little children on the Course," wrote the correspondent to *The Crayon*; "they have been sent home to England. One never loses the idea of exile which hangs round the

English in India." The desire to hand them over to relatives in England must have been a very strong one, for it was a financial burden as well an emotional one. While it is not known how much the Fultons, Gillhunts, Horsleys and Hudsons paid for their children's passage, it would have amounted to several hundreds of pounds. As was usual, the parents negotiated with the captain, who kept all the money, that being one of the perquisites of the commander of an East Indiaman.

Children who did travel with their parents naturally shared the same accommodation. When itinerant lawyer William Hickey sailed back to England on the *Nassau* in 1779, his fellow passengers included "Mr. George Smith and wife, and three lovely children, who were to occupy the roundhouse." This meant that the Smith family had the whole sternward half of the poop cabin, which must have cost an enormous sum, as William Hickey himself paid the equivalent of £500 for just a screened-off section of the forward part of the poop, the cuddy.

The situation was different for the children travelling on the *Friendship,* because they were in the care of servants. Cabins—or perhaps a dormitory—were established in the steerage, immediately forward of the Great Cabin, and their *ayahs* would have berthed with them. Hopefully the mates, who had their cabins in the same area, and the seamen, who had to work around them when they were playing on the quarterdeck, were all men who enjoyed the company of children.

Hugh Reid listed two *ayahs*. The woman who looked after the Fulton and Gillhunt girls was "a native servant named Goloul." Interestingly, the nanny for the Horsley children was "a native servant named Mrs Robinson." By deduction, she was the native Indian wife of one of the passengers, Captain George A. Robinson of the Second European Regiment of infantry, who had been given leave from his post as military auditor-general to go home on furlough. That she had come on board as a servant was a subterfuge, and more evidence of Hugh Reid's flexibility. So-called "black" wives were not allowed on Honourable East India Company ships; it is on record that a Bombay merchant managed to get his Indian wife home only by bribing the ship's commander with the enormous sum of five thousand pounds. How much Hugh Reid was paid is unknown, but the ruse must have been aided and abetted by the Horsleys, who were evidently Captain Robinson's friends.

Robinson might have preferred to sleep in the steerage with his wife, but the regulations also stipulated that he, as an army officer returning home, should have a berth in the Great Cabin. This he had to share with two others—the eminent Dr John Laird, who had been an East India Company army surgeon since February 1771, and was now the First Member of the Medical Board, and Captain G. Davis of the 29th Light Dragoons.

All three would have paid the set Company rate for their passage—2,000 sicca rupees (the silver-rich coins that were the currency in Bengal), the equivalent of £200. Another expense was their cabin furniture, which they had to supply themselves. They may have slung their cots in company, or had the Great Cabin partitioned with thin wooden screens—but, whatever the choice, it meant that Hugh Reid had already installed his own furniture in the poop cabin, where he and Eleanor had the starboard side of the roundhouse.

The larboard side of the roundhouse would have been reserved for Miss Eliza Loftie. Though airy and well-lit, and with good access to both the stern gallery and the quarter gallery, it had the disadvantage of being very noisy. This was partly because of the thuds and shouts of the seamen working on the mizzen rigging above, but mostly because the poop deck—the roof of the cabin—was the poultry yard, and when grain was thrown into the coops the thunder of pecking beaks was like a squall of hail.

It was customary, however, for single ladies to be allotted a space close to the captain's cabin. As Mary Martha Sherwood, wife of Captain Henry Sherwood of the 53rd Foot, noted on the *Devonshire* in 1805, the ship's commander "is always supposed to be the guardian for the time being of the ladies under his care." One of Mary Martha Sherwood's fellow passengers—a "Miss L—"—misunderstood Captain Murray's gallantry when he was merely following orders, and jumped to the conclusion that he meant to marry her. Luckily, because Eleanor was with him, Hugh Reid did not risk this embarrassment. It was also nice for Eleanor to have Eliza Loftie's company when she walked on the stern gallery, or relaxed in her cabin or in the cuddy.

The cuddy—the forward half of the poop cabin—was now the formal dining room. Couches would have been placed there, along with Reid's dresser, but the dominant feature was the dining table. Here, meals were taken by all the passengers—except, of course, the children, who ate with the servants in the steerage, under the presiding eye of the new third mate, James Mitchell. At the third mate's table, too, were the clerks brought along by Dr Laird and

Captain Robinson, these being Charles Wales and Richard Bridges.

On Company ships the seating at the cuddy table was regulated by rules and long tradition. Captain Reid's place was in the middle, facing the glassed doors that led to the quarterdeck, with Eleanor and Eliza Loftie to either side of him. Dr Laird and Captain Robinson, being the two senior passengers, would flank the two ladies, and opposite Dr Laird his friend, Captain Davis, the Light Dragoon officer, would be placed. Beside Davis was the surgeon-cum-passenger, Dr Dumerque, and alongside the doctor either the first mate, John Muirhead, or the second mate, John Macdonald, depending which was the officer on duty on deck.

This system was so rigid that any alterations demanded by a passenger could lead to endless trouble. In October 1811, Lady Maria Nugent, who was sailing to Calcutta on the *Baring,* requested to be moved from her place at the captain's elbow to the other side of the table, as the light reflected from the sails was hurting her eyes. Despite this apparently reasonable request, an army officer, Captain Midwinter, refused to give up his seat, which led to such a fuss that Captain Midwinter and his wife retired to their cabin space in a huff.

Infuriated, the testy Captain Templar retaliated by banishing them to the third mate's table in the steerage for the rest of the voyage. Embarrassed by the general fuss and Templar's ranting, Lady Maria insisted on dining in her own cabin from then on, and her friend, Lady Charlotte Murray, made up her mind to keep her company there. As a result, only one lady passenger—coincidentally Eleanor Reid, who was travelling to Calcutta with Hugh—

was left to grace a table that was surrounded by variously embarrassed or angry men.

Dining on the *Friendship* on the homeward passage in 1800 and 1801 was not likely to be so stressful, the table being much smaller than on the regular East Indiamen. That there were only nine to serve also meant that there was only one steward, a Portuguese by the name of Rossa. The small number certainly did not mean that formality was abandoned, however. While breakfast, at eight in the morning, was a hurried affair involving tea, toast, cold meat and ship's biscuit, everyone was expected to dress for dinner, which was held at two in the afternoon. For the men, this meant uniform, so that Reid and his officers, in their blue cutaway coats with white waistcoats over white breeches (black boots or breeches were strictly forbidden, unless in deep mourning), made a nice contrast to the scarlet sported by the soldiers. Eliza Loftie and Eleanor

would have worn gracefully draped muslin, probably sprigged, with puffed sleeves high on their arms. Each would be shod in dainty slippers, and either wear a gauze turban or have small, fanciful decorations in her high-piled hair.

The meal was elaborate to match the dressing-up, and surprisingly like dinner in Calcutta, considering the shipboard ingredients. Hugh Reid often recorded in his logbook that the cook "killed a Hog for the Europeans and a sheep for the Lascars," and shipboard sheep and pigs were slaughtered for the cabin, too, along with many hens and ducks. There were at least three courses, followed by dessert, and accompanied by beer and wine. On the *Sir Edward Hughes* in February 1797, Lady Anne Barnard listed a menu involving "pease soup," a roasted leg of mutton, roast fowls, corned beef, a ham, mutton chops, stewed cabbage and potatoes, "Removed by an enormous Plumb Pudding." Homeward bound passengers were apt to demand the curries they had become fond of in India—indeed, there were so many old India hands on the outward voyage of the *Baring* that Lady Maria Nugent recorded a plea from the captain to borrow her *ayah,* so she could teach the cook how to make a curry.

Just as at home or in Calcutta, the ladies withdrew once the table was cleared, leaving the men to their tobacco and the decanter. This last might make several tours of the table or just one, depending on the liberality of the captain, who was the provider of all food and drink. Once he had replaced the stopper, with a nod and a pointedly polite, "Good afternoon," the men took the hint and removed themselves, to pass the time as best they could until the much more informal tea at six.

This was just a drink (made from putrid water, as the voyage dragged on) and a snack, because there was yet another meal to come, which was supper, at nine. This was a simple meal, contrived from leftovers from dinner, often turned into soups or lobscouse, which was a sea-dish of chopped cold meat stewed up with cracker crumbs, often known as hash. If it had a pastry top and had been baked in the oven, it was known as hash with an awning. After the ladies had withdrawn from the supper table the decanter made just one round, and then all lanterns were blown out, so that everyone was forced to grope his way through the gloom to bed. There had to be a curfew, because England was at war.

Hugh Reid must have contemplated the arrangements for departure with compressed lips, as the senior captain in the outgoing convoy was the impatient Salkeld, the same man who had so callously abandoned the *Friendship* in the privateer-ridden Atlantic. Again, Joseph Salkeld was in command of the *Minerva* – as the *Bombay Courier* noted on January 7, 1801, "The Honorable Company's Freighted ships *Minerva,* Captain Salkeld, *Highland Chief,* Captain Greenway, *Friendship,* Capt. Reid and *Varuna,* Captain Farrer left their Pilots, all well on the 11th instant, with a fine favourable breeze." Eleanor also records that the country ship *Santa Cruz,* commanded by Captain John Collie, would sail in company as far as Ceylon.

The Company's elderly frigate *Nonsuch,* commanded by Captain Canning, was to escort them through the head of the Bay of Bengal. as far as the latitude of Madras. This support was more illusory than real, for not only was the *Nonsuch* battered and weatherworn, having just returned from a fruitless hunt for the captured Indiaman *Kent,* but she had just survived a running battle with *La Confiance,* where Canning had held his fire in case the vibration shattered the planks—the twenty-year-old ship's timbers were so fragile that she collapsed into a pile of kindling when put into drydock later that year.

Once the *Nonsuch* had turned back for the Sand Heads, the extra ships would be on their own, with the unreliable Salkeld their commodore, and in very dangerous waters. too. Over the two months of October and November, Robert Surcouf's *Confiance* had taken four prizes, including the East Indies country ship *Prize* of Calcutta. In November the 14-gun *General Malartic,* "commanded by citizen Jean Duterte"—also operating out of the Isle de France—had attacked the Company ship *Phoenix,* commanded by her owner, William Moffatt. Duterte, having very recently captured the East Indies country ship *Mermaid,* which he had sent back into port after stripping her of everything valuable, was confident of another prize. Captain Moffatt, however, was too wily to be easily deceived and taken.

According to his report, the *Malartic* was flying English colours, and hailed the *Phoenix* in the English language, but nonetheless his suspicions were aroused, as the other vessel was in a shot-torn state, and he already knew that a French privateer had just "fought a long and desperate action with an American ship, supposed the *Rebecca,* from Calcutta." So, instead of tamely hauling aback, he readied his ship for action. The troops and officers of the 88th regiment he was carrying to Calcutta were ordered to keep out of sight in the waist of the ship, and the whole complement was armed. Aided by the male passengers and the seamen, the soldiers not only repelled the French boarders, but stormed the *General Malartic* and seized her—a gallant action that earned Captain Moffatt a ceremonial sword.

To all appearances, however, Eleanor Reid was not at all worried about the grave risks that lay in wait in hostile seas—though her husband often recorded exercising the guns during the voyage, it went unmentioned in her journal. Nor did she seem to notice it when the boatswain "discovered a dangerous leak" on February 1, 1801, forcing Reid to order the ship brought to, putting her in this vulnerable position so that a stiffened and tarred tarpaulin could be drawn over the leak, and baize nailed over it. Neither did she seem to be aware of how often the crew was set to repairing the sails, which were wearing thin and going rotten—or that urgent repairs had to be carried out while the ship was at St Helena, including the replacement of the main topmast, along with all its rigging. Attack threatened as the coast of England was raised. "At 9 a.m.

saw a fleet to the SWest, a Ship from which gave Chace to us," wrote Reid on May 21, when the convoy was on the verge of arriving in the Downs. They were rescued by the Royal Navy frigate *Endymion*—but Eleanor did not seem to notice that, either. Instead, she had company to enjoy, and entertaining stories to hear. And that is where her journal is taken up again.

As Messrs. Hudson, Bacon, and Co. had done all the repairs the ship required, they provided a comfortable vessel to take us down to Saugor. Two of Mrs. Hudson's sons were going home under our care, and their father intended accompanying them down the river. On the 6th of December 1800, we left Calcutta; we had omitted seeing the Black Hole so often described by travellers; we often, however, passed the monument erected in memory of the wretched sufferers at the west side of the writer's buildings, which forms one side of Tank Square. In the centre of the square is a fine piece of water, which supplies the inhabitants at all seasons of the year.

As the afternoon was very fine, we had an opportunity of again beholding the villas as we passed down Garden Reach, but they did not interest us as first. This is the case with almost every thing we are accustomed to have, either in view, or in possession. The next day we reached Fultah, where we landed, and had an excellent dinner at the tavern, the only house of entertainment between Calcutta and Saugor. In the evening we again embarked in the accommodation boat, and next day reached the *Friendship* at Saugor, without accident.

On the 9th, Mr. Charles Law came on board to dispatch the ship; he solicited this appointment in consequence of his sister in law going home with us to England. This business being finished, we were joined by all the passengers in the evening, *viz.*, Miss Eliza Loftie, Capt. George Robinson, Capt. G. Davis, Dr. John Laird, Mr. Charles Dumerque, and the children, three boys and five girls, with their native servants, ayahs, &c.

The Hon. Company's ship *Nonsuch* was appointed to convoy the fleet to a certain distance; the ships ready to sail with us were the *Minerva,* Capt. Salkeld; the *Varana,* Capt. Farrer, and the *Highland Chief,* Capt. Greenaway; also the *Santa Cruz,* Capt. John Collie, who was to keep company until we were off the Island of Ceylon.

On the 11th December we left Saugor Roads, without losing any of our men by tigers, although boats from the ship had landed on the island almost every day. The next morning we discharged our pilot, just three months from the day we received one on board on our entrance to the port. A few days after we sailed we became somewhat settled, and soon formed ourselves at ease with each other; conversation, without stiffness or reserve, was kept up at table among our agreeable party, nor did it fail during the whole voyage. Capt. Robinson was a well-informed agreeable man, and had seen much service in India, particularly under Lord Cornwallis, whom he served as military secretary; he was now returning to join his family in England. Dr. Laird was a particular friend of Capt Robinson, and a most worthy man, much esteemed by many he had left behind; he also had seen much service with the army under General Sir Eyre Coote, whom he attended until his death.

His memory was sadly impaired, particularly respecting any recent event; but of any thing concerning the army, or occurrences of former times, he could give the most minute account. This loss of memory was attributed to the consequences of a tiger hunt, the history of which I shall give you. Mr. Robinson, himself, and a party of gentlemen, had agreed to spend a little time with a friend at a place called Couti, not far from Kedgeree, where they enjoyed the manly sport of bear hunting, and were generally successful. One morning they went out as usual, and left an elderly gentleman and a young man as his companion; these two had strolled from the bungalow on foot, enjoying the cool morning air. Nothing interrupted their pleasure until they passed an opening in the jungle, when their ears were assailed with a most hideous growl; upon turning to the spot whence the sound issued, they were horror-struck at seeing a large royal tiger worrying at the throat of a poor cow he had just seized.

They instantly started back towards the house, thinking every moment they should be attacked by the tiger. The young man very soon out-ran the elder, who called lustily for him to stand and look at the tiger in the face, assuring him it would not then attack them; at length the young man slacked his pace, and let the elder come up with him, who seizing his coat, cried, "now we are equal, you young dog, run for your life." They reached the house in safety, which without doubt they owed to the prey which had already occupied the animal's attention. Measures were now concerted for his destruction; accordingly next day a large party sallied forth, well mounted upon elephants who were trained for such an encounter. They were very soon at the place where the tiger lay concealed: they partly surrounded him but nothing could induce him to leave the cover. They fired many shots in all directions, and were in hopes they had killed him.

The elephant upon which Dr. Laird was mounted being more bold than the rest, advanced to the jungle, when, just as he entered, the tiger sprang upon his neck; the doctor instantly fired his piece, and the furious animal quitted his hold, but the elephant was so frightened that he turned and set off at a rate which made it impossible for Dr. Laird to dismount until he came to a river, where in consequence of his apprehension that the elephant would ford, he dropped off behind, and hurt himself considerably with the fall; this however was not the worst, he now had to find his way back to the house, which was upwards of five miles distant, in a scorching sun: he was immediately seized with a jungle fever, from the effects of which his memory never recovered.

The tiger was killed, but the party lost several gentlemen by fever before they returned to Calcutta, in consequence of which, neither Dr. Laird or Mr. Robinson ever attended another hunting party while they remained in India.

We had the finest weather down the bay; the *Nonsuch* left us about latitude 16, and the *Santa Cruz* about latitude 10 north, leaving our squadron of four ships to take care of themselves, the *Minerva* being appointed commodore. We crossed the equator on the 28th December, without meeting any of those distressing calms so prevalent between the Brazil and Guinea coasts.

Nothing occurred worth noticing until the 6th of January 1801, when about 11 P.M. the greatest panic seized all on board. We were alarmed by a grinding of the ship's bottom, as if she had struck on a coral bank, attended with a rumbling noise, and most violent tremulous motion of the vessel. The captain instantly ordered the lead to be thrown out, but no bottom could be found with a hundred fathoms of line; the pump was then tried, to see if the ship were leaky in consequence of the shock, but she was found as tight as ever.

There was a fine light breeze at the time, and the night not so dark but that the other three ships could be seen at no great distance; we were in about nine degrees south latitude, and 92 east longitude, and upwards of five hundred miles from any known land. We were left to conjecture concerning this singular occurrence, but most of those on board concluded it must have been occasioned by an earthquake. Capt. R— gave the best description of the sensation by which he was awakened: he compared the agitation of the ship to that which would be experienced if a number of anchors were dropped from different parts of her at the same instant, and the noise to that which the cables would make in running out. When we compared notes with the other ships, we found they had been alarmed in the same manner; indeed one of them had guns ready to make signals of danger. There can be no doubt that it was caused by some convulsion at the bottom near where the ship passed.

We now got into the strong south-east trade winds, and made great progress towards the Cape of Good Hope, off which place the *Varuna* parted from us, as she was ordered to land some stores there, and to re-join us at St. Helena. Five days after this the *Minerva* and *Highland Chief* parted, and left us to come on by ourselves. This was very unjustifiable on the part of our commodore: but as his ship sailed much faster than ours, he no doubt gave a sufficient reason in his logbook.

We arrived however in safety at St. Helena on the 1st of March; the other ships had only arrived two days before. As Capt. Robinson was intimate with Major G., commanding the garrison here, he was so good as to procure accommodations for us all at his house, where we were very comfortable as long as the ship remained. I frequently saw my old friend Mrs. Porteous. from Orange Grove; we had some pleasant rides to Longwood, and dined with the Rev. Mr. W. a brother of Mrs. G., whose house was situated in a most romantic part of the Island, from whence we commanded the most magnificent views of rugged nature.

On the 9th of March we were much gratified by the arrival of H. M.'s ship *Buffalo,* from Port Jackson, having on board our old and worthy friend Gov. Hunter, with his nephew and niece, Capt. and Mrs. Kent; they had come from the Cape in company with the *Varuna,* to convoy us to England. Now all was bustle once more, preparing for our departure for our native land.

Longwood House, from Fowler's Views

As Gov. H. had the direction of the ships, he intended touching at the Island of Ascension to procure some turtle; accordingly on the 16th of March we sailed from St. Helena, and in five days anchored at the island of Ascension. It appeared as if recently burnt to a brown cinder; not the smallest verdure could be seen from where the ship lay. Before dark a boat was sent from each ship to assist in turning the turtle, as it was agreed to share them among the different ships.

Next day our friends from the *Buffalo* dined with us, and in the evening it was proposed that the ladies should land, just to have it to say that they had been upon the island. This proposal did not meet my husband's approbation: however we persevered, and got a wetting without having the gratification of landing at all; as the boat was nearly swamped in the surf. Mrs. K. was much alarmed; and had it not been for the exertions of her brother, Lieut. B. K., who was on shore with the seamen, our adventure might have ended seriously. As an aggravation of our disappointment, when we came on board no one pitied us; they all said we could have expected nothing else, from the great surf that continually rolled on the shore.

Next day, when the turtle was divided, three came to our share; they were immense creatures, weighing upwards of 400 pounds each. Our people brought on board several buckets full of turtle eggs, which they found buried in the sand; they were perfectly round, about the size of a small orange, with a soft flexible skin; they also brought off a number of little turtles, about the size of small crabs, and a number of tropic birds, who were so stupid as to suffer themselves to be taken by hand when sitting upon the rocks.

All being ready, we left the island on the 23d of March, and proceeded with a fine strong trade-wind towards the Equator, which we crossed on the 28th of March; from that time until the 3d of April we had much unsettled weather, with squalls, thunder and lightning, and almost constant rain. This was expected about these latitudes: however we now got into the regular north-east trade winds, about four degrees north, and proceeded steadily on, in a north-west direction, until we came to about 23° north, and 37° west, where we fell in with a vast quantity of gulph weed, which at times was so thick in all directions, as to have frightened people unacquainted with its appearance. We were several days sailing through these fields of floating marine substance, and caught many branches of it; they were extremely elegant, and greatly resembled some land plants. Many very curious marine animals were found adhering to these branches.

About the 27th degree of latitude we were clear of the sea-weed, and then began to get into the variable winds, which enabled us to get round the Azores, or Western Islands, but had much bad weather, the ship at times taking in great quantities of water over the decks. This continued until we arrived in soundings off Scilly, where we encountered a most severe gale, in which a poor fellow named Hunt, a seaman, had both thighs broken by the falling of the arm-chest. The limbs were immediately set by Doctor Laird, and Mr Dumerque with so much skill and success (notwithstanding the violent motion of the ship) that when the man was afterwards taken to the London Hospital, the surgeons there said the operation did great credit to those who had performed it: the man perfectly recovered, and sailed afterwards with the captain to India. The passengers kindly made up a purse of 30 guineas for this poor fellow.

On the 21st of May we fell in with a large fleet from the Mediterranean, who joined convoy, much to our annoyance, as many of them sailed very heavily, and detained us. We had very thick weather on entering the British Channel. One night a large ship, supposed to be a frigate, ran on board the *Highland Chief*: they were sailing in opposite directions, and the bower anchors of the *Highland Chief* hooked into a port of the frigate, and as the ships were going fast through the water, the anchor was carried away. The cable being bent, very soon all ran out at the hawse-hole, and lucky it was that the end of the cable was not made fast, as had that been the case some serious mischief must assuredly have happened; as it was, the *Highland Chief* received so much damage from the shock that she was obliged to be towed into Plymouth.

The weather continuing very foggy, obliged us to keep our bell continually tolling, for fear of running foul of ships coming the contrary way; and as the fleet that joined us consisted of 150 sail, nothing was heard but the blowing of horns, beating of drums, and tinkling of bells, to keep clear of each other; but the fog signals from the men of war, made by the report of guns, were so well understood, either by the number, or by quick or slow time, that the ships could alter their course to any point of the compass. We may say that we entered the English channel in the dark, as during five days we could not see a mile from the ship, and sailed upwards of 300 miles in this way. However, on the morning of the 24th of May we had the heartfelt satisfaction of once more seeing our native land; the chalky cliffs of the Isle of Wight could not be mistaken.

Shipping at Spithead

As the wind was easterly, a signal was made for the convoy to put into Spithead, where we anchored about two in the afternoon. Mr. Dumerque was sent to London with the dispatches; at which time Capt. Robinson [with Mrs Robinson and the Horsley children], Doctor Laird, and Capt. Davis took the opportunity of going to town also.

As I did not intend leaving the ship until she arrived in the river Thames, Miss Loftie remained with me; we stayed here four days, and no custom-house boat or officer came on board of us; what a fine opportunity we had of smuggling! My husband, however, had put that out of our power, by shewing all our presents, &c., before we left Calcutta.

On the 28th the *Lapwing* frigate made the signal for convoy to the eastward, in consequence of which we proceeded, and passed through the Downs next day, having no occasion to anchor, as the other ships were obliged to do, for their poor seamen to be pressed. The few European seamen we had were hid away, and the boarding officers, seeing so many black faces on board, did not suspect us.

The next day we entered the river Thames, and were met by my brother-in-law, Mr. Thomas Reid, who had procured a very fine sailing boat to take us to town; this was a joyful meeting indeed, rendered doubly so to me when I learned that my beloved parents and all my family were well.

Next day, the 2d of June, we arrived in London, after an absence of two years and three days, with thankful hearts to a merciful God, who had permitted us to return in safety to our native land, having traversed a space of upwards of thirty-seven thousand miles without the smallest accident. It was particularly gratifying to my husband to receive letters from the friends of those poor men who embarked from Ireland, expressive of their sincere thanks for the great kindness and humanity shewn to them on the passage, and observing that they had mentioned that the only hardship they experienced was the necessary confinement, which the laws of their country and the safety of the ship required.

I now conclude my remarks upon my first voyage, which I am conscious requires much correction and revision.

London from Deptford, 1730

Seven

Afterward : June 1801-November 1853

While Eleanor was catching up with her family—her parents, William and Janet Barclay, her brothers, William, Andrew and George Dallas Barclay, her sisters, Margaret and Jane, and her brother-in-law, Richard Porter—Hugh Reid was supervising the unloading of the *Friendship*, the gunpowder in her magazine being taken out first. Then, having handed in his homeward voyage rosters, and testifying that they were "True and Correct Lists of the Ships Company and Passengers to the Best of my knowledge and belief" (though they include neither Eleanor's name, nor that of the seaman she called Hunt), Reid followed his wife into town.

East India House, T.H. Shepherd

There was much that was novel to see and hear. Napoleon Bonaparte, who had been created the first consul of France, now controlled the whole of Italy, so that the Mediterranean and Straits of Gibraltar were more dangerous than ever. Horatio Nelson, hero of the Battle of the Nile and now a vice-admiral, had created a sensation by flaunting the buxom and beautiful Emma, wife of the staid Sir William Hamilton, as his mistress.

Even more importantly to Hugh, Nelson had ensured that the Baltic Sea remained open to British shipping, by disobeying orders to withdraw ("Damn me if I do!" he growled, and put his telescope to his blind eye), instead leading his squadron through heavy fire from shore batteries to sink the Danish fleet.

Sale Room at Lloyds

Closer to home, there was a new East India House in Leadenhall Lane, which had been ceremoniously opened in April 1800. Naturally, in view of his five percent share, Captain Reid was interested in the auction of the goods he had carried on behalf of the Company. This was held in the great space known as the General Court Room, which was arranged as a semi-circular amphitheatre with tiered seats, where the director in charge of the proceedings sat at a long table. There was also his private trade to dispose of, while reporting to the ship-owners was a priority.

Hugh Reid's command of the *Friendship* was not renewed. Whether it was his choice or a decision made by the Mangles brothers is unknown, but it was certainly an amicable arrangement, as their association continued for many years. Instead, the command was given to a Captain J. Smith, and the *Friendship* was put back into the West Indies trade.

Reid branched out on his own, spending the proceeds of the voyage on a Quebec-built ship named *Phoenix*. He most probably negotiated the deal at Lloyds Coffee House, on the northwest corner of the Royal Exchange, though his meeting place of choice was the Jerusalem Coffee House on Cornhill, where the captains of East Indiamen gathered to exchange gossip, anecdotes and hints, and to read the Asiatic journals.

At first glance, buying the *Phoenix* was a step down in his career, as she was such a small ship, registered at just 176 tons, even smaller than the notorious *Bounty*. But, for her size, the *Phoenix* could carry a lot of cargo. Under the single berth deck, where all the complement of the ship lived, there was a thirteen-foot hold, braced with solid beams. The *Phoenix* was newly coppered and rated A1, too, so Reid obviously considered her a good investment.

According to *Lloyds List*, Reid took his departure with a cargo for the Cape of Good Hope in December that same year, 1801. Whether Eleanor sailed with him is unknown. About that time, Hugh Reid gave his address as Wellclose Square, a respectable precinct in East London where many sea captains made their homes, and Eleanor may have stayed there.

In view of her loyalty and courage, though, it is more likely that she did keep him company, particularly as there is no record of him bringing the *Phoenix* back to London. Instead, Captain Reid went into the country trade, plying the Indian Ocean between South Africa and the Orient.

Eleanor's accommodations in the little *Phoenix* would have been both novel and uncomfortable. There was no poop cabin, and no stern gallery. It is likely that she slept with her husband in a stateroom off the starboard quarter, where a gun could be part of the furniture. Most probably a settee and the captain's chart desk would fit in there, too, so movement had to be careful, particularly in a rough sea.

The Great Cabin was furnished with the captain's table, where Eleanor would eat her meals in the company of whichever one of the two mates was not on duty on deck. The small number of seamen would berth forward on the same deck, and eat off a swinging table, or prop their plates on their knees as they sat—and, to add the spice of danger to the mix, Captain Reid would have carried a letter of marque, giving him the right to fight enemy ships as a privateer.

The experience was not to last for long. In January 1803 the Asiatic newspapers noted the "safe arrival in the river of the ship *Phoenix,* Captain Hugh Reid, from the Cape of Good Hope, which she left the 21st September." He had come to Calcutta to take over a much grander command, as the *Asiatic Mirror* reported on 9 February—

> *Yesterday at half past two o'clock was launched from the yard of Messrs. Hudson, Bacon and Co. on this side of the water, a well finished ship of 540 Tons burthen, named the* Mangles, *to be commanded by Captain Hugh Reid, late of the* Phoenix. *A great part of her Cargo is ready, and will sail for England, early in next month.*

Not only did Hugh Reid have the command of the new ship, but he was a part owner, too. Two other owners were the men who had given their name to the vessel, John and James Mangles, while Hugh's brother, Thomas Reid, had also invested in the *Mangles*.

The sixth share was the usual builder's investment, made as a gesture of faith in his product, and was registered to John Bannister Hudson, who gave his London address as St Helen's, Bishopsgate.

As promised by the paper, departure swiftly followed. The *Mangles* left Bengal on March 26, 1803, and made port at Cape Town on June 20. Hugh Reid did not meet with the usual jovial reception there, however. The Cape of Good Hope was no longer friendly territory, having been returned to Dutch control in February, as part of the uneasy ceasefire that had been negotiated with Treaty of Amiens.

Exactly one month later, the ship reached St Helena, where there was more unsettling news—that the Treaty of Amiens had collapsed, and the war with France had resumed. Sailing north through the Atlantic must have been nerve-wracking, as the enemy privateers were at work with new enthusiasm.

The *Mangles* was reported at Cork on 19 September. After unloading the Irish part of her cargo, Reid sailed for the Downs, getting there on October 2, 1803. Accordingly, Eleanor arrived home just in time to welcome the arrival of twin nieces, Hannah and Eleanor, born to Margaret and Richard Porter in November.

HMS Culloden*, anon, pen and wash*

It was a quick turn-around, as the instruction for the return voyage was to join a large convoy of East Indiamen. Because of the resumption of war, the convoy was to be escorted all the way to the Bay of Bengal—and by no less than the great 72-gun HMS *Culloden,* veteran of four great battles, including the Glorious First of June. The equally battle-hardened Sir Edward Pellew, one of Nelson's Band of Brothers, was the commodore.

But, when the *Mangles* arrived at Portsmouth, in early August, 1804, it was to find that the convoy was gone, having sailed on 10 July, and that the next convoy to India was not due until September. However, by going into Falmouth, Captain Reid was able to join a small group of North America-bound merchantmen and South Seas whaleships that was leaving there on August 19, escorted by the 32-gun frigate *Orpheus*. Luckily, the *Mangles* was a fast sailer, and fortunately, too, when Captain Reid arrived at Madeira it was to find that Pellew's convoy was there.

Forthwith, the extra ship *Mangles* joined the other East Indiamen—*United Kingdom,* Captain John Pelly, *Baring,* Captain Dixon Meadows, *Worcester,* Captain Searles Wood, *Airly Castle,* Captain John Mackintosh, *Duke of Montrose,* Captain John Paterson, *Lord Hawkesbury,* Captain James Timbrell, *Sovereign,* Captain Richard Meriton, *Alexander,* Captain John Francklin, and *Monarch,* Captain Stephen Hawes. And, according to Robert Hay, who was one of the seamen on the *Culloden,* the passage to the Bay of Bengal was very pleasant.

Sir Edward Pellew, a large, convivial man who "knew the advantages of cheerfulness in a ship's company," encouraged fiddling and dancing—"if there happened to be more dancers than could get conveniently within the sound of Bob's fiddle, the admiral's band was ordered up." The echo of music over the sparkling waters was so beguiling that one of the captains, who had a number of lady passengers on board, brought his ship alongside so that they could enjoy the lively sounds—unfortunately, as he came too close, and his spritsail yard snagged in the *Culloden*'s main rigging. The stray Indiaman was "boomed off" by seamen armed with studding-sail booms, but it was an embarrassment that would take some living down.

It is impossible to tell if it was Hugh Reid's *Mangles* that got tangled up with the *Culloden,* though he was certainly carrying a number of ladies. One of these, by great coincidence, was the same Mrs Eliza Fay who wrote the early letters descriptive of daily life in Calcutta. She was a sad little figure now, returning to Bengal after ventures in millinery and shipping that had left her bankrupt. Other women were Mrs Wybrow, the wife of a navy surgeon, who was travelling with her husband, Mrs. S. Herman, who was also with her husband, and the wife of a German missionary, Mrs. Gerricke, who was joining her husband in Calcutta. The fifth, if she was there, was Eleanor.

One of the male passengers was "Mr A. Barclay, of the Royal Navy," who could well have been Eleanor's second-oldest brother, Andrew. If so, he appears to have started a new career, commanding ships in the local trade, as a Captain Andrew Barclay "of the country service" took passage back to England on the *Admiral Cockburn* in 1818. There was also a cadet by the name of Pearson, plus two shipmasters named Hitchings and Humphries, who described themselves as free mariners (meaning they had a licence to reside in India), and "Mr C. Manini, a native."

"The Extra Ship *Mangles*, Captain Reid, which was prevented leaving England in company with the Ships, lately arrived under convoy of the *Culloden*," announced the *Bombay Courier* on December 19, 1804. Evidently the ship was off the Sand Heads at the time, for in the Calcutta supplement of January 31, 1805, it was further revealed that Reid (or his pilot) had had the bad luck to run aground on the way up the Hooghly River, but without reporting any injury to the ship.

Anchored safely off Calcutta, and with his incoming cargo unloaded, Hugh Reid returned to the country trade, this time voyaging as far as Canton and Macao, in China. On January 10, 1806, he was reported at Penang, from China, with one passenger, Henry Stone (the man who had married Dr Roxburgh's beautiful daughter Mary), and on April 4, 1806, he arrived in Calcutta "with some damage."

Though the cause of the damage was not described, there were hazards aplenty in the Bay of Bengal, including enemy action. That same month, the *Calcutta Gazette* noted the capture of both the frigate *Atlanta* and the Company privateer *Napoleon,* and reported also that the Honourable Company's ship *Admiral Gardner* had been attacked by the privateer *Bellona,* and had lost five men in the action.

"The *Caroline,* Captain [Nicholas] Surcouf, the *Henrietta,* and three other small privateers" were fitting out at Mauritius, as the *Calcutta Gazette* revealed on April 17, 1806; "and were said to be destined for the Sand-heads." The *Henrietta* was a 70-ton brig with 25 officers and two 18-pounder carronades, "painted black, with white top-cloths." The 80-ton lateen-rigged *Caroline* was reputed to be very fast. Manned by a crew of sixty, she mounted ten guns. Nicholas Surcouf, commander of the *Caroline,* was the brother of Robert Surcouf, whose prizes had included the *Kent.* Since then, Robert had retired, but now, even more ominously, there was gossip that he was about to return to the Bay of Bengal. Whispers said that he had com-missioned a 20-gun corvette, *Revenant*—"Ghost"—and was on the verge of leaving St Malo, France.

The gossip was right. After manning the *Revenant* with a 192-strong crew, Robert Surcouf sailed from St Malo in March 1807, and arrived at the Isle de France in June, leaving a trail of seized ships and burned ships behind him. At the beginning of September, after an interval of being fêted by the inhabitants and refitting his ship, he set out to pillage the Bay of Bengal.

Within mere days had snared his first captures. As the *Bombay Courier* gloomily commented on October 14, "Five ships have already become the prey of the *Revenant.*" And one of them was the *Mangles.*

According to the report, on September 26, 1807, Robert Surcouf seized the 800-ton, 12-gun *Trafalgar*, with ten thousand sacks of rice in her holds, "and immediately after boarded and took the *Mangles*." The *Mangles* had 11,000 bags of rice in her holds, and was also carrying an assorted cargo of mirrors, furniture and books. Two days later, Surcouf captured the 12-gun *Admiral Applin*, with 9,500 bags of rice, and on October 2, he took the *Suzanna*, Captain Taylor, with 5,500 bags of rice and a between decks cargo of sailcloth. As the editor of the *Bombay Courier* wryly observed, "we are concerned to add that the former good fortune of this dashing adventurer seems to have attended his return to the Indian seas." The prizes were sent into Mauritius, while the *Revenant* continued her cruise, capturing and ransacking six more ships before returning to port in early January.

By sheer good luck, though, Hugh Reid had escaped Surcouf's clutches. He had handed over the command of the *Mangles* just six months before, meaning that he and Eleanor—if she was sailing—had only narrowly missed finding themselves prisoners of the French. Instead, the unfortunate shipmaster had been Captain John Galloway.

The handover of the command of the *Mangles* was not because Reid had lost his nerve, but because he had a new ship on the stocks. "On Sunday last," reported the *Asiatic Register,* "was launched from Mr White's building slip at Howrah, the new ship intended for Captain Hugh Reid—

> *This fine specimen of Calcutta naval architecture, made her* début *under the name of the* "Providence." *Her entrée into the Hooghly afforded a grand spectacle. The length of her ways being considerable, and her descent gradual, she glided along with an impetuosity rapidly increasing, till she triumphantly floated on the stream.*

The date of the launch was May 31, 1807. While Isaac White was the shipwright, according to the registration the builder of the *Providence* was Matthew Smith, an energetic newcomer to the Howrah shipbuilding industry who was working on establishing slips of his own. Accordingly, the *Providence* was a top-quality job, being an advertisement for his new business. Rated at 630 tons, she was nearly 130 feet in length, with lofty decks, the headroom in the Great Cabin being well over six feet.

The *Providence* sailed down the Hooghly River on August 9, 1807, where Hugh Reid had the bad luck to run aground again. However, the *Bombay Courier* commented, it was confidently expected she would get off unscathed, as she was only in ballast, and the weather was good. Once he had taken on his cargo, Reid sailed her to Macao, on the first of at least two voyages between India and China. On February 21, 1809, Reid's name appeared in the paper again, when the *Providence* arrived at the Hooghly River from Macao.

Shipping on the Pearl River, from Nordhoff

His passengers were all army officers—Colonel Weguelin, Major Robertson, Captains Blackenhagen and Stewart, Lieutenants Auriol, Walker, Watson and Smith, and Mr. Hogg, surgeon. Once they were on shore, he moored the *Providence* off Howrah to be refreshed and reloaded, and in June he sailed downriver to Diamond Harbour, to take on the last of the cargo and receive passengers. This, too, was accomplished quickly, as Reid took his departure from Saugor on 25 July.

For him, and for Eleanor—as surely she was there—it was time to go home.

East Indiaman taking on a pilot at the Downs

On January 27, 1810, the *Providence* saluted the fort at St Helena, and on April 16 the ship was reported in the Downs. If Eleanor had indeed accompanied her husband on the *Mangles* in August 1804, she had been away for six momentous years. Naturally, there were changes in her family situation. Her sister, Margaret, had borne four more babies—Janet, named after their mother, William, after their oldest brother, Hugh Reid, after Eleanor's dashing husband, and Thomas, perhaps named after Hugh's brother. There was more exciting family news—Eleanor's youngest brother, George Dallas Barclay, had performed so bravely as a midshipman on *Mars* during the Battle of Trafalgar that he was promoted to the rank of lieutenant.

There had been changes in the political and social scenery, too. Napoleon, now Emperor, was master of all of continental Europe save Russia. Though Nelson's tactics at Trafalgar had assured Britain supremacy of the sea, the brilliant, much-loved admiral was dead. Britain's hero was now Arthur Wellesley, who was now embarked on the conquest of the Portuguese and Spanish peninsula, and had just won a decisive battle at Talavera.

Despite Napoleon's enforced embargo on British ships and goods, England was in the middle of a commercial explosion, and in London, the town mansions built by the newly rich were pressing against the boundaries of Westminster. Accordingly, the Surveyor-General for Crown Lands had decided to open up the 500-acre expanse of Regent's Park, once a forest, but now a wasteland, because the trees had been felled for Britain's shipping. A competition was being staged to determine the grandest, most dramatic and most impressive design for the new district, and the chatter in the salons predicted that the eminent architect John Nash was bound to win. In the taverns and coffee houses, on the other hand, men openly wondered about the sanity of the monarch, King George III.

Of more immediate importance to Captain Reid was news he picked up at the Jerusalem Coffee House—that the Royal Navy had suffered a humiliating defeat at the Isle de France, in a failed attempt to prevent French privateers from preying on shipping in the Bay of Bengal. Grande Port had been successfully invaded by a British landing party on August 13, 1810, but four French frigates had managed to break past the British blockade, and sneak into the anchorage through the maze of channels and sandbanks. When the British commodore, Captain Samuel Pym, ordered four of his frigates to follow and attack, two became grounded and had to be scuttled and burned to save them from the French. Another was captured, and the fourth, which could not get within broadside range, was eventually forced to surrender. The disastrous action was the most devastating naval defeat of the wars against the French.

So the French corsairs were still sailing unimpeded from their haven in Mauritius, to blaze their destructive paths across the Indian Ocean. It was a grim thought, and one that should have been good reason for Captain Reid to decide to retire from the sea. For a while it looked likely, as he offered the command of the *Providence* to a Scot, who, by strange coincidence, had the same name as Eleanor's brother, Andrew Barclay, though it is unlikely that they were related.

Born in Fife in 1759, this Andrew Barclay was eleven years older than Hugh Reid, but, while he had a long record as an officer on East India Company ships, he had never risen to the rank of captain. Nevertheless, Hugh Reid had seen something of his quality in India, because Barclay recorded in his memoirs that he "received a letter from Captain Reid, owner of the ship *Providence,* a fine vessel of 650 tons, mounting 16 guns, as a Letter of Marque, or Privateer and merchantman at the same time, able to defend herself if attacked, asking me if I would take a one-fourth share of the ship, and go out as captain of her myself: to which I agreed, and immediately took the command, as she was ready for a voyage to India."

Andrew Barclay was in Scotland visiting family at the time, but he packed at once, and headed back to London. The *Providence* left Portsmouth on September 7, 1810—for Cork, where Barclay loaded Irish prisoners for New South Wales. It was a repeat of the *Friendship* voyage, one that Reid had declined to make himself. But he had not decided to retire, either.

Instead, on July 27, 1811, he and Eleanor sailed from Portsmouth as passengers on the East Indiaman *Baring*. As the *Bombay Courier* recorded on February 1, 1812, after noting the ship's safe arrival at Calcutta, there were four ladies in the passenger list. Of first importance was Lady Maria Nugent, the wife of Field Marshall Sir George Nugent, who had come to take up his post as the new Commander-in-Chief. Second was Lady Maria's friend, Lady Charlotte Murray, wife of Lieutenant-Colonel Murray, while of more minor standing were Mrs Ann Midwinter, wife of Captain Midwinter, and Mrs Eleanor Reid, whose husband was "Captain Hugh Reid," of the "country shipping service."

Hugh Reid had come to Calcutta on behalf of John Mangles, to supervise the construction of the 1,200-ton *Vansittart* at the yard of John Gilmore & Company. The job was the equivalent to the golden handshake of later times, being a recognition of his fine work in the past, and the path to his retirement. He was not just a part owner of this new ship, but the managing owner, too, the power behind the design, construction and outfitting of one of the aristocrats of the sea. And the task would not end when the *Vansittart* was safely and grandly afloat—as the ship's "husband," he would negotiate a charter, supervise her loading, and ship her officers and crew.

That the new ship should be built in India instead of England was another outcome of the protracted conflict in Europe. The government had put restrictions on the building of large East India ships, because their "scantling of timber is equal to that of line of battle ships," and it was obvious which should have priority. The Directors of the Honourable Company gave way to the demands of the Admiralty, but their specifications for Calcutta-built ships were very detailed indeed, in pursuit of continued quality. *Vansittart*'s keel was to be 133 feet, 7 inches, her breadth 42 feet, 4 inches, and her hold 17 feet, 1 inch, while her decks were to be lofty—6 feet, 4 inches between decks, and 6 feet, 7 inches in the roundhouse. Naturally, she was to be built of teak, and the Company's high standards were to be adhered to throughout.

Where Hugh and Eleanor stayed is unknown, but their days would have been typical of European Calcutta. As Lady Maria Nugent put it, it was "a diary of engagements, and the business of society." In the early mornings, Hugh went over to Howrah, while Eleanor rode out in a carriage with lady friends. Then, while Hugh watched the keel laid and the framing rise, Eleanor received visitors at home, or went out to tiffin parties, where, as Lady Maria recorded, there could as many as twenty about the table.

There was also the responsibility of organising the domestics and making sure that dinner would be ready at two. By then, Hugh would be back from the shipyard for this main meal of the day, at which there was usually a good number of guests, the Nugents once entertaining fifty. Then came the familiar routine of siesta, bathing and dressing as the afternoon heat subsided, the ride on the Course, the paying of calls and receiving of visitors, and the late tiffin, which, for the men, wound up with a lengthy spell at the table talking business over Madeira, while the women gossiped and played cards in another room. The routine only altered on Sundays, when the Reids worshipped at the chapel in Lal Bazaar, presided over by the Scottish London Society missionary, Reverend Nathaniel Forsyth.

For Hugh, there were old friends to encounter, one being an echo from his adventurous past. About the end of the year, he was unexpectedly reunited with Thomas Watkin Court, who was one of the three country captains who had supported Prince Nuku—Court had commanded the *Sultan* during the battle for Bacan and Tidore, when Hugh Reid had been first officer on the *Duke of Clarence*. Surprisingly, Court was now the owner of the *Mangles,* which had been ransomed at the Isle de France for the sum of 15,000 silver dollars. Reid and the Mangles brothers had not suffered greatly when the *Mangles* had been seized, as it had been insured for 150,000 rupees, but still, it was only natural for Hugh to be interested in the strange outcome. Not long after that, Court sold the ship to Sheik Gollaum Hassan of Calcutta, for an undisclosed sum.

Eighteen months drifted by, while hull and decks were planked, and frames were formed for the quarter galleries and stern galleries. The part of the hull that would be under water was sheathed and tarred, paid and caulked, and finished off with copper. It was not until November 10, 1813, that the *Asiatic Mirror* was able to announce that yet another great ship had been launched "at the dock yard of Messieurs Gilmore and Co."

Echoed the *Bombay Courier*—

> *Yesterday was launched from the Dock yard of Messrs. Gilmore and Company, the new ship of 1200 tons, built for the service of the East India Company; and to be commanded by Captain Hugh Reid. Sir George Nugent did Captain Reid the honour to preside at the ceremony of naming this ship. His Excellency, attended by his Suite and many other gentlemen, arrived at the Yard half past one o'clock, and at a quarter past two, the preparations for the launch being nearly completed, His Excellency ascended a platform raised for the occasion, in front of the ship and but a few feet distant from the bow. From this platform the ceremony was conducted. The shores being removed, the arrangements completed, and the screws which were placed under the bows being in action, the ship began to move: at this instant Sir George flung the flask of wine up the bows, and saluted the majestic pile by the name of the* Vansittart*: – at the same instant the Band of His Majesty's 24th, which was stationed near the platform, struck up "Rule Britannia."*

As usual, the assemblage was then entertained in the apartments above the shipyard, where a great tiffin of superior foodstuffs was waiting, along with sufficient wine for a long series of toasts. According to the *Bombay Courier*, these totalled a dozen or more, starting with the toast to the King, and progressing through the Queen and the rest of the Royal Family to the East India Company, the

Governor General, Sir George Nugent, and anyone else important whose name popped into the toastmaster's mind. All this culminated in a ball, where those who could still stand would dance until dawn.

That, of course, was not the end of work on the *Vansittart.* There was a great deal more to be done before she could sail—rigging, furnishing, decorating. Glass had to be put in the windows, and deadlights fastened beside those windows so they could be closed in heavy weather. There were lockers and guns and doors to install; capstans to secure and decks to be planed to a perfect finish; there was the installation of coops and pens for the shipboard livestock. The embellishments had to be supervised, too—the magnificent carving and gilding that was part of the reason East Indiamen were known as Monarchs of the Sea, and here in Calcutta it was carried out by gifted Asian artists. And, of course, there was the rigging of several miles of rope.

On New Year's Day, 1814, the ship was sailed down the river to be loaded. On March 5, 1814, the *Bombay Courier* reported, "By a letter dated from on board the *Vansittart,* Captain Reid at the Sandheads on the 8th instant, we learn that she was then quitting the Pilot, and that all the Passengers were well. The *Vansittart,* though drawing more than 24 feet, sailed remarkable well, and could pass the other ships in company with ease." She was part of a 10-ship convoy, *Lloyds List* later noting that the regular ships *Streatham, Devonshire, William Pitt* and *Marchioness of Exeter,* the extra ships *Moffatt* and *Batavia,* the *Ganges,* country ship, and the licensed ships *General Kyd, Vansittart,* and *Lady Flora* had assembled at Saugor Island. The fleet headed first for Point de Galle, Ceylon, and then steered for St Helena, picking up their escort, HMS *Semiramis*, on the way.

For Captain Reid, the 24-gun *Semiramis* proved a bigger threat than the enemy privateers. On passage through the Atlantic, he somehow ran afoul of *Semiramis*, an accident that led to an embarrassing court case. "In the Court of Exchequer, yesterday, Mangles and others, Proprietors, and Captain Reid, part Proprietor and Commander of the *Vansittart* extra Indiaman, were sued by Mr Jervis, Counsel for the Crown, for compensation for injury done to H.M.S. *Semiramis*, on the voyage from the Cape of Good Hope, by the *Vansittart* running foul of her," quoted the *Bombay Courier* from a report the editor had received, dated July 13, 1816–

> *It was an invariable rule, and formed part of the sailing instructions given to every ship of a Fleet, to prevent the danger of two vessels getting on board each other in contrary tacks: – the vessels on the starboard tack to keep the wind – those on the lar-board tack to bear up. The* Vansittart *not obeying this signal, occasioned the accident. The* Semiramis *lost her bowsprit, fore mast, main-top-mast, and had her main mast sprung.*

In a word, Reid had almost sunk the convoy escort. "A verdict was given against the defendant," the report concluded. The Crown Counsel, Mr. J. Gaselee, would fix the charges at a later date.

Despite this belated blot on his record, Hugh Reid enjoyed a pleasant retirement. Rich with the returns from past indulgences and current investments, he was able to move into a recently built house in Bernard Street, in the fashionably artistic Bloomsbury precinct of London. One of their neighbours was Eleanor's second-eldest brother,

Captain Andrew Barclay. There, Hugh and Eleanor lived a staid and quiet, but sociable life, worshipping at St Pancras Church (where there is now a simple memorial to them both), and playing aunt and uncle to Margaret and Richard Porter's large family.

Then came the marriage of Eleanor's youngest sister, Jane, to Robert Campbell, in 1816, and after that the wedding of her youngest brother, George Dallas (the young hero of the Battle of Trafalgar) to Mary Ann Prickett. Two of his eight children—Eleanor, born 1821, and Hugh Reid, born about 1829 or 1830—were named after them. A favourite, it seems, was his daughter Janet, born in 1822. Sadly, at about the same time, Hugh lost his brother, Thomas, Eleanor's "revered" brother-in-law, who died on September 20, 1821, aged fifty-four.

Hugh and Eleanor kept up their interest in India. When their pastor in Calcutta died, they sent money for a stone to be erected over the spot at the mission at Chinsurah where his ashes had been buried. As specified, the inscription read, "To the Memory of the Rev. Nathaniel Forsythe, of Smalholmbank, Lochmoben in Scotland, Missionary, who arrived in Calcutta Dec. 1798, and after a laborious, holy and exemplary life, died at Chandemagore in February 1816, aged 47 years. This stone is erected by Captain Hugh Reid of London. The deceased is affectionately remembered by his friends, as the most faithful and zealous Protestant minister in Chinsurah."

Hugh also sponsored Christian women who wished to settle and teach in Calcutta, by guaranteeing the £400 bond required by the East India Company—Mrs Ann Harris in 1818, and Mrs Elizabeth Corrie and Miss Anne Chatfield in 1829.

And, meantime, an editor at the Jerusalem Coffee House had persuaded Eleanor to allow the publication of the journal she had kept on the *Friendship*, which came out in the *Asiatic Journal* in 1819 and 1820, and so she became that most fashionable of middle-class women, a published author. In 1823, however, she moved from Bloomsbury, that haven of writers. Hugh had bought one of the first residences of Regent Park, at number 16, Cornwall Terrace. Captain Andrew Barclay moved too, investing in a house in the same complex, while Eleanor's brother-in-law, Richard Porter, bought a house at 19 Regent Street, just around the corner.

For all these men, having such a prestigious address was a symbol of their affluence and solid respectability.

Cornwall Terrace, T.H. Shepherd

Then, for Eleanor, tragedy struck. The same *Asiatic Journal* that had published her journal posted her husband's death notice: "June 21, 1832—At Cornwall Terrace, Regent's Park, aged 62 years, Capt. Hugh Reid: an upright, warm-hearted, and benevolent man. His loss is deeply deplored by his disconsolate widow and a numerous circle of friends." Nine days later, on June 30, Hugh was buried in the churchyard at St Pancras, where the register testifies him to be aged sixty-two years, five months.

The first clause in his Will is an interesting one, because of his express wish that Eleanor should not marry again. "I wish after all my lawful debts are discharged I bequeath to my beloved wife Eleanor wishing her to remain single, the sum of ten thousand pounds sterling to be at her own disposal," it runs, and then makes sure that she will never be without a house over her head. "I also bequeath to my wife Eleanor this house furniture plate books and all other goods & chattels also the residue of whatsoever other property I may be possessed of at the time of my demise after the following legacies are paid—"

William Barclay, "oldest brother of my wife," received one hundred pounds plus the interest of the thousand pounds Hugh had invested at three percent, and when he died it was to pass on to his wife Elizabeth, and then divided among his children. Captain Andrew Barclay, who had evidently never married, received one hundred pounds as well, as did Richard Porter, while the children of Richard and "Margaret Porter late sister of my wife" shared the interest of one thousand pounds. Jane, who had married Robert Campbell, had not had children, so the interest of one thousand pounds that she received was to be distributed among the children of "our brother-in-law George Dallas Barclay" when she passed away. George Dallas himself received the standard one hundred pounds plus the interest on one thousand, which was to be passed on to his children at his death, too. Helen, the widow of Hugh's brother Thomas, was the receive one hundred pounds each year while she lived, an annuity that was to revert to Eleanor at her death.

Even with all that money given away, Eleanor was still a very wealthy woman. According to her own Will, written in 1849, Hugh had left her many treasures, including gold chains and a diamond brooch, silver vases, several large paintings, and a miniature of himself. She was also the personal owner of a house at number 4, Ulster Terrace, Regent's Park, where evidently her sister, Jane Campbell, lived. Eleanor did not move in with her, instead staying in the Cornwall Terrace house—but not alone, because both the census records of the time and her own Will indicate that she informally adopted George Dallas's daughter Janet Margaret Barclay, who was about ten years old at the time. Janet, who became her companion, eventually inherited the house, along with all its chattels, plus the residue of the fortune once the host of nieces and nephews had been given their share.

Eleanor did not die at 16 Cornwall Terrace. Instead she passed away in Brighton, at the good age (for those times) of seventy-five. Evidently she was suffering from some illness, because she was under the care of the respected Dr James Wilson, an ex-East India Company surgeon who now had offices in Regency Square. Her body was carried to London, where she was buried beside her husband in the churchyard at St Pancras, on a grey, foggy first of November, in the year 1853.

St Pancras, 1822

Acknowledgements

Throughout the research for this fascinating project, I have found lively interest and active help from many informed people. I would particularly like to thank Helen O'Dea, genealogist, for producing such a detailed picture of Eleanor Barclay Reid's genealogy, plus her marriage and death certificates.

Librarians in Australia have been amazing: I owe much to Gillian Simpson and her team at the Vaughan Evans Library, Australian National Maritime Museum; to the entire team at the State Library of New South Wales and the Mitchell Library; and also to Janette Pelosi at the State Records Authority of New South Wales, for answering my emailed questions so comprehensively. Also in Australia, I owe thanks to Perry McIntyre at the Global Irish Studies Centre, University of New South Wales, for her interest.

Elsewhere, Rick Spilman was very helpful with technical details of the lengthening of the *Friendship*, and the problems of her sailing qualities, while Andreas von Mach was a source of very useful ship details, and Bill Wells produced contemporary newspaper reports. All three are members of Marhst-L, an international electronic discussion group that is sponsored and administered by the Marine Museum of the Great Lakes at Kingston, Ontario, Canada, with the assistance of Queen's University at Kingston, and which has provided both inspiration and information.

Other interested and helpful members were John Harland, Martin Evans, Nicholas Blake, Peter Beeston, Bill Bunting, and Don Seltzer, whom I thank for their comments and advice. And finally, plaudits to my husband, Ron, who listened patiently to endless draft passages, produced sketches, and created the wonderful cover image.

Annotated Bibliography

Logbooks

Marquis Cornwallis, 1 February to 1 November 1796. State Library of New South Wales, MLMSS 7491, safe 1/242. Readily available in both album and transcript views on the SLNSW website, under the title, "Log Book of the ship Marquis Cornwallis."

Friendship, 10 May 1800 to 17 July 1801. Originally held at National Archives, Kew, now at the British Library, L/MAR/B/358 B. Australian Joint Copying Project microfilm 1624, State Library of New South Wales. While much of this is too faded to be legible, entries after arrival at Calcutta are reasonably clear.

Books

Addison, Midshipman Thomas. Journals of the East India Company's Service, 1801-1829, extracts, published in, *The Naval Miscellany,* edited by John Knox Laughton, printed for the Navy Records Society, 1902.

Anon. Gleanings in Africa ... London, 1805. Collection of letters written during the British occupation of the Cape of Good Hope, mostly emancipist, but with some interesting descriptions. Available online.

Barclay, Captain Andrew. *Life of Captain Andrew Barclay of Cambock, near Launceston, Van Diemen's Land / written from his own dictation at Cambock, February 19, 1836 to Thomas Scott.* Printed by Thomas Grant, probably about 1854. This Andrew Barclay was not Eleanor's brother. His short memoir follows the same general pattern as the career that is listed in Hardy and Farrington (*q.v.*), but has self-serving anecdotes that seem apocryphal.

There is also much missed out—for instance, Barclay preferred not to mention that he carried convicts to Australia, perhaps because he eventually settled and flourished in Tasmania.

Barnard, Lady Anne. *The Cape Journals of Lady Anne Barnard 1797-1798.* Edited by A.M. Lewin Robinson, with Margaret Lenta and Dorothy Driver. Cape Town: Van Riebeeck Society 1994. Wonderful descriptions of the passage to the Cape of Good Hope on the *Sir Edward Hughes,* and an interesting, discursive journal of her first months in Cape Town, with frequent tart comments about local society. A 2-volume sequel, *The Cape Diaries of Lady Anne Barnard 1799-1800,* was edited by Margaret Lenta and Basil Le Cordeur, and published by the same press in 1999. The arrival of the *Friendship* and the visit of the Reids were unmentioned, Lady Anne being out of town at the time, but these journals were still a very important source for the commentaries.

Bateson, Charles. *The Convict Ships 1787-1868.* Sydney: AH & AW Reed, 1974 (first published in Glasgow in 1959). Excellent histories of ships that carried convicts to Australia at some time in their career, including *Friendship, Mangles* and *Providence.*

Becke, Louis, and Walter Jeffery. *The Naval Pioneers of Australia.* London, John Murray, 1899. Gossipy description of early Australia, more focused on the social scene than the title would suggest. Good accounts of Dampier's explorations and Hunter's voyage on the *Waaksamheyd.* Available online.

Bowen, H. V., with Margarette Lincoln and Nigel Rigby (editors). *The Worlds of the East India Company.* London:

Boydell, 2002. The papers consulted in greatest detail were "The English East India Company and India," by Om Prakash (1-17), and "Establishing the Sea Routes to India and China: Stages in the Development of Hydrographical Knowledge," by Andrew S. Cook (119-136).

Bowen, H. V., with John McAleer and Robert J. Blyth. *Monsoon Traders: the maritime world of the East India Company.* London: Scala, 2011. Beautifully illustrated monograph, produced to accompany the opening of a new permanent Asian gallery at the National Maritime Museum.

Brice, R. K. H. *A History of the Bengal Pilot Service.* A compilation of data accumulated over many years by Captain G. T. Labey, and edited by Captain Brice in 1963. Published online in 2009. Both Labey and Brice were old Hooghly River pilots. Rambling and hard to follow, but well worth the effort.

Brooke, T. H. *A History of the Island of St Helena ... to the Year 1806.* London, 1808. Written by the secretary to the colony. Available online.

Bulley, Anne. *The Bombay Country Ships 1790-1833.* New York: Routledge, 2013. As the author notes, "Bombay and Bengal were a world apart," but there is a great deal of relevance to Reid's career in this ground-breaking study.

Chaplin, Arnold. *A St. Helena Who's Who...* New York, 1919. Focused on Napoleon, but otherwise useful, being a good supplement to Brooke's *History* (*q.v.*). Available online.

Chatterton, E. Keble. *The Old East Indiamen.* London, 1914. Anecdotal history, popular for many years. Available online. Also *Ventures and Voyages* (London, Neptune Library, 1935 repr. of 1928 edition). Useful illustrations.

Clark, Arthur C. *The Clipper Ship Era.* New York: Putnam, 1920. Some early background and illustrations.

Collingridge de Tourcey, George. *The First Discovery of Australia and New Guinea.* 1906. Collingridge was a prominent Australian woodcut-engraver and journalist, with a passion for maritime history. This book was written for New South Wales schools, and though it was not adopted by the system, it provides an excellent overview. Available online.

Compton, Herbert (editor). *A Master Mariner, being the life and adventures of Captain Robert William Eastwick.* London: Fisher Unwin, 1891

Cotton, Sir Evan. *East Indiamen: the East India Company's Maritime Service.* Batchworth Press, 1949. This wide-ranging discussion is a major source for the story of the East Indiamen. Though dated, and supplanted in many respects by Sutton (*q.v.*), it is still reliable and relevant.

Daniell, Thomas & William. *A picturesque voyage to India by way of China.* London, 1810. William was Thomas Daniell's nephew. Both men were artists who scraped a living and the money for further travel out of painting gorgeous pictures of India and the Orient and assembling them in a book. The plates were made by Indian craftsmen.

Dawson, L. S. *Memoirs of Hydrography...* Eastbourne, UK, 1883. Potted histories of the first surveyors, including the captains of the First Fleet transports, and Thomas Forrest 1774-76. Available online.

Delaney, John. *Strait Through: Magellan to Cook and the Pacific.* Princeton, New Jersey: Princeton University Library, 2010. Illustrated with wonderful old maps, accompanied by good text descriptions.

Druett, Joan. *Petticoat Whalers, Whaling Wives at Sea 1820-1920.* University Press of New England, 2001. This, with *Hen Frigates, Wives of Merchant Captains Under Sail,* which was published in New York by Simon & Schuster in 1998, was the source of domestic details of the shipboard life of a captain's wife. The chapter "Sex and the Seafaring Wife" (pp. 67-88, *Hen Frigates*) is particularly relevant.

Egan, Pierce, illustrated by Thomas Rowlandson, et al. *Real Life in London, or the Rambles and Adventures of Bob Tally-Ho...*London, 1821, 1822.

Elmes, James. *Metropolitan Improvements, or London in the Nineteenth Century.* Illustrated with plates by T.H. Shepherd. London, 1828. The complete guide to pre-Victorian London.

Farrington, Anthony. *A Biographical Index of East India Company Maritime Service Officers 1600-1834.* London: British Library, 1999. An invaluable index, compiled from India Office Records. NB.: the seafaring histories of Hugh Reid and Hugh Atkins Reid, who were two different men, were mistakenly combined. Also see Farrington's *Catalogue of East India Company Ships' Journals and Logs 1600-1834* (published by the British Library at the same time) for another excellent resource, particularly when combined with Nicholson's *Log of*

Logs. (Includes the interesting note that John Roberts, not Michael Hogan, commanded the *Marquis Cornwallis* on the homebound voyage 1796.)

Farrington, Anthony. *Trading Places: The East India Company and Asia, 1600-1834*. Exhibition catalogue, well illustrated. London: British Library, 2002.

Fay, Eliza. *The Original Letters from India of Mrs Eliza Fay*. Edited by Walter Kelly Firminger. India, 1908. Originally published 1817, in Calcutta. The letters in the first part of the book describe travel to and from Calcutta, and impressions of places and people there, 1779-1782. The second part is a series of letters written to a Mrs. L— in 1815, briefly sketching out three more voyages, beginning 1784 and ending in 1795. Eliza Fay passed away before her account was up to date, so the voyage on the *Mangles* in 1804 was not described. The book is available online.

Findlay, A. G. *A Directory for the Navigation of the Pacific Ocean...* London, 1851. Part of a series covering all the oceans of the world, updated every now and then. Online.

Fletcher, R. A. *Warships and their story*. London: Cassell, 1911.

Folkard, H.C. *The Sailing Boat...* London, 1870. Detailed descriptions of small boats all over the world, with explanatory sketches. Available online.

Forrest, Captain Thomas. *A voyage to New Guinea and the Moluccas ...* London, 1779. A racy firsthand account of an eighteenth century foray into the seas about New Guinea and the Spice Islands. Available online.

Fraser, James Baillie. *Views of Calcutta and its Environs.* London, 1824. Scottish travel writer and artist. Wonderfully detailed aquatints, many focused on shipping in the river.

Fry, Howard T. *Alexander Dalrymple and the Expansion of British Trade.* London: Frank Cass, 1970. The section "The British in the East Indies, 1761-1805" (136-165) is a useful study of British attempts to encroach on the Dutch dominance in the Spice Islands.

Griffin, Andrew. *London, Bengal, the China Trade and the Unfrequented Extremities of Asia: the East India Company's Settlement in New Guinea, 1793-95.* British Library Board: British Library Journal 96. An excellent study of Captain John Hayes and his exploits in New Guinea and the Spice Islands. Available online.

Grove, Richard H. *Green Imperialism: Colonial Expansion, Tropical Island Edens...* Cambridge, UK: University Press, 1995. Very useful and well presented study of the fashion for acclimatisation and transfer of landscapes.

Hackman, Rowan. *Ships of the East India Company.* World Ship Society, 2001. A detailed and reliable listing from India Office records.

Hall, Mr & Mrs S. C. *Ireland, its Scenery, Character &c.* London, 1841. Atmospheric illustrations. Available online.

Hardy, Horatio Charles. *A Register of Ships Employed in the Service of the Honorable the United East India Company...* London, 1811. The basic source of data for the study of East Indiamen. Includes voyages of regular ships with lists of officers, agents, and Thames pilots, and regulations concerning indulgences, salaries, uniforms. Available online.

Hay, Robert. *Landsman Hay.* Journal at sea, including HMS *Culloden* on convoy to India, 1804. Edited by A. Vincent McInerney. London: Seaforth, 2010. Fluent and fascinating account of life on Nelson-era warships, written from an unusual perspective.

Hezel, Francis X. *The First Taint of Civilization: A History of the Caroline and Marshall Islands...* Honolulu: University of Hawaii Press, 1983. A superb and highly readable account of early European contacts in Micronesia. Includes a rousing account of McCluer's adventures in Palau.

Hickey, William. *Memoirs of William Hickey.* Edited by Alfred Spencer. 4 vv. London: Hurst & Blackett. 1913-25. Hickey was a ne'er-do-well lawyer who travelled widely, and who left a vast and fascinating memoir, available online. There is also a version edited by Peter Quennell (Hutchinson, 1960).

Hunter, John. *An Historical Journal...* London, 1792.

Kindersley, Jemima. *Letters from the Island of Teneriffe, Brazil, the Cape of Good Hope, and the East Indies.* London, 1777. Interesting account of a woman's experiences in India, particularly when read in combination with Eliza Fay's letters. Parts are online at the website "The Travel Letters of Mrs. Kindersley."

Lee, Ida. *Commodore Sir John Hayes, His Voyage and Life.* London: Longman, Green, 1912. Available online. Dated but valuable account of Hayes's adventures in the Spice Islands.

Losty, J. P. *Calcutta, City of Palaces.* London: Arnold Publishers for the British Library, 1990. Beautifully illustrated book, with excellent descriptions of daily life in European Calcutta.

Nagle, Jacob. *The Nagle Journal, A diary of the life of Jacob Nagle, sailor ...* Edited by John C. Dann. New York: Weidenfeld & Nicolson, 1988. Well designed publication, with a discursive, most informative and readable commentary.

Nordhoff, Charles. *Life on the Ocean.* Cincinnati, USA, 1874.

Nugent, Lady Maria. *A Journal from the Year 1811 till the Year 1815, including a voyage...* 2 vv. London, 1839. Interesting description of her passage to India on the *Baring*, but with no mention of Eleanor Reid, either then or later, though it is likely that Eleanor was one of the women invited to her cabin on board, and to tiffin parties in Calcutta, respectable women being so scarce. Good descriptions, too, of social life in Calcutta.

O'Brian, Patrick. *Joseph Banks, A Life.* Chicago: University Press, 1987. Well written and well researched by a staunch admirer of Banks.

Oulton, Walley Chamberlin. *The Traveller's Guide; or, English Itinerary...* London, 1805. Details of Eleanor's journey to Waterford came from this. Available online.

Paine, Lincoln. *Ships of the World...*New York: Houghton-Mifflin, 1997. Attractively produced encyclopaedia, characterised by thorough scholarship.

Parkinson, C. Northcote. *Trade in the Eastern Seas...* Cambridge, UK: University Press, 1937. Rousing and anecdotal. Ship details are not reliable, but a basic source that is available online.

Pinkerton, J. *Voyages and Travels in all Parts of the World.* London, 1808-14. Includes engravings of Malacca by Edward Hawke Locker, an English watercolourist who was secretary to Admiral Pellew during HMS *Culloden*'s sojourn in the East Indies.

Plowden, Francis. *An Historical Review of the State of Ireland...* Philadelphia, 1806. Volume II, part II has a detailed description of the 1798 Rebellion and its aftermath. Available online.

Roberts, Mrs. Emma. "The East India Voyager." Serialised in *Parbury's Oriental Herald,* vol. one, 1837: pp 2-7 (choice of a cabin); 73-79 (ladies' attire); 177-85 (children in India; useful hobbies; gardening; food; management of servants; behaving with propriety); 273-281, 396-403, 493-500 (grandmotherly advice to outward bound cadets). Available online.

Saunders, Graham. *A History of Brunei.* New York: Routledge, 1994. While focused on Borneo, this study has useful background for the Forrest expedition to New Guinea.

Shepherd, Thomas H. *London and its Environs in the Nineteenth Century...* London 1831. Potted descriptions of landmarks, with many detailed etchings.

Sherwood, Mary Martha. *The Life and Times of Mrs Sherwood (1775-1851) from the diaries of Captain and Mrs Sherwood.* Edited by F. J. Harvey Darton. London, 1910. Interesting account of the passage to India by an army officer's wife.

Solvyns, François Balthazar. *A Collection of Two Hundred and Fifty Coloured Etchings: Descriptive of the Manners, Customs and Dresses of the Hindoos.* Calcutta, 1796, 1799. Wonderful artwork, available online.

Stevens, Robert White. *On the Stowage of Ships and their Cargoes.* London: Longmans, 1871. An invaluable resource, available online, and commonly known as "Stevens on stowage." Along with Reid's logbook, this was the source of the description of the stowing of sugar, saltpetre, bales of fabric, and indigo on the *Friendship* in Calcutta.

Styles, Michael H. *Captain Hogan: Sailor, Merchant Diplomat on Six Continents.* Virginia, USA: Six Continent Horizons, 2003. An interesting, though one-sided, account of Michael Hogan's chequered life. *cf.* the entry in the *Australian Dictionary of Biography*, which is more candid and perhaps more reliable.

Sutton, Jean. *The East India Company's Maritime Service 1746-1834: Masters of the Eastern Seas.* London: Boydell, 2010. This is the story of the Larkins family, shipmasters and managing owners. Not directly relevant to the Reids' story, but a very good book, with much that was useful. An excellent sequel to Sutton's *Lords of the East: The East India Company and its Ships* (London: Conway Maritime, 1981), which is the prime source for a study of the background and functioning of the ships of the Honourable East India Company, being thoroughly reliable as well as very readable.

Tench, Watkin. *A Narrative of the Expedition to Botany Bay.* London, 1789. Watkin was a marine officer. The book, a tremendous success at the time, is now available free, online.

Trusler, John. *The London Advisor and Guide...* London, 1786. Itineraries for travel, and hints for getting around the city in Georgian times. Available online.

Weinreb, Ben, with Christopher Hibbert. *The London Encyclopaedia.* London: Macmillan, 1983. Indispensible history of London streets, squares, and landmarks.

Whitaker, Anne-Maree. *Unfinished Revolution.* NSW, Australia: Crossing Press, 1994. Valuable study of the transportation of United Irishmen and the aftermath in New South Wales and Norfolk Island.

Widjojo, Muridan Satrio. *Cross-cultural alliance-making and local resistance in Maluku during the revolt of Prince Nuku, c.1780-1810.* Doctoral thesis, Department of History, Faculty of Arts, Leiden University, 2007. A .pdf of this superb study of the Prince Nuku rebellion can be downloaded from the Leiden Repository.

Newspapers, directories, dictionaries, encyclopaedias and journals

Alphabetical List of the Honourable East India Company's Bengal Civil Servants.... Dodwell and Miles. London, 1839. Outside the book's timeline, but still useful. Available online.

Asiatic Journal and Monthly Register... volumes 1-34, 1816-1841.

Asiatic Annual Register or a View of the History of Hindustan, 7 vv., 1800-1809. The launch of the *Providence* is described in volume 10, in the entry for 2 June 1807.

Australian Dictionary of Biography: biographies of, Capt. Edward Abbott, Alexander Dalrymple, Major Francis Grose, Dr John Harris, Capt. Michael Hogan, Capt. John Hunter, Rev. Richard Johnson, Bt. Major George Johnston, Capt. William Kent, John Macarthur, Lt. Col. William Paterson.

Bombay Courier: 15/03/1800 (ships at St Helena); 12/04/1800 (ships at Cape of Good Hope); 25/10/1800 (Reid's account of the *Walker*'s boarding by natives); 17/01/1801 (departure of *Friendship*); 15/01/1803 (*Phoenix*, Reid, from Cape of Good Hope); 12/04/1803 (launch of *Mangles*); 19/12/1804 (*Mangles* sailed from Falmouth); 10/01/1806 (*Mangles* at Penang); 27/05/1806 (*Mangles* arrived in Calcutta); 10/06/1807 (launch of *Providence*); 12/09/1807 (*Providence* on sandbank); 7/11/1807 (Surcouf); 14/10/1807 (*Revenant*'s captures); 11/03/1809 (*Providence* passenger list); 1/02/1812 (*Baring* passenger list); 4/12/1814 (launch of *Vansittart*); 5/3/1814 (departure of *Vansittart*); 1/02/1817 (court case in London re *Vansittart* and *Semiramis*).

East-India Register and Directory... John Mathison and Alexander Way Mason. London, 1803

Historical Records of New South Wales. Vol. I part II (Phillip): pp. 372, 382-85 (voyage of the *Supply* to Batavia); Hunter's report of the voyage of the *Waaksamheyd,* p. 617; vol. IV (Hunter-King): p. 148 (*Friendship* arrival), 165 (*Friendship* manifest).

Life, 22 May 1944: "The Gilberts & Marshalls," by Samuel Eliot Morison. Highly readable story of the passages of Captain Gilbert and Captain Marshall through the islands named after them. Available online.

Lloyds List. Various. 1796-1818.

Lloyds Register. Various. 1796-1818.

Log of Logs. Created by Ian Nicolson. Three volumes. Covers ships sailing in Australasian waters 1788-1990. What makes it particularly valuable is the metadata attached to each entry, giving location of logs and papers, and listing places visited. Canberra: Roebuck Society, 1990, 1993, 1998. Available online as three .pdf files.

New Gresham encyclopaedia. London, 1922.

Popular Science Monthly, 1874. Natural history drawings.

The Crayon, Vol. 2, No. 13 (Sep. 26, 1855), pp. 192-193. Available online through jstor.

The Universal Politician, and Periodical Reporter ... by a society of gentlemen. November 1796. Pages 337 and 351 have the reports of the capture and recapture of the *Friendship*.

Websites

As URLs go out of date, titles of websites are given instead.

"Books, Boxes and Boats." Includes links to *Lloyds List* and *Lloyds Register*.

"Eighteenth Century Collections." Available only at subscribing libraries, so was browsed at the State

Library of New South Wales. Includes the *Bombay Courier.*

"FIBIS" – Families in British India Society. Searchable database, plus lists of books and journals, and links to relevant websites, some free, others not.

"Free Settler or Felon." Excellent resource for looking up convict ships and convict ancestors. Partially interactive.

"Mariners and Ships in Australian Waters."

"Primer on Eighteenth Century Women's Fashion by Kristen Koster."

"Sentenced Beyond the Seas: Australia's Early Convict Records." This includes a transcript of, and a link to, "Return of male convicts embarked on the 'Friendship' transport, New Geneva, Ireland, 1799 August 24 - 1800 February 16": National Library of Australia, MS 144.

"Thoroughbred Heritage, Breeders and Breeding: The British East India Company in Early Australia."

Eleanor Barclay Reid's Family

William BARCLAY was married to **Janet HARDIE** on 11 Oct 1767 at Edinburgh, Midlothian, Scotland.

Children:

William Barclay. Birth date unknown. Eleanor's oldest brother, according to Hugh Reid's Will.

Andrew Barclay bap. 5 Jul 1770, St Cuthbert's Midlothian, Scotland. Recorded in Eleanor's Will as Captain Barclay, and in the Will of his brother George Dallas Barclay (Probate 28/04/1834) as Captain Andrew Barclay.

Margaret Barclay Porter, bap. 19 Nov 1772, St Cuthbert's Midlothian, Scotland, married **Richard Porter** at St Mary's, Marylebone on 23 Jun 1799. Witnesses: Thomas Reid, William Barclay (sen.), William Barclay (jnr.), John Calvert, Stephen Knight. (Stephen Knight married Elizabeth Porter at the same time.) Richard Porter was b. 29 August 1773, and buried at St. Sepulchre, London, on 3 November 1848. According to Hugh Reid's Will of 1827, Richard Porter lived at 19 Regent Street, London. He and Margaret had 12 children, the youngest born 1813. Most were baptized at St. Martin in the Fields in what appears to be a mass christening: **Eleanor** [and] **Hannah Porter** (b. 7 Nov. 1803, bap. 1812); **Janet Porter**

(b. 1 Sept. 1805, bap. 1812;); **William John Porter** (b. 17 Sept. 1806, bap. 31 Dec. 1812; died 1886 in Burma); **Hugh Reid Porter** (b. 14 Dec. 1807, bap. 1812) **Thomas Porter** (b. 1808, bap. 31 Dec 1812); **Mary Ann Porter** (b. 16 Dec. 1811, bap. 1812); **Richard Porter** (n.d. bap. 1812; probate 1848).

Eleanor Barclay Reid, b. 1777 or 1778 (census records), married **Hugh Reid** at St Mary le Bone on 16 September 1798, witnessed by **William Barclay** and **Thomas Reid**. According to the *Gentleman's Magazine* of 1832, Hugh Reid died June 21, 1832 at Regent's Park. Service/burial: St Pancras Parish Chapel, Camden 30/06/1832. Age 62y 5mo.. Eleanor Reid died in October 1853. She was under the care of Dr. James Wilson, MD (Edinburgh 1832), formerly an HEIC surgeon, of Regency Square, Brighton. Service/burial: St Pancras Parish Chapel, Camden 01/11/1853. Age 75. There is a memorial "Captain HUGH REID, 1832, and his wife ELEANOR, 1853" on the East Wall, North Section, of St Pancras Church.

George Dallas Barclay, b. 8 June 1782 in London, bap. at London Wall Scotch Church on 7 July 1782. George Dallas Barclay married **Mary Ann Prickett** (b. to John and Elizabeth Prickett on 29 Nov. 1801), on 24 January 1821 at St. Leonard's Shoreditch Church, London. George Dallas Barclay died in Yarmouth, Norfolk, on 25 Feb. 1834, "after a severe and protracted illness," aged 51. His children: **George Reid Barclay** (bap. 24 May 1820); **Andrew William Barclay** (bap. 24 May 1820 too, but not necessarily twins); **Eleanor Barclay** (b. 20 Mar. 1821, bap. 13 May 1821); **Robert Campbell Barclay** (bap. 24 May 1824; died during the Indian Mutiny of

1857-59, and is buried at St. Paul's, Calcutta, under the mass memorial, "died during the mutiny of the native troops and subsequent operations from 1857 to 1859; some on the field of battle; some by the hands of their own followers; others by disease; all doing their duty. This monument has been erected by their fellow officers." He was Bt. Major, 68th Regiment, Native Infantry.): **Janet Margaret Barclay** (bap. 22 Oct. 1822 [but may be 1827], who was Eleanor's companion after Eleanor was widowed (1841 and 1851 census); **Isabella Barclay** (b. 11 July 1826, died 8 Feb. 1831); **Mary Ann Barclay** (bap. 9 June 1828); **Hugh Reid Barclay** (bap. 15 Feb. 1830).

Jane Barclay Campbell (according to Eleanor's Will, her dear sister), birth date unknown. She married **Robert Campbell** at St. George the Martyr, Southwark, Surrey, on 1 Jan. 1816.

INDEX

Old Salt Press

Old Salt Press is an independent press catering to those who love books about ships and the sea. We are an association of writers working together to produce the very best of nautical and maritime fiction and non-fiction. We invite you to join us as we go down to the sea in books.

New Release

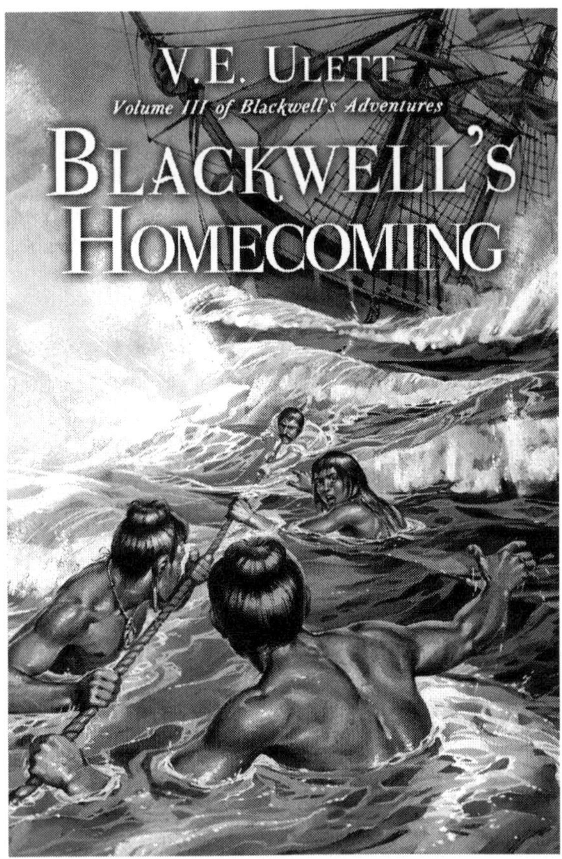

In a multigenerational saga of love, war and betrayal, Captain Blackwell and Mercedes continue their voyage in Volume III of Blackwell's Adventures. The Blackwell family's eventful journey from England to Hawaii, by way of the new and tempestuous nations of Brazil and Chile, provides an intimate portrait of family conflicts and loyalties in the late Georgian Age. *Blackwell's Homecoming* is an evocation of the dangers and rewards of desire. ISBN 978-0-9882360-7-3

New Release

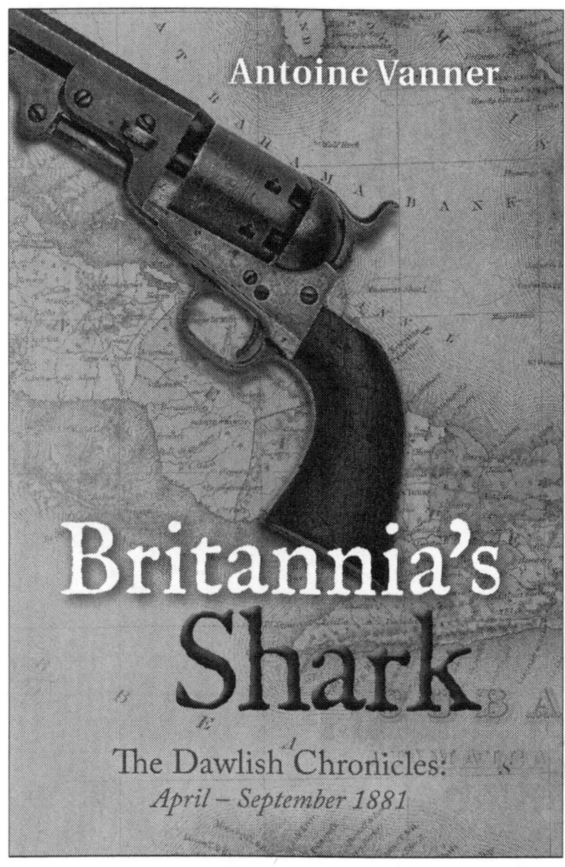

It is the year 1881, and a daring act of piracy draws ambitious British navy officer, Nicholas Dawlish, into a deadly maelstrom of intrigue and revolution. In a headlong adventure, Dawlish and his beloved wife, Florence, voyage from the excesses of America's Gilded Age to the fevered squalor of an island ruled by savage tyranny. Manipulated ruthlessly from London by the shadowy Admiral Topcliffe, Nicholas and Florence must make strange alliances if they are to survive—and prevail. ISBN 978-09922636-9-0

New Release

In 1870, on the medium clipper ship *Alahambra,* the last man hoisted aboard in Sydney is the drunken shantyman, Jack Barlow. On a ship with a dying captain and a murderous mate, Barlow struggles with a tragic past, a troubled present and an uncertain future, at the same time guiding *Alahambra* through Southern Ocean ice and the horror of an Atlantic hurricane.

Based on a true story, *The Shantyman* is a gripping tale of survival against all odds at sea and ashore, and the challenge of facing a past that can never be wholly left behind.
ISBN 978-09941152-2-5

Proudly produced by Old Salt Press

HELL AROUND THE HORN by Rick Spilman. A nautical thriller set in the last days of sail. ISBN: 978-09882360-1-1

TURN A BLIND EYE by Alaric Bond. England is at war with Napoleon, but smuggling is rife on the south coast of England. ISBN: 978-09882360-3-5

TORRID ZONE by Alaric Bond. She's a tired ship with a worn-out crew, yet HMS *Scylla* must venture once again into enemy-ridden seas. The sixth in the Fighting Sail series. ISBN: 978-09882360-9-7

CAPTAIN BLACKWELL'S PRIZE by V.E. Ulett. A romantic adventure from the days of wooden ships and iron men. ISBN: 978-09882360-6-6

CAPTAIN BLACKWELL'S PARADISE by V.E. Ulett. Book number two in the rousing Blackwell series. ISBN: 978-0988236059

THE ELEPHANT VOYAGE by Joan Druett. The rescue of six castaways in the sub-Antarctic leads to international controversy. ISBN: 978-09922588-4-9

THE BECKONING ICE by Joan Druett. Wiki Coffin battles a vicious murderer in the icy sub-Antarctic. The fifth in the Wiki Coffin maritime mystery series. ISBN: 978-09922588-3-2

Made in the USA
San Bernardino, CA
26 March 2017